PLATO AND ARISTOTLE'S ETHICS

This volume, emanating from the Fourth Keeling Colloquium in Ancient Philosophy, presents essays and comments by nine outstanding scholars of ancient philosophy, which examine the influence of Plato on the development of Aristotle's ethics. The essays focus on the role of pleasure in happiness and the good life (Christopher Taylor and Sarah Broadie), the irreducibility of ethical concepts to value-neutral concepts (Anthony Price and Sarah Broadie), the relation of virtue to happiness (Roger Crisp and Christopher Rowe, Terry Irwin and Sir Anthony Kenny), the role of the requirement of self-sufficiency in determining the content of happiness (John Cooper and Sir Anthony Kenny), and the question of whether the just man should be a participant in the political life of his city (Richard Kraut and Christopher Rowe).

ASHGATE KEELING SERIES IN ANCIENT PHILOSOPHY

The *Ashgate Keeling Series in Ancient Philosophy* presents edited collections of leading international research which illustrate and explore ways in which ancient and modern philosophy interact. Drawing on original papers presented at the S.V. Keeling Memorial Lectures and Colloquia at University College London, this series incorporates contributions from the Anglo-American philosophical tradition and from continental Europe, and brings together scholars internationally recognised for their work on ancient philosophy as well as those whose primary work in areas of contemporary philosophy speaks of the importance of ancient philosophy in modern philosophical research and study. Each book in the series will appeal to upper-level and graduate students and academic researchers worldwide – both those who are interested in ancient philosophy and those who are working in the relevant areas of contemporary philosophy.

Plato and Aristotle's Ethics

Edited by
ROBERT HEINAMAN
University College London

ASHGATE

Published by
Ashgate Publishing Limited
Gower House
Croft Road
Aldershot
Hampshire GU11 3HR
England

Ashgate Publishing Company
Suite 420
101 Cherry Street
Burlington, VT 05401-4405
USA

Ashgate website: http://www.ashgate.com

British Library Cataloguing in Publication Data
Plato and Aristotle's ethics. – (Ashgate Keeling series in
  ancient philosophy)
  1. Plato – Ethics 2. Aristotle, 384-322 B.C. – Ethics
  3. Aristotle, 384-322 B.C. 4. Plato – Influence
  I. Heinaman, Robert
  170.9'22

Library of Congress Cataloging-in-Publication Data
Plato and Aristotle's ethics / edited by Robert Heinaman.
        p. cm. – (Ashgate Keeling series in ancient philosophy)
    Includes indexes.
    ISBN 0-7546-3403-5 (alk. paper)
      1. Plato–Ethics. 2. Aristotle–Ethics. 3. Ethics, Ancient. I. Heinaman, Robert.
      II. Series.

B398.E8P59 2003
170'.92'238–dc21

2002043698

ISBN 0 7546 3403 5

Printed and bound in Great Britain by Biddles Ltd *www.biddles.co.uk*

Contents

List of Contributors

Sarah Broadie is Professor of Philosophy at St. Andrews University.

John M. Cooper is Stuart Professor of Philosophy at Princeton University.

Roger Crisp is Uehiro Fellow and Tutor in Philosophy at St. Anne's College, Oxford.

T.H. Irwin is Susan Linn Sage Professor of Philosophy at Cornell University.

Sir Anthony Kenny is former Master of Balliol College, Oxford.

Richard Kraut is Charles and Emma Morrison Professor in the Humanities at Northwestern University.

A.W. Price is Reader in Philosophy at Birkbeck College, London.

Christopher Rowe is Professor of Greek at Durham University, and currently holds a Leverhulme Personal Research Professorship.

C.C.W. Taylor is Fellow and Tutor in Philosophy at Corpus Christi College, Oxford, and Professor of Philosophy at Oxford University.

Introduction

Robert Heinaman

Plato, Aristotle and Kant are generally considered to have been the greatest philosophers who ever lived. All made enduring contributions to the study of ethics, and Aristotle and Kant in particular continue to have a profound effect on contemporary discussions of moral philosophy. As chance would have it, Aristotle was a student of Plato, being a member of the latter's school, the Academy, for the final twenty years of Plato's life. The impact of Plato on Aristotle's philosophy can hardly be exaggerated. In November of 2002, nine outstanding scholars of ancient philosophy gathered at University College London to discuss some aspects of the complicated story of the relation of Aristotle's ethics to Plato's ethics, how Aristotle reacted to and was influenced by Plato's ethical views. This volume contains the record of that colloquium, including the remarks of commentators on the principal papers. The remainder of this introduction outlines some of the main points of those papers.

Christopher Taylor's paper, 'Pleasure: Aristotle's Response to Plato', focuses on Aristotle's attempts to explain the nature of pleasure and its role in the good life. Aristotle believes that pleasure is an important part of the good life for a human being. His discussion of pleasure is mainly concerned with arguing that pleasure is a good rather than something evil or indifferent. But Plato's account of the nature of pleasure was ill suited to supporting the position of Aristotle. Plato understood pleasure to be either the replenishment of a bodily deficiency to its normal state or the awareness of such replenishment. If pleasure thus essentially involves a bodily deficiency – an evil – it is hard to see how pleasure can be part of the good life. Surely the person who lives well is the person who avoids evils, not the person afflicted by evils which he is able to remove.

Another problem with the replenishment model is that it only applies in a straightforward way to the pleasures of eating and drinking. If we try to extend it to sexual pleasure, for example, the model will describe the desire for sex as the perceived lack of sexual activity, and the pleasure as the making good of that lack. But we have a deficiency or lack here only because the perceived activity is regarded as good. And any account of why sexual activity is worthwhile would have to include the point that it is pleasant. But then in this case the application of the replenishment model presupposes a prior account of what makes the activity pleasant, whereas it was precisely an account of pleasure that the replenishment model was supposed to provide.

Aristotle replaces the replenishment model with the view that pleasure is the exercise of natural capacities in appropriate conditions. All animals have certain capacities the exercise of which constitutes what it is for that kind of animal to lead a life. When those capacities are exercised in appropriate conditions, or when the exercise of the capacity is unimpeded, that exercise of the capacity is pleasure.

Unlike the replenishment model, this analysis supports Aristotle's view that pleasure is an important part of the good life. He thinks that the good life consists in the exercise of rational capacities. Hence, such a life will be intrinsically pleasant.

However, such a life is intrinsically pleasant only when the rational capacities are exercised in the *appropriate* conditions. But what are the appropriate conditions? A problem for Aristotle's account is that it seems that any adequate answer to this question must include the condition that the activity is pleasant to the agent – rendering his account circular. If the description of those appropriate conditions cannot on pain of circularity include reference to the pleasantness of the activity we might appeal to the idea of natural functioning: if, for example, an animal is naturally adapted to eating some type of food, Aristotle might say that a healthy specimen of that type of animal will enjoy eating that food. But this is an inadequate account of pleasure: there is no reason why the animal must enjoy the food since there is no reason why nutritious food must taste good and provide pleasure.

There are two important unclarities in Aristotle's position. First, is his definition a definition of enjoyment, the *enjoying* of a pleasure, or a definition of what is enjoyed, the *pleasure* that is enjoyed? Secondly, taking the enjoyment of food as an example, is the unimpeded exercise the exercise of the capacity to be nourished, or the exercise of the capacity to be aware of being nourished? The possible answers to these questions give us four possible interpretations of Aristotle's definition:

1. What we enjoy when we enjoy food (e.g.) is unimpededly being nourished.
2. Enjoying food is unimpededly being nourished.
3. What we enjoy when we enjoy food is unimpededly perceiving our being nourished.
4. Enjoying food is unimpededly perceiving our being nourished.

The exercise of the capacity to be nourished is to be nourished, a change in the body from one condition to another. If this were what Aristotle's definition intended to identify with either enjoyment or what is enjoyed there would be a serious problem. For then what is defined is a change whereas Aristotle argues that pleasure is not change but another kind of event: an activity. Changes are spread out over time and thus take time to complete, developing through distinguishable stages. But in *Nicomachean Ethics* X.3-4 Aristotle argues that pleasure is an activity, which is not spread out over time and, unlike a change, is complete as soon as it exists. This suggests that 1 and 2 should be rejected as interpretations of Aristotle's claim.

Another point that must be taken into account is that Aristotle regularly speaks of enjoying changes such as housebuilding. We might say this shows that in denying that pleasure is a change Aristotle is denying that enjoyment is a change, not that what is enjoyed is a change. However, Aristotle nowhere clearly distinguishes the questions 'what is enjoyment?' and 'what is it that we enjoy?'.

Previously Taylor thought that the solution was to maintain that Aristotle does not distinguish the questions, that the exercise of a capacity is sometimes an activity and sometimes a change. Under the description 'the exercise of the capacity to build' every change is also an activity, and it is under that description that the event is enjoyed. However, this idea, that it is *qua* the exercise of the capacity to build that the event is enjoyed, is also absent from the text.

David Bostock proposes instead that Aristotle divides human pleasures into two broad types, pleasure in thought and pleasure in perception. Both thought and perception are activities, and Aristotle's references to taking pleasure in changes should be understood as references to the pleasure in perceiving changes. Then Aristotle rejects theses 1 and 2 and accepts either 3 or 4. Bostock affirms 3 and maintains that perception and thought are always the objects of enjoyment, but the textual evidence is compatible with 4 and the identification of pleasures with perceptions and thoughts.

In the case of the pleasure to be found in the good life, does Aristotle think that the virtuous agent enjoys being aware, in thought and/or perception, of acting virtuously, or is the enjoyment to be identified with the thought and/or perception of acting virtuously?

Nicomachean Ethics VII identifies pleasure with unimpeded activity, while Book X does not speak in those terms but rather identifies pleasure as something that supervenes on activity. This change may reflect an 'increased awareness' by Aristotle of the difference between the questions of what is enjoyed, and what is enjoyment. The Book VII account will apply to both, while if Aristotle had come to see enjoyment of an activity as a kind of awareness of the activity, then it would be difficult to identify the enjoyment with the activity. 'I suggest, then, that the virtuous agent is aware in thought of what the content of his or her good *proairesis* [choice] is, and in perception that the description of the action fits the content of that *proairesis*, and that those thoughts and perceptions are inseparable from the agent's enjoyment of virtuous activity' (19).

In 'The Irreducibility of the Ethical in Plato and Aristotle', Anthony Price argues that one of the lessons that Aristotle learned from Plato is that it is an error to think that the correct application of ethical concepts such as 'brave' or 'just' must be explicable in terms of value-neutral concepts. As is illustrated by the failure of the *Laches*' proposed definition of courage as 'standing fast and facing the enemy', modern day readers can take it as a general lesson of the Platonic dialogues' search for definitions of moral concepts that such definitions cannot succeed if they are framed in value-free terms alone. Unlike attitude-independent neutral and concrete terms, moral concepts involve 'attitudes whose interconnections, and significance in life, constantly provoke reflection, dissension, and revision' (29).

However, Plato's own explanation of the failure of such definitions is less general, for he is concerned above all with trying to define the virtues. Virtue is always beneficial to the virtuous person. To call an action *courageous* or *just* is to make a practical judgement that the action in question is good for the agent and hence *the thing to do*. But there is no concrete description of an action that could always in every circumstance specify what the thing to do is. So moral descriptions could not be reduced to neutral concepts.

Aristotle takes over this idea. When, for example, he defines the brave man as one 'who faces and who fears the right things and from the right motive, in the right way, and at the right time', as one who 'feels and acts according to the merits of the case and in whatever way the *logos* directs', he is giving an account of brave action whose satisfaction by any particular action can only be judged with the help of practical wisdom. It cannot be reduced to some value-free paraphrase specifying types of concrete action.

What, then, makes it the case that an action is courageous? The application of an ethical description is supervenient on the satisfaction by the action or person of a value-neutral concrete description. For example, it is because an action is the *returning of a loan* that it is *just*. For Plato, goodness is essentially tied to mathematical relations of proportion, order and harmony. As opposed to such a single 'thin' account of the good, Aristotle offers a multiple 'thick' account of the good: there is not a single property of *good*, but what it is for something to be good will vary between different categories. For example, in some case it may be that for an action to be good is for it to be brave.

Plato's and Aristotle's conceptions of ethical practice are based on the irreducibility of the ethical as well as their views of the good. The virtuous action lies in a mean between excess and deficiency and can only be identified by insight into the details of a particular situation.

Aristotle adopts Plato's belief in egocentric eudaimonism, the belief that the end for the sake of which we always act is our own happiness. But while Plato sees the Form of the Good as the ultimate good and the source of the goodness of other good things, for Aristotle it is *eudaimonia* that is the ultimate good and the source of the goodness of other things.

To close, Price questions the contrast which has been drawn by John McDowell between the positions of Plato and Aristotle on the question of how morality is to be justified. According to McDowell, whereas Plato attempts to respond to those who reject morality, Aristotle takes it for granted that his audience already accepts morality. But this is a false contrast. The *Republic*'s argument is in fact addressed to those already educated in morality. Its defence of justice is based on the claim that justice delivers an inner peace and harmony that is essential to happiness. But while Plato describes the democratic man as living a disordered life, it is a life with which the vulgar are content. Hence, the disorder of such a life which excludes the possibility of genuine happiness is not, apparently, something that can be grasped by those who are not already committed to morality. As for Aristotle, *Nicomachean Ethics* IX.4 offers a justification for morality that is externalist.

Using 'Socrates' to refer to the character that appears in Plato's dialogues, Roger Crisp argues in his paper 'Socrates and Aristotle on Happiness and Virtue' that Socrates' views on the relation of virtue to happiness in the early dialogues produced some friction within his position which led to the possible rejection of eudaimonism; and that the position of the later Aristotle returns to the eudaimonism of the early Socrates.

The early Socrates accepted both of the following claims:

Psychological Eudaimonism: each person, when acting rationally, pursues her own perceived greatest happiness.

Rational Eudaimonism: each person has strongest reason to pursue her own greatest happiness.

People believe that it is worthwhile to pursue their own good, and so we can explain their actions in terms of pursuit of their own good. That is why Socrates adopts eudaimonism.

Socrates also accepts moralism, the view that virtue is a constituent of happiness. Though happiness has other constituents as well – for example, health – Socrates still believes that virtue on its own is sufficient for happiness. The value of other goods is trivial in comparison to the value of virtue, but their presence may increase happiness.

While some have tried to weaken Socrates' claim that nothing bad can happen to the good person, Crisp thinks such a dilution is unwarranted. The good man may lose health or other goods, but the gods will be sure to compensate the good man for such a loss by future good things which at least match in goodness the earlier evil. Thus, it is always best for a person to choose justice.

We should distinguish between

Monistic Rational Eudaimonism: Each person has ultimate reason only to pursue her greatest happiness,

and

Pluralistic Rational Eudaimonism: Each person has an ultimate reason to pursue her greatest happiness, alongside at least one other ultimate reason.

Socrates accepts the pluralistic version of rational eudaimonism, for he believes that both divine commands and morality are two sources of ultimate reasons for action. This opens up the possibility of conflict between one's ultimate reasons for action. But Socrates believes that, in fact, the reasons for action deriving from these different sources will not conflict with one another since obedience to god is virtuous and god directs an agent to his greatest good.

While Socrates agrees with egoists such as Thrasymachus that it is rational to pursue one's own happiness, he thinks that they have failed to appreciate the importance of virtue for happiness – that virtue is sufficient for happiness and nothing else is good without virtue.

If one were to put a greater emphasis than Socrates does on the importance of non-moral goods for happiness, then rational eudaimonism might require one to do what is immoral in pursuit of one's own happiness. In response one could say that non-moral action would not be recommended by rational eudaimonism because it would lead to punishment by the gods which would outweigh any value in the goods secured by immoral action. One never sacrifices by doing what is virtuous.

But the internal tensions in Socrates' own position emerge in the case of the philosopher-rulers in Plato's *Republic* who sacrifice themselves in agreeing to do what is just by ruling. And if this sacrifice were to be compensated for later by the gods, it would seem that it could only be by providing them with contemplation in the after life. But they could have expected to be able to engage in contemplation after death in any case. Here then we appear to have a clash between rational eudaimonism and the demands of justice, where justice requires self-sacrifice.

The views of the early Aristotle are similar to those of Socrates: he is committed to moralism and pluralism about happiness, and agrees that there are non-eudaimonistic reasons for action based on the interests of other people. As the *Republic* allows for the possibility of self-sacrifice, so Aristotle's position makes it possible that action based on concern 'for others and not oneself' (*Rhetoric* 1367a5) may be a case in which justice requires self-sacrifice.

But the later Aristotle, like the early Socrates, rejects the possibility of morality conflicting with happiness. The *Nicomachean Ethics* retains his commitment to Psychological Eudaimonism and Rational Eudaimonism. How would he respond to a rational eudaimonist such as Thrasymachus who claimed that vicious behavior can be in an agent's self-interest? While Aristotle retains Socrates' moralism he rejects pluralism: happiness is virtuous activity alone and the only good. Since there are no goods other than virtuous behavior there are no goods that could be secured by engaging in non-virtuous behavior.

It is not clear what Aristotle would say about the case of the philosopher's descent into the cave. Contemplation is an exercise of a virtue and therefore a moral constituent of happiness. If so, Aristotle might allow that philosophers could justly refuse to rule since contemplation would be moral behavior. But this is consistent with claiming that in the world as it is the mixed life is better than the life of contemplation. Then the philosopher sacrifices nothing in agreeing to participate in politics. Happiness is the exercise of virtue, and both contemplation and virtuous action count as exercises of virtue. There is nothing for virtue to conflict with.

Since non-eudaimonistic reasons are grounded on virtue, Aristotle can allow such reasons yet retain rational eudaimonism and the position that it is always best for the agent to choose virtue.

In the *Republic* Plato argues for certain claims about the relation between virtue, non-moral goods and happiness, including:

> *The Comparative Thesis*: From the point of view of happiness, virtue is always to be chosen over all non-moral goods, individually and collectively,

and

The Dominance Thesis: Virtue is the dominant component of happiness: it is always to be chosen over every other component of happiness, individually and collectively.

These are theses for which Plato argues in the *Republic* in response to Glaucon's challenge to prove that justice pays. Surprisingly, Aristotle has little to say about them directly. In his paper, 'Glaucon's Challenge: Does Aristotle Change his Mind?', Terry Irwin examines the *Magna Moralia*, the *Eudemian Ethics* and the *Nicomachean Ethics* in order to tease out Aristotle's position on these questions. For each treatise he considers what it says about (1) happiness, (2) magnanimity and (3) self-love. On all of these topics, he says, we can see that each treatise is committed to a consistent view regarding Glaucon's challenge, and, further, we can see that Aristotle' position changes over time.

Magna Moralia. (1) Here Aristotle rejects the view that virtue is sufficient for happiness since he thinks that happiness is a comprehensive good including non-moral goods as well as virtue. Since virtue does not guarantee the presence of other goods, virtue is not sufficient for happiness. Nor does Aristotle affirm that virtue must always be more important for happiness than non-moral goods. The Comparative and Dominance Theses are not affirmed by Aristotle.

(2) Magnanimity is the virtue that determines the virtuous person's attitude to external evils. It is reasonable to think that the *Magna Moralia* rejects Socrates' view that ill fortune is a matter of indifference as long as one is not oneself responsible for it. In rejecting this Socratic attitude as appropriate to magnanimity, Aristotle could be understood to reject the Comparative Thesis and the Dominance Thesis.

(3) Understanding the self-lover as someone who 'does everything for his own sake in things that concern expediency' (*MM* 1212a29-30), it is the vicious person and not the virtuous person who is a self-lover. When it comes to choosing the fine, however, it is the virtuous person who loves himself most. But this shows him to be a lover of the good, not a self-lover, since he will love himself only insofar as he is good. He is above all a lover of the good, which is not necessarily identical with his own good.

This entails the rejection of the *Eudaimonist Thesis*, the claim that I only have sufficient reason to do what is just rather than what is unjust if I will be happier by doing what is just rather than what is unjust.

Eudemian Ethics. (1) Defining happiness as living virtuously, happiness also requires completeness. Hence, virtue is not sufficient for happiness since it is complete only with external goods. But nothing is said to commit Aristotle one way or the other on the Dominance Thesis.

(2) The magnanimous man achieves large scale successes deserving much honour and requiring the possession of the external goods needed for success. Nothing is suggested about magnanimity and one's attitude to ill fortune. The question of whether the just person who suffers dishonour would be better off if he were less just and received more honour is not discussed, so nothing is implied about the Comparative Thesis or the Dominance Thesis.

(3) There is no discussion of self-love in *Eudemian Ethics*, but it commits him to a rejection of the *MM*'s account of self-love. For it adopts eudaimonism, saying that the rational agent posits happiness as the goal guiding all his actions. This is not consistent with the non-eudaimonist account of self-love found in *MM*.

Aristotle does not accept that the just person is happy when tortured, so he rejects the sufficiency of virtue for happiness. And there is no affirmation of the Comparative Thesis since he does not suggest that the tortured virtuous person is happier than the vicious person who is not tortured.

The *Nicomachean Ethics*. (1) Aristotle claims that happiness depends on external circumstances, hence Aristotle rejects the *Sufficiency Thesis*: virtue is not sufficient for happiness. He accepts the *Stability Thesis*, that one ought to do what is virtuous whatever the cost in non-moral goods. Since he accepts Eudaimonism and thinks that any rational action is the best means to securing an agent's own happiness, he is committed to the Comparative Thesis and the Dominance Thesis.

(2) The magnanimous man is calm in the face of misfortune because his character as expressed in virtuous actions is more important than any loss. The magnanimous man properly evaluates external goods, and does not regard them as of great importance. But neither are they of *no* importance. So Aristotle rejects the Sufficiency Thesis in favour of the Dominance Thesis.

(3) Viciousness is such a wretched condition – the vicious man cannot be a friend to others or even himself – that we are always better off in choosing virtue over vice, whatever the result may be with regard to external goods. This commits Aristotle to the Dominance Thesis.

Irwin concludes that the evidence suggests that in the *Nicomachean Ethics* Aristotle changes his mind about the Comparative Thesis and Dominance Theses and, unlike in the *Magna Moralia* and the *Eudemian Ethics*, agrees with these claims from Plato's *Republic*.

In the *Philebus* Plato investigates the question: what is *the* good for human beings, what is it in a life that makes that life happy? Plato argued that it could not be identified with any constituent of human life by appealing to the criteria of finality and self-sufficiency which, in his view, the good must satisfy. In 'Plato and Aristotle on "Finality" and "(Self-)Sufficiency"' John Cooper argues that Aristotle, in seeking to identity the good, uses criteria based on those of finality and self-sufficiency from the *Philebus*, but uses them to draw a conclusion directly contrary to the conclusion of Plato.

In *Philebus* 20b-23b it is argued that neither pleasure nor reason can be identified with *the* good because neither, on its own, is sufficient or the most final good. Both a life of reason without pleasure and a life of pleasure without reason would need (*prosdein*) something further to be a life worth choosing: the life of reason would be devoid of pleasure and the life of pleasure would be devoid of reason. This shows that both pleasure without reason and reason without pleasure – by lacking a good – would not be 'sufficient'. Hence, for either sort of life there would be a further end beyond what it had, and hence neither life would contain the final good. Only a mixed life containing both goods would be worth choosing and contain the good. Taking a life to be constituted by activities and experiences, the *Philebus* concludes that the good cannot be identified with constituents such as reason or pleasure. Rather, the good is identified with a property of a life, the beautiful and truthful way in which the constituents of a life are harmonized.

While building on the argument of the *Philebus*, Aristotle also modifies the criterion of sufficiency in such a way that a very different conclusion is the result. The unqualifiedly final end, Aristotle explains, is one that is worth choosing for itself and never worth choosing for the sake of something else. Further, the unqualifiedly final good must be, not sufficient (*hikanon*) as Plato understood that requirement, but *self*-sufficient (*autarkês*): 'on its own [it] makes life choiceworthy and lacking in nothing' (*NE* 1097b14-15), which Aristotle understands to mean 'lacking in nothing *needed for choiceworthiness*' (129). Aristotle does not believe that *eudaimonia* needs nothing further since he allows that it needs external goods – friends, wealth, etc. But it needs nothing further to be choiceworthy. Later identifying the good which constitutes *eudaimonia* as contemplative activity, Cooper asserts that, for Aristotle, it alone makes a life worth choosing, and in that sense is the most choiceworthy good. The possession of further goods does not make *eudaimonia* itself more choiceworthy, even if those goods make the life of the happy man who has them more choiceworthy as well as better. Nor is contemplative activity itself more choiceworthy when it is made better through the help of fellow-workers. As the most choiceworthy good, *eudaimonia* or contemplative activity alone determines the role of other goods in the life of the person who has them, and it is only for the sake of it that other goods are worth choosing.

Thus, Aristotle rejects the *Philebus*' inference that since the life of reason without pleasure lacks something, such a life is not worth choosing. And contemplative activity can be *the* good even though it is a constituent of a human life.

How can contemplation be seen as the greatest human good without undermining morality? We must construct an answer to this question since Aristotle himself never addresses it. Other goods are worth choosing in particular cases only in relation to contemplative activity, *eudaimonia*. It is the moral virtue of the virtuous man that determines how and when he chooses those other goods, but the value of the choice itself is higher than the value of the goods chosen. In this way moral virtue is of higher value than the chosen goods.

Since moral virtue is subordinate in value to contemplation, it follows that to be done correctly, the choice of goods must be done in the knowledge that contemplation is superior to the choosing of those goods. With this picture, there is no room for the question of whether we should omit a morally virtuous action in order to contemplate instead. On this view, 'moral virtue and contemplative virtue, and the goods that I have been calling independent, are related to one another so to speak each *en bloc*, as values of different orders or at different levels. Thus moral value is subordinated to contemplative activity as a kind of value, or in terms of the values that they are. Nonetheless, it is moral virtue, and only it, that tells us what is rationally required of us, or permitted, to do' (146).

In 'Justice in Plato and Aristotle: Withdrawal *versus* Engagement', Richard Kraut argues that in an important respect Aristotle's political orientation differs from Plato's. Whereas Plato advises his readers to withdraw from political affairs, Aristotle thinks that justice demands the opposite, the participation of the just man in politics.

Apart from fulfilling his basic duties as a citizen, Socrates played no role in the public affairs of Athens because he believed that it would have led to his death and produce no benefit for himself or the city. Likewise in the *Republic*, Plato twice points out that, in ordinary circumstances, justice requires the citizen to 'do his own' by playing no role in the corrupt affairs of politics in a democracy: it is only by destroying one's own soul that one can attain success in the political life of a city such as Athens. Salvation for one's own soul requires withdrawal. Only in the highly unlikely circumstances of Plato's ideal city would it be proper to engage in political life.

Unlike Plato, Aristotle tells his students that they must examine all political systems. And unlike Plato, Aristotle advises his readers on how to seek to improve any political situation they happen to find themselves in, even the most dire. Aristotle thereby abandons the Platonic view that the corruption of one's soul must follow from engagement with ordinary political affairs. While Aristotle retains Plato's belief that the aim of political action should be the improvement of the souls of the citizens in a city, he believes that that should be the goal of politics for *all* cities, not merely for the ideal city. Perhaps most citizens guided by most constitutions can only achieve a limited degree of virtue, but that is still a worthwhile goal. Citizens do not need to be perfected in order to be improved and benefited.

Kraut then goes on to argue that this difference between Plato and Aristotle reflects differences in their conceptions of justice. Plato's definition of justice as doing one's own in the *Republic* allows a just person to withdraw from politics whereas Aristotle's account of justice in *Nicomachean Ethics* V disallows such a withdrawal. On Plato's understanding, one can do one's own in social isolation, as when someone with a well-ordered soul refrains from eating too much cake because that would harm his body. On Plato's definition, this act of temperance is also an act of justice. Similarly a philosopher contemplating the Forms is doing what is just. Hence, Plato can say that one doing such things but not participating in politics is doing what is just, is 'doing his own'.

Aristotle takes a dismissive attitude to Plato's account of justice. He thinks that justice is a virtue that is essentially concerned with a person's relations to other people. Unlike Plato with his belief in the Forms, Aristotle does not think that there are any non-sensible objects that are just or unjust. Hence, neither can any relation we stand in to such objects be regarded as just or unjust.

Plato thought that the attempt to reform cities living under oligarchic or democratic constitutions will inevitably fail and will only lead to the corruption of the aspiring reformer's soul. So there can be no moral objection to philosophers refraining from such attempts. By contrast, Aristotle thinks that it is important to distinguish different degrees of injustice in cities, and that many can indeed be improved without threatening one's own virtue. Those who refuse to do anything to improve a city when they are in a position to do so are unjust. On Aristotle's definition the just person is lawful and equal. This last property is the ability to make correct judgements about the distribution of goods, and Aristotle assumes that this virtue operates in political contexts, such as the assembly or the law courts. The just person, then, will engage with the political life of his city.

Chapter 1

Pleasure: Aristotle's Response to Plato

C.C.W. Taylor

Aristotle discusses pleasure in the context of lively debate both about its nature and about its value, of which we have evidence in his own writings and those of others, above all of Plato.[1] For him the question of value predominates. His treatment of the topic belongs to the ethical treatises, not to his discussion of the soul and its faculties, and while both principal discussions include accounts of the nature of pleasure those accounts are subordinated to his evaluative interests; his primary concern is to give pleasure its proper place in his account of the best form of human life, and it is because that concern requires a proper understanding of what pleasure is that the account of its nature engages his attention.

Aristotle's survey of current views on the value of pleasure reveals a wide range of conflicting opinions, from Eudoxus' identification of pleasure with the good at one extreme to, at the other, the denial that any pleasure is good, either in itself or incidentally. This diversity does not lend itself to the eirenic project mentioned in *Eudemian Ethics* (hereafter *EE*) I.6 of showing that every opinion possesses some truth. While some apparent conflicts can be reconciled some theses have simply to be rejected, the best that can be done for them being an explanation of how people have come to hold them (*Nicomachean Ethics* (hereafter *NE*) 1154a21-b20). Aristotle himself is firmly committed from the outset to the view that pleasure is an inseparable attribute of the best life. The *EE* begins from the unargued claims (a) that the good is *eudaimonia* and (b) that *eudaimonia* is the finest, best and pleasantest of all things (1214a1-8). In *NE* thesis (a) is first declared to be established by universal consent (1095a17-20) and later established by an argument to the effect that *eudaimonia* alone fulfils the formal criteria of the good, viz. those of being sought for its own sake alone and of being self-sufficient (1097a15-b21). A further argument leads to the substantive account of human good as 'activity of the soul in accordance with excellence', i.e. the excellent realization of specifically human capacities (1097b22-1098a20). This is confirmed by a number of arguments to the effect that that kind of activity possesses some agreed marks of the good life; one such mark is

---

[1] For discussion see J.C.B. Gosling and C.C.W. Taylor, *The Greeks on Pleasure* (Oxford: Clarendon Press, 1982) (hereafter referred to as GT).

that the life of excellent activity is intrinsically pleasant (1099a7-28), leading to the position which is the starting-point of *EE*, that the good life is finest, best and pleasantest (1099a23-31). The thesis that the life of excellent activity is intrinsically pleasant seems partly to rest on the basic intuition that a wholly satisfactory life must be pleasant (otherwise it would lack a feature which counts significantly towards its being worthwhile), but is also supported by a thesis which is less obviously part of common evaluative consciousness, viz. that 'the person who does not enjoy fine actions is not good' (1099a17-18). Though Aristotle does say that no one would call a person just unless that person enjoyed acting justly (a18-19), it is not obvious that that is an unbiased report of actual contemporary Greek usage, independent of his own substantive view, derived from his account of the psychology of virtue and the process of habituation necessary to inculcate virtue, that it would not be *correct* to call anyone virtuous who did not enjoy acting virtuously.

Given this prior commitment to the intrinsic pleasantness of the good life, Aristotle's discussion of pleasure has two main functions. First he has to rebut arguments which purport to establish that pleasure cannot contribute to the good life, either because pleasure is bad, or because it is not good. This defensive strategy will lead him to give an account of pleasure in so far as he seeks to show that those who expel pleasure from the good life do so because they have mistaken views of what pleasure is. Further, his own account of pleasure should provide some additional positive arguments in support of the thesis that pleasure is at least inseparable from the good life.

The contents of the discussions of pleasure in *NE* bear out these suggestions. As is well known, the work contains two treatments of the topic, VII.11-14 and X.1-5, with a certain degree of overlap in subject-matter, but no cross-references, either explicit or implicit, in either direction. They are clearly two independent discussions which owe their position in the text of *NE* to the hand of an editor, possibly Aristotle himself but more plausibly a later redactor, and since *NE* VII is one of the Books common to both versions of the *Ethics*, it is generally assumed that its discussion of pleasure belongs originally to *EE*, and further that that discussion is earlier than the one in *NE* X. (I shall return to the question of the temporal relation of the two discussions at the end of this paper.) The discussion of Book VII is very largely devoted to the examination, leading to the rebuttal, of arguments hostile to pleasure, to which is appended a brief statement of Aristotle's positive view. In Book X, by contrast, the positive view is set out much more elaborately, while the anti-hedonist arguments appear as arguments against a thesis which is absent from VII, namely Eudoxus' thesis that pleasure is the good. Most of these arguments are rebutted, but Eudoxus' thesis is not explicitly endorsed, and the ensuing discussion *appears* to point rather to pleasure's being an inseparable aspect (or perhaps accompaniment) of the good than to its being the good itself.

I shall not attempt to deal with all the issues raised in these complex passages, confining myself instead to a single central issue. Both passages contain criticism of a certain view of the nature of pleasure, seen as foundational to many of the arguments hostile to pleasure which Aristotle is attempting to rebut. This is the view of pleasure as a perceived process of replenishment of a natural lack, and thereby a return from a state of deficiency, where something necessary to the proper functioning of the organism is lacking, to a state of equilibrium and thus of normal function. The terminology in which this view is stated is not always so specific as that which I have just used. At 1152b12-14 the first argument for the position that no pleasure is good is stated as follows: 'every pleasure is a perceived coming into being (*genesis*) of a natural state, but no coming into being is of the same kind as its completion, e.g. no process of building is the same kind of thing as a house'. While 'perceived coming into being of a natural state' is less specific than 'replenishment of a natural lack', the discussion of 1152b25-1153a7 strongly suggests that replenishments of lacks are at least paradigm cases of the pleasures described by the theory; the examples mentioned include cases in which nature is 'replenished' (1153a2-6), which are contrasted with cases like pleasure in thinking, where there is neither distress nor desire, 'because one's nature is not deficient' (1152b36-1153a2). (The *genesis* terminology and its application to cases of physiological deficiency recall Plato, *Philebus* 53c-54e, where the view of certain clever people that pleasure is always a process of coming to be, never a state of being, is applied to the pleasures of eating and drinking to reduce to absurdity the claim that the good life is the one devoted to those pleasures.) Similarly in Book X we have at 1173a29-b20 a series of arguments against the theory that pleasure is a process of change (*kinêsis*) and a coming into being, arguments which have some overlap with those from Book VII just mentioned. Here too the only kind of process mentioned is that of replenishment, the theory is said (b13-15) to be based on consideration of the pleasure and distress associated with food and drink (*trophê*), and the concluding argument is that the pleasures of thought etc. which involve no distress cannot be processes of coming to be 'since there has been no lack of which there could come to be replenishment' (b15-20). The evidence therefore suggests that the account of pleasure as the perceived coming into being of a natural state is not an alternative theory to that of pleasure as the perceived replenishment of a natural lack, but merely a less specific designation of that very theory.

The theory is familiar from well-known passages of Plato, notably *Gorgias* 494-7, *Republic* 585d-e and *Philebus* 31-2. The paradigm cases are those of pleasures in the satisfaction of bodily-based appetites, especially those for food, drink and sex. The *Gorgias* passage illustrates the simplest stage of the theory. Bodily appetite is either identified with or seen as arising from bodily deficiency, which is experienced as unpleasant. This unpleasant consciousness (*lupê*) prompts the agent to make good the deficiency, and the process of filling up the deficiency (*anaplêrôsis*) is experienced as pleasant. There are a number of unclarities even at this stage. First, it is unclear whether distress and pleasure are literally identified with physical deficiency and physical replenishment respectively, or are thought of as effects of those physical conditions. It is implied, though not explicitly stated, that pleasure and distress involve awareness, but it is not clear whether that is awareness of physical deprivation and replenishment, or awareness of pleasure and distress themselves. If the former, is the thought that (a) pleasure and distress are the awareness of those physical conditions, or (b) that those conditions, given that the agent is aware of them, are pleasure and distress?[2] A further set of problems arises from the assimilation of sexual desire to the model of hunger and thirst. In the latter two cases bodily desire can plausibly be seen as a response to physiological deficiency, dehydration, lack of protein, carbohydrate etc., and physiological deficiency can be identified as such by its reference to bodily functioning; without appropriate solid and liquid nourishment bodily function is impaired, and pleasure is (or is a response to) the process of restoring proper functioning. But sexual desire cannot plausibly be seen as a response to a physiological deficiency which impairs bodily functioning; either it is simply a response to a lack of sexual pleasure, in which case the physiological model loses its explanatory force, or else it is a response to a lack of sexual activity, which is itself conceived of either as a precondition of proper bodily functioning, or (perhaps more plausibly) as part of that functioning.[3]

The application of the theory to sexual pleasure can thus be seen as an extension (in one way or another) from the cases where it has the clearest application. Given one kind of extension, desire is seen in both kinds of case as a response to a deficiency, and pleasure as bound up with the making good of that deficiency, though it is only in the primary cases that the deficient items can be identified as constituents of the organism, whose mutual adjustment is a precondition of correct functioning. Given the other kind, desire is a response to deficiency in some cases and excess in others, and pleasure is a response to the restoration of equilibrium in both. A further extension is exhibited by the application to mental pleasures in *Republic* IX; as hunger and thirst are states of bodily deprivation, and bodily pleasures are the making good of those lacks, so ignorance or lack of understanding can be seen as states of mental deprivation, and the making good of those lacks in learning as mental pleasures. Here too the question arises of what it is that is lacking; is it a precondition of proper mental functioning, which would assimilate the mental case to those of hunger and thirst, or is it that functioning itself, which would rather assimilate it to the sexual case? If the acquisition of knowledge or understanding is thought of as a prerequisite of the exercise of those faculties, then the model of hunger and thirst is appropriate. But if the soul is seen as lacking understanding of some subject-matter, then making good that lack would appear to consist in coming to have that understanding, which is not a process identifiable as completed prior to the exercise of understanding. One might think of the dissatisfaction of someone trying to make sense of a complex pattern, say a visual or musical pattern; that dissatisfaction is alleviated when and only when one has come to see the pattern, and one has come to

---

[2] If (b) is the case, then awareness of physical deprivation and of replenishment is awareness of (respectively) distress and of pleasure.

[3] A more plausible theory of sexual pleasure would result if the specific notion of deficiency were replaced by the more general notion of imbalance. Sexual desire could then be seen, not implausibly, as a response to an excess of some physiological component (in modern terms a hormonal imbalance, e.g. an excessive level of testosterone), and pleasure a response to the restoration of the balance via the discharge of the excess in the process of copulation. In this case too we have an extension of the original model, though in a different direction from that suggested in the preceding paragraph.

see it when and only when one has seen it. So having come to see it is not a prerequisite of seeing it.

There are, then, some unexpected complexities in the replenishment model of pleasure, not only in its extension to mental pleasures, but also in its application to those very cases of bodily-based appetites which originally suggest it. But even setting these complexities aside, the model has a general feature which makes it particularly problematic for someone who, like Aristotle, seeks to assure the place of pleasure in the good life. For according to the model pleasure is seen as something essentially remedial, as bound up with (to use a deliberately vague expression) the process of getting rid of an imperfect and undesirable state. It seems at best an alleviation of the troubles of the human condition; consequently it is hard to see how pleasure thus conceived could have any role in the ideally good life, much less be a necessary feature of it. Hence it is not surprising to find Aristotle in *NE* VII citing arguments which rely on this model in support of the theses that no pleasure is good (1152b12-15) and that pleasure is not the good (1152b22-3).

A possible response to this objection would be to accept that the constant fluctuation of deficiency/desire and replenishment/pleasure is a necessary feature of human life. The ideally good life, envisaged as free from deficiency and its associated distress, is not a possible human life, though perhaps it might be possible for some other creature, such as a god (provided that the god is conceived non-anthropomorphically). Yet traditionally the life of the gods was regarded as blessed (*makarios*) in the highest degree, and the blessed life as supremely pleasant (*NE* 1152b5-7). If the replenishment model is accepted, either those traditional beliefs would have to be abandoned, or the model would have to be construed as a model of human pleasure only, and divine pleasure conceived as something altogether different. On either account the defence of pleasure which the model allows is comparatively weak; pleasure is not something to be hoped for or aspired to for its own sake, but is at best something to be welcomed as an amelioration of our imperfect condition.[4] And even that welcome, it would seem, should be qualified; for if pleasure is essentially remedial, arising when a deficiency is remedied, would we not do better to avoid those deficiencies in the first place than to seek to remedy them? As Socrates argues against Callicles, it would surely be the height of irrationality to seek to have an itch in order to have the pleasure of scratching it (*Gorgias* 494c-d), yet on the replenishment model that ought to be a paradigm of a pleasure. Even if one distinguishes necessary pleasures, i.e. those arising from deficiencies whose satisfaction is necessary for human life, from unnecessary, the tendency of the model will be to favour asceticism. For the strategy recommended by the model will be to remedy only those deficiencies which cannot be avoided, and any deficiency whose satisfaction is not necessary for survival can, it seems, be avoided by eliminating the desire which generates the deficiency. Thus to someone subject to sexual desire lack of sexual activity is perceived as a deficiency; but if one ceases to want sex one no longer feels the lack of it.

---

[4] Cf. Glaucon's account of justice in *Republic* II.

The replenishment model is not, then, well adapted to assure the place of pleasure in the good life. It also has some independent defects. First, as Plato had pointed out (*Republic* 584b, *Philebus* 51b-52b) many kinds of pleasures are not preceded by episodes of desire. So I can enjoy e.g. the smell of a rose, or a beautiful view, or memories of childhood holidays, without previously having desired to have, or felt any lack of those experiences. The scent is wafted through the open window, the view is disclosed at the crest of the hill, the pleasant memories simply occur to me, all without any antecedent longings. Here the phenomenology gives no support to the replenishment theory. Of course that does not refute the theory, since not all deficiencies make themselves apparent in desire; I may suffer from vitamin C deficiency without any desire to take vitamin C (or indeed without any awareness of the deficiency). But if the replenishment theory is not supported by the phenomenology in these cases, the onus must be on the proponent of the theory to show why the cases are best described in terms of the theory. In the vitamin C example physiological theory enables us to identify the deficiency independently of phenomenology; proper bodily functioning requires a certain level of vitamin C, and failure to maintain that level reveals itself in various symptoms, which may have nothing to do with desire for substances containing vitamin C. But in the cases of pleasure cited above nothing analogous allows us to identify any unfelt lack; why should we suppose that my delight in the scent of the rose is prompted by the making good of a deficiency of which I was unaware, however that deficiency is to be identified (on the problem of identification see below)? One might perhaps adopt that theory as the best explanation, or, at the extreme, in default of any other possible explanation; both strategies require examination of possible alternatives, and a more careful examination of the replenishment model itself.

Earlier we saw that the most plausible application of that model to sexual pleasure was the following: the model postulates that sexual activity is necessary to a worthwhile life, and consequently explains the experience of the lack of it as unpleasant, and the experience of the making good of that lack as pleasant.[5] In this case the notion of lack or deficiency is derivative from that of worthwhile activity, indeed the lack is precisely the lack of a worthwhile activity. Now while we should not expect any single answer to the question 'What makes an activity worthwhile?', it seems undeniable that one feature which makes at least some activities (to some extent) worthwhile is that those activities are enjoyable, and equally undeniable that sex is worthwhile at least partly because it is enjoyable. It follows that we do not give a complete account of sexual pleasure by describing it as the making good (or as arising from the making good) of a lack of sexual activity. For the perception of the absence of sex as a lack presupposes that sex is seen as worthwhile, and it is seen as worthwhile at least partly in so far as it is seen as enjoyable. So even in such a central

---

[5] Here the postulation is that of the theorist who is seeking to explain why humans and other animals find sex pleasant. The subject, whether human or non-human, which experiences pleasure need not (and in the non-human case presumably does not) itself endorse or even entertain that postulation. Instead the theory has to include the further postulation of a natural nisus towards a life satisfactory or worthwhile for creatures of that kind, such that the lack of conditions necessary for that life is experienced as unpleasant.

case as that of sexual pleasure, the deficiency/replenishment model presupposes a prior account of what it is that makes sex enjoyable. This is so even in the case of a sort of pleasure which is typically preceded by an episode of felt desire. The necessity of such an account is even more clearly apparent in the kinds of case considered above, where there is no preceding desire. And given such an account, the positing of an unfelt lack appears quite otiose. For what is that supposed lack a lack of? Either it is just a lack of pleasure, in which case the 'theory' reduces to the tautology that pleasure is the making good of a lack of pleasure, or else it is a lack of whatever it is that makes e.g. smelling the rose pleasant (alternatively, a lack of whatever that pleasure consists in). But in that case the explanatory work is being done by that account, whatever it is, not by the posited lack. Aristotle's own response to the deficiency/replenishment model can be seen as making this point.

That model now appears to have got things the wrong way round. It seeks to give a general account of pleasure via the notion of making good a deficiency, but in most cases the deficiency can be specified only as a deficiency of pleasure, or as a deficiency of whatever features it is in virtue of which things are pleasant. In a few cases indeed, but only a few, the deficiency can be specified independently of pleasure, e.g. hunger and thirst, to which we might add what might be classified as addictive pleasures, e.g. the pleasures of nicotine, alcohol and other drugs. In the case of the first two effective bodily functioning demands an appropriate level of nutrition; in the addictive cases an acquired habit leads to a situation in which a given level of the drug is demanded. In either type of case deficiency is experienced as a craving, and the making good of the deficiency is experienced as the pleasure of satisfying the craving. It is important to distinguish the peculiar nature of addictive pleasures from non-addictive pleasures in the same kind of object; the pleasure of satisfying a craving for alcohol is distinct from the simple enjoyment of alcoholic drinks, as is made clear by the fact that either kind of pleasure may be experienced without the other. Addictions, and consequently addictive pleasures, are pathological, a manifestation of the malfunctioning of the organism. In fact there appear to be comparatively few non-pathological pleasures which the deficiency/replenishment model actually fits; in addition to the pleasures of satisfying hunger and thirst the pleasure of getting warm when one has been cold is the one which springs most readily to mind.

This suggests that the theorist who wishes to defend the status of pleasure as a necessary constituent of the good life has two options. Such a theorist, we assume, will not seek to defend pathological pleasures. They have no role in the good life, and the explanation of the way in which they are pleasant, and why they are, will presumably reveal them to be a special case, perhaps counted as pleasures because of some resemblances to the normal or standard case. For the standard case itself one alternative open to the theorist is that of recognizing two irreducibly different kinds of pleasure, one of which fits the deficiency/replenishment model, and has comparatively few members, the other, which does not fit that model, containing all the rest. The other alternative is that of devising a single account which applies to all. Aristotle chooses the second alternative.

On this account the factor common to all pleasures is the exercise of natural capacities in appropriate conditions. The basic idea is that pleasures are appropriate to the different species of animals; every species has capacities for activities which constitute its specific life, and when those capacities are exercised (i.e. when the corresponding activities are undertaken) in the appropriate conditions their exercise is pleasant to the individual member of the species (*NE* 1176a3-8). So since it is constitutive of the life of some kinds of dogs to chase hares, when the conditions for chasing are appropriate (e.g. both dog and hare are healthy, the ground is not too rough, the scent is good) then the dog will enjoy chasing the hare.[6] Human life is constituted by the capacities shared with animals, growth, reproduction, nutrition, perception and locomotion (the first three also shared with vegetables), with the addition of the specifically human capacity for thought; hence some human pleasures, notably those in food, drink and sex, are kinds of pleasures which animals also enjoy, while intellectual pleasures are specific to humans. Pleasures are common only at the generic level; thus animals of every kind enjoy food and sex, but each kind of animal enjoys its specific kind(s) of food, while rejecting the kinds which other species enjoy, and each kind enjoys sex only with members of its own species. Again, non-human animals enjoy the exercise of perceptual capacities only instrumentally (e.g. the lion enjoys the scent of the deer as a sign of its approaching meal (*NE* 1118a16-23)), whereas humans enjoy them intrinsically; i.e. aesthetic enjoyment is a specifically human kind of pleasure.

This analysis has the advantage of applying as well to cases which fit the deficiency/replenishment account as to those which do not. Taking our previous cases as examples of the latter, the exercise of the sensory capacities (smell and sight) and of memory are constitutive of specifically human life, and will therefore be in appropriate circumstances pleasant. (On the problems of identifying appropriate circumstances see below.) The principal problem in the application of the deficiency/replenishment analysis to intellectual pleasures was that that analysis applied straightforwardly to the pleasure of acquiring knowledge or understanding, but not so straightforwardly to the pleasure of exercising those capacities. That problem now disappears, since both kinds of intellectual activity are characteristically human. Turning to the cases of the pleasures of satisfying hunger and thirst, the crucial point is that those drives belong to a natural pattern of animal activity, which, since humans are a species of animals, is *ipso facto* part of the natural pattern of human activity. Unlike addictions, hunger and thirst are not pathological conditions; on the contrary, they are essential elements in the proper functioning of the animal's capacities to seek and acquire nourishment. There is something wrong with an animal which is not hungry when it is short of food or not thirsty when dehydrated (if the cat refuses to eat or drink for days on end you take it to the vet), and also with an animal which wants food when it is not hungry or drink when it is not thirsty. Satisfying one's hunger and slaking one's thirst are perfectly genuine cases of pleasure; the crucial point for Aristotle is that they count as such in so far as they fall under the general classification of the appropriate exercise of natural capacities.

---

[6] It is not clear whether this analysis would commit Aristotle to agreeing with the hunting lobby that hares etc. enjoy being hunted; if not, it must presumably be because fear inhibits the pleasure which the prey would otherwise feel in exercising its specific capacity for flight.

The point that on the Aristotelian analysis the pleasures of satisfying hunger and thirst are genuine pleasures is worth emphasizing, since it brings out a divergence between Aristotle and Plato. At *Republic* 583c-585a Socrates argues that the great majority of bodily 'pleasures', viz. those which involve the replenishment of some deficiency, are not in fact pleasures at all; they are rather processes of escape from distress, which people mistake for genuine pleasures through lack of experience of the latter. Again at *Philebus* 44a-b a similar view is attributed to 'people who are said to be very expert about nature', and is given qualified approval by Socrates. Plato appears to accept this argument as showing that genuine pleasure must be free of any element of distress, since later in the *Philebus* (51e-52a) Socrates admits the pleasures of learning among genuine pleasures subject to the proviso that 'they do not involve any actual hunger for learning, and that there is no distress from the start through hunger for knowledge'.[7] The claim that most bodily 'pleasures' are not in fact instances of pleasure, since in those cases the process of getting rid of the distress arising from bodily deficiency is mistaken for genuine pleasure, appears to embody a confusion. Even if it is granted (i) that the state of bodily deficiency (e.g. hunger) is unpleasant and (ii) that the state of having got rid of that deficiency (e.g. having satisfied one's hunger) is neither pleasant nor unpleasant, it does not follow that the process of transition from the state of deficiency to the state of repletion is not really pleasant.[8] Aristotle's analysis allows him to escape this error; the process of transition from deficiency to repletion is the process in which the nutritional capacity is appropriately exercised, and is therefore standardly pleasant. Equally, the analysis points away from the mistaken belief that states of repletion (as distinct from processes of replenishment) are neutral between pleasure and pain. For those states are as much part of the pattern of the exercise of natural capacities as are the processes which give rise to them, and are therefore, like the latter, naturally experienced as pleasant.

The attractions of this analysis, given Aristotle's project of vindicating the claims of pleasure to a place in the best life, are obvious. Since the best human life consists in the excellent exercise of specifically human, i.e. rational capacities, it follows immediately from the analysis that that life must be, not merely pleasant, but intrinsically pleasant, i.e. pleasant just in virtue of being the kind of life that it is; 'their life (i.e. the life of those who exercise rational capacities excellently) has no need of pleasure as a sort of adornment, but it has pleasure in itself' (*NE* 1099a15-16). At the same time the wide diversity of human capacities and activities, answering to a corresponding diversity of human interests, gives a ready explanation of the diversity of kinds of pleasure, and of the observation that what is pleasant to

---

[7] Trans. J.C.B. Gosling, *Plato* Philebus (Oxford: Clarendon Press, 1975).

[8] In fact both (i) and (ii) are highly questionable. Not all cases of bodily deficiency are unpleasant, first because in some cases the person who has the deficiency is not aware of it, and secondly because even when one is conscious of the deficiency, moderate degrees of hunger and thirst, particularly when one expects to satisfy them within a fairly short time, need not be experienced as unpleasant. And states of having satisfied desires grounded in bodily deficiencies, such as being replete having been hungry, or being warm having been cold, are paradigms of pleasant states.

one person may be unpleasant or neutral to another. Capacities are developed to different degrees in different individuals; so someone with a gift for mathematics will naturally enjoy doing mathematics, whereas for someone whose mathematical capacity is undeveloped the activity will be burdensome.

Though appealing, the analysis faces some major problems. Perhaps the most pressing is this. Pleasure is or arises from the exercise of natural capacities in good or appropriate conditions, but it is problematic whether it is possible to identify appropriate conditions without including among them the condition that the activity is pleasant to the agent. If so, the analysis is viciously circular. Some of Aristotle's formulations do indeed expose him to this criticism. Thus he asserts that 'To each person that kind of thing is pleasant which he is called "a lover of", e.g. a horse to the horse-lover, and a spectacle to the lover of spectacles' (*NE* 1099a8-10). Of course it is a truism that people enjoy the kind of things they are keen on, but it is a truism because it is at least a necessary condition for being keen on something that one should enjoy the activities appropriate to that thing. And if being keen on a certain activity is one of the conditions necessary for undertaking that activity in good or appropriate conditions, and thereby for taking pleasure in that activity, then it follows that pleasure itself is one of the necessary conditions for pleasure.

Aristotle might reply that it is possible to identify good or appropriate conditions independently of pleasure, by appeal to the notion of the natural functioning of the species. Thus if a certain species is naturally adapted to eat a certain kind of food, he might claim that a healthy individual of that species will enjoy nutritious samples of that food, provided that there are no interfering factors such as cold, fear or contamination of the food; this view is suggested, though not explicitly spelled out, at *NE* 1176a3-9. But that claim is open to counter-examples; a diet might be perfectly nutritious but unpalatable, perhaps because the ingredients are lacking in flavour, or because it palls through lack of variety. Aristotle might attempt to deal with these counter-examples by appeal to his principle that, in cases of pleasure (as generally in cases of perceptual appearances), the criterion of truth is how things seem to the *spoudaios*, the person in good condition (*NE* 1099a21-4, 1113a29-33, 1166a12-13, 1173b22-5, 1176a16-19). So, just as we count honey as really sweet because it tastes sweet to the healthy person, even though it may taste bitter to someone who is ill, we judge the pleasantness of the nutritious diet by how it tastes to the person whose appetite itself is healthy, not pampered or jaded. But this move makes it clear that the analysis can be protected against the possibility of counter-examples only at the price of circularity. For if you do not count as having a healthy appetite unless you enjoy healthy food, then the claim that healthy food is really pleasant because it tastes so to the person with a healthy appetite is self-guaranteeing, because vacuous.

The variety of human tastes and interests reinforces this difficulty. Aristotle counts pleasure in the exercise of the senses as a paradigm of human pleasure. Since for him sense perception is the realization of a sensory capacity by its appropriate object, sensory pleasure requires that both the capacity and the object should be in good condition. On the side of the capacity the requirement is that the sensory apparatus should be functioning well, while on the side of the object the requirement is variously expressed: 'every kind of perception is exercised on a perceptual object, and the perfect exercise is that of perception in good condition exercised on the finest (*kalliston*) of the objects falling under the perception' (*NE* 1174b14-16); ... 'in the case of each kind of perception the best exercise is that of the one in best condition exercised on the best (*kratiston*) of the objects falling under it' (b18-19); ... 'there is pleasure of every kind of perception, and also of thought and speculation, and the pleasantest is the most perfect, and the most perfect is the pleasure of the faculty in good condition exercised on the best (*spoudaiotaton*) of the objects falling under it' (b20-23). The problem is to understand what Aristotle means by the quoted adjectives, 'finest' and 'best'. The requirement that the sensory apparatus be working to perfection seems naturally matched by the requirement that the object be such as to stimulate perfect exercise, e.g. that perfect sight be stimulated by maximally visible objects (in terms of Aristotle's theory, colours). But that condition is manifestly insufficient to guarantee that the perception is pleasant; as Anthony Kenny memorably points out 'the most sensitive nose in the world put in front of the most powerfully smelling manure in the world will not necessarily find the experience pleasant'.[9] Nor need the absence of pleasure be attributed, as Kenny's example might perhaps suggest, to the sense's being overpowered by the object, as the eyes can be dazzled by too bright light; an object might be maximally visible or smellable, i.e. most clearly detected by the sense over the widest range of conditions, without the perception's being pleasant. But if the finest and best objects are not the maximally perceptible objects, what are they? It is tempting to suggest that they are the most beautiful objects, but 'beautiful', unlike the Greek *kalon*, has natural application only to the objects of sight and hearing. It is hard to know how to understand 'beautiful smell', 'beautiful taste' and 'beautiful tactile sensation', unless 'beautiful' is understood as 'delightful', in which case the object's being fine and good is not independent of its being pleasant. Aristotle's thesis is clearly intended to apply to all the sense modalities; so the object's being *kalon* or *spoudaion* is its being fine-looking, fine-tasting etc.; and the difficulty that those attributes are not applicable independently of the percipient's pleasure in the appearance becomes general. Clearly, it will be hopeless to appeal to the judgement of the *spoudaios* to determine which sensory object is *spoudaion*. For the analysis of sensory pleasure requires that both faculty and object should be in good condition; but if the object's being in good condition just is its seeming pleasant to the person whose faculties are in good condition then its being in good condition is identical with its being pleasant, and so cannot be part of the analysis or explanatory account of its being pleasant. Further, either the good condition of the sense-faculty includes its judging the right things pleasant, or it does not. If the former, the account is doubly vacuous, since one can neither identify good objects without appeal to a faculty in good condition, nor vice versa. But if the latter, then the account breaks down. For it is clearly possible that two people with perfect hearing, as measured by auditory testing, might disagree on which sounds are pleasant and which unpleasant, one adoring the bagpipes and detesting church bells, the other hating the former and loving the latter.

---

[9] *Action, Emotion and Will* (London: Routledge & Kegan Paul; New York: Humanities Press, 1963), 149.

Such diversity can be accommodated within a general account of pleasure as (arising from) the exercise, in good conditions, of the activities characteristic of the species only by the acknowledgement that it is characteristic of humans, unlike members of other species, to have different interests and preferences from one another, with the consequence that the description of good conditions for the exercise of the activity must include the condition that that exercise satisfies the agent's preferences, interests etc. That is not to revert to the deficiency/replenishment account of pleasure, since a preference or an interest is not a deficiency. Preferences etc. can indeed give rise to deficiencies. Thus a keen sailor obliged to live far from suitable water is likely to find life frustrating. But in that case the deficiency presupposes the preference, and is identified in terms of it; one lacks what one needs (viz. accessible water) in order to satisfy one's preference (viz. for sailing), and in consequence of that lack one's life is lacking something (viz. sailing) required to make it satisfactory. It is not the case, as the deficiency/replenishment account maintains, that the preference is either the deficiency itself, or the awareness of the deficiency. The moral is that neither the notions of deficiency and replenishment nor those of activities proper to members of a species offer a reductive account of pleasure. Any account of pleasure must make room for notions of wanting, preference, interest etc., but those notions do not offer the prospect of reduction, since pleasure itself figures in any account of them. (Being keen on sailing involves enjoying sailing, being pleased at the prospect of a sailing trip etc., subject to all the usual qualifications.)

At *NE* 1153a12-15 Aristotle sums up his rejection of the deficiency/replenishment account of pleasure in these words: 'Therefore it is not correct to say that pleasure is a perceived process of coming into being; rather one should say that it is the actualization of the natural state, and instead of "perceived" one should say "unimpeded"'. I take the requirement that the actualization should be 'unimpeded' to sum up the absence of obstacles, both internal and external, to the exercise of the capacity in appropriate conditions. That exercise could be 'impeded' by the inappropriate condition of the object, e.g. unpalatable food, or by the inappropriate condition of the subject, e.g. anxiety, loss of appetite, or both. Understanding 'unimpeded' in this broad sense, I take Aristotle to be offering as an improvement on the replenishment account the account of pleasure as the unimpeded actualization of a natural capacity. Thus understood his account raises two interrelated questions. First, is it an account of what we enjoy, or take pleasure in, or is it an account of what enjoyment is? That is to say, is Aristotle saying that what we enjoy is always the unimpeded exercise of a natural capacity, or that enjoyment (= pleasure) is the unimpeded exercise of a natural capacity? Secondly, what unimpeded exercise is he talking about? Taking the enjoyment of food as an example, is he talking about the unimpeded exercise of the capacity to take in nourishment (the nutritive capacity) or of the unimpeded exercise of the capacity to be aware of taking in nourishment, a perceptual capacity, perhaps to be identified with the sense of taste or of touch (see below)?

In advance of answers to these questions we have four possible interpretations of Aristotle's account:

1. What we enjoy when we enjoy food is unimpededly taking in nourishment.
2. Enjoying food is unimpededly taking in nourishment.
3. What we enjoy when we enjoy food is unimpededly perceiving taking in nourishment.
4. Enjoying food is unimpededly perceiving our taking in nourishment.

We must, of course, allow for the possibility that the account is undifferentiated between some (or conceivably all) of these alternatives. Thus if Aristotle does not distinguish between an account of what is enjoyed and an account of what enjoyment is, then (1) and (2) would collapse into one another, as would (3) and (4). That would apparently present a straight choice between an undifferentiated account of the pleasure of food as the unimpeded exercise of the nutritive capacity and an undifferentiated account of it as the exercise of a perceptual capacity. But if the former presupposes awareness of the exercise of the nutritive capacity as a necessary condition of pleasure (i.e. enjoying food/what we enjoy when we enjoy food is unimpededly taking in nourishment, provided that one is aware of doing so) the gap between the two rival accounts is narrowed.[10] Another possibility is that Aristotle does distinguish between an account of what is enjoyed and an account of what enjoyment is, and offers both. Thus (1) and (4) above are not only consistent with one another, but together offer a reasonably plausible comprehensive account of enjoyment and its objects; generalized it would claim that what we enjoy is the unimpeded exercise of natural capacities, and that enjoyment is the awareness of that exercise.

There is a well-known difficulty confronting the attribution of theses (1) and (2) to Aristotle. This is that absorbing nourishment is a process (*kinêsis*) which goes from a beginning to an end through a series of stages, takes time to complete, is not complete till it is over, can be interrupted and takes place quickly or slowly. But in *NE* X.3-4 Aristotle argues that none of those marks of processes is true of pleasure, which is something whole and complete, like sight; the point is that pleasure, like sight, is complete as soon as it has occurred, unlike processes such as building which approach completion in a series of stages and achieve it only when the process is over. Hence at least by the time of writing *NE* X Aristotle appears firmly committed to the thesis that no pleasure is a *kinêsis*, and hence to rejecting theses (1) and (2). As regards Book VII, though the arguments for that conclusion are lacking, Aristotle appears to accept the conclusion itself; for he asserts (1153a9-12) that pleasures are not processes of coming to be (nor do all involve any such process) but activities and an end-state (sc. the state in which a process of coming to be is completed), and that they occur not when something is coming to be but when something (sc. a capacity) is utilized. A few lines later (a15-17) he says that the reason that people think that pleasure is a coming to be is that they think an activity is a coming to be, whereas they are different. So here, as in Book X, it appears that no pleasure is a *kinêsis*.

---

[10] Cf. n. 2 above.

This result in turn faces an equally well-known difficulty on the other side, viz. that at various places Aristotle speaks either explicitly or implicitly of processes such as building, writing and calculating, which are plainly *kinêseis* by the criteria of *NE* X.3-4, as things which are enjoyed (1173a15, b30, 1174a6, 1175a12-17, a34-5, b18). A possible way out of this difficulty relies on the distinction between theses (1) and (2) above. In these cases what is enjoyed is the process carried out in the appropriate conditions; so the devotee of building enjoys unimpeded building. What is denied in both discussions of pleasure is not that claim about what is enjoyed, but the corresponding claim about what enjoyment is, in this case the claim that enjoying building just is building unimpededly. Given that denial, and the positive claim that pleasure is not (a) *kinêsis* or *genesis* but (an) *energeia*, the enjoyment of building would have to be some *energeia* supervening on the building itself, perhaps perception or awareness of the building, as suggested in thesis (4).

An obvious objection to that way out of the difficulty is that Aristotle nowhere explicitly distinguishes the two questions 'What is enjoyment?' and 'What kinds of things do people enjoy?'. A fortiori, he never points out that the insistence that pleasure is never a *kinêsis*, but always an *energeia*, applies to the first question only, and that in at least some cases one correctly answers the second question by citing some *kinêseis* such as building or assimilating nourishment. Throughout he presents the discussion as if there were a single question 'What is pleasure?', to which 'Pleasure is (a) perceived *genesis/kinêsis*' and 'Pleasure is (an) unimpeded *energeia*' are conflicting answers. The distinction of question (1) from question (2) (as of (3) from (4)) is not, then, grounded directly in the text; it emerges from a process of sympathetic interpretation, as a distinction which offers Aristotle a way out of a difficulty. Hence if that difficulty can be resolved by an interpretation which remains closer to the text, by avoiding the appeal to that distinction, that interpretation is to be preferred.

In GT we propose an alternative solution, which has at least the advantage of not requiring the distinction of questions (1) and (2). There is a single undifferentiated question, 'What is pleasure?', to which the unitary answer is 'Pleasure is the unimpeded exercise of capacity'. Thus the pleasure of thinking is the unimpeded exercise of the capacity to think, and of building the unimpeded exercise of the capacity to build. Some capacities, such as the capacity to see, are exercised in acts which are themselves *energeiai* by the criteria of X.4 (and also by the grammatical criteria of *Metaphysics* IX.6). Others, such as the capacity to build, are exercised in acts which are *kinêseis* by those criteria, since every act of building proceeds by stages, is not complete till it is over etc. But every stage in the process of building is also an exercise of building capacity (i.e. an *energeia*), and it is under the latter description that it is enjoyed. Hence the answer to 'What is enjoyed in building?' is 'The unimpeded exercise of building capacity', and the answer to 'What is enjoying building?' is 'Enjoying building is exercising building capacity unimpededly'.

David Bostock dismisses this suggestion, saying that 'it is completely obvious that this is not Aristotle's view of the matter'.[11] Aristotle, he maintains, makes it quite

---

[11] 'Pleasure and Activity in Aristotle's *Ethics*', *Phronesis* 33 (1988), 251-72. The quotations

clear both in *NE* and in *Metaphysics* that walking and building simply are processes (= *kinêsis*) 'no matter what one's motive might be for undertaking' them. (The question of motive is obviously irrelevant; an act of walking is an exercise of the capacity to walk irrespective of one's motive for walking.) Bostock apparently takes the fact that these simply are processes as sufficient to establish that it cannot be the case that they are enjoyed qua exercises of their respective capacities. But he gives no argument for this conclusion, nor is it clear how it is supposed to follow. It would, of course, follow if 'simply are processes' implies 'are processes and nothing else, hence not exercises of capacities'; but it is abundantly clear from Aristotle's general account of capacities and their exercise that that is simply false. Walking, building etc., and in general things that people do, are all exercises of capacities. We still require an argument to establish that it cannot be Aristotle's view that it is qua exercises of capacities, not qua processes, that they are enjoyed.[12]

Bostock's dismissal of this view is therefore too swift. Stronger reasons for scepticism are provided by considerations similar to those applied above to the distinction between theses (1) and (2), viz. that the thesis that processes are enjoyed not qua processes but qua exercises of capacity is also extraneous to the texts, and is simply imported to resolve a difficulty. After all, the use of the 'qua' terminology (in its Greek original *hêi*) is a standard piece of Aristotelian technicality. If what he means is that the process of building e.g. a house is enjoyed not qua building a house but qua the exercise of the capacity of building, why should he not say precisely that? As above, sympathetic interpretation should be subordinated to fidelity to the text. Bostock's own solution of the difficulty can justly claim superiority in that respect, since it is closely based on the text. His claim is that Aristotle thinks that there are just two kinds of specifically human pleasure, viz. pleasure in thought and pleasure in the exercise of the senses. These are *energeiai* by the various criteria of *NE* and *Metaphysics* IX, and are listed among the examples of *energeiai* in the latter passage (1048b23-4, 33-4). What are loosely described as pleasures in or of activities such as eating or building are in fact pleasures in or of the associated thoughts and perceptions. The following quotation expresses the central point (271):

> We do, of course, speak of enjoying eating and drinking, just as we also speak of enjoying building, or writing, or hosts of other things which Aristotle will say are processes. But in all cases, as I interpret him, his view is that the place where the pleasure is to be found is in the associated thoughts and perceptions. Thus the builder may enjoy seeing his wall go up so straightly and so cleanly, as he may also enjoy the feel of the trowel in his hand, and the bodily sensations produced by the effortless exercise of his muscles. He may also enjoy first anticipating and then

---

are from 262-3. See also his *Aristotle's Ethics* (Oxford: Clarendon Press, 2000), 160-65.

[12] One might defend Bostock by arguing that Aristotle holds that, while one indeed exercises the capacity to build, the building and the exercise of the capacity to build are two distinct (though presumably spatio-temporally concurrent) entities, in modern terminology distinct events, not, as I have assumed, one entity with two non-equivalent descriptions. I know of no evidence justifying the attribution to Aristotle of such a theory, but cannot pursue the question here.

contemplating the completed building. In these thoughts and perceptions there may be pleasure, but *not* in the actual process of building. And Aristotle's fundamental thought here is that pleasure takes place in the mind, but one can hardly say this of building, any more than of eating and drinking.

In support of this claim Bostock points to the fact that the account of pleasure in *NE* X.4, which is said to make clear what sort of thing it is (1174a13-14), is in fact an account of the pleasures of perception and thought (1174b14-26, b33-1175a1). As he points out, in that chapter Aristotle ties pleasure closely to life (1175a10-21); it is significant that the examples of the activities which constitute life are thought and hearing (sc. hearing music), since this section thereby illustrates Aristotle's claim at 1170a16-19 (repeated more emphatically at a33-b1) that human life consists primarily in perception and thought. One might add the fact that the discussion in X.5 of the different kinds of human pleasures is introduced by the remark that the pleasures of thought are different from those of perception, and the different kinds of pleasure (sc. of thought, of perception, or perhaps of both[13]) from one another (1175a26-8), which suggests that no other kinds of pleasure need to be considered.

Another passage which supports Bostock's analysis is the account of *sôphrosunê* (temperance or moderation) at *NE* III.10. The virtue is a proper disposition towards the pleasures of food, drink and sex. Its sphere is delimited via a classification of pleasures first into 'psychic' (exemplified by the pleasures of ambition, learning, and telling and listening to stories) and bodily, and then via a division of the latter. The principle of classification of bodily pleasures is according to the various senses. The pleasures appropriate to *sôphrosunê* are distinguished from those of sight (the examples cited are pleasures in colours, shapes and drawing), hearing (pleasure in music and acting) and smell, allowing them to be identified as pleasures of touch and taste; Aristotle actually says 'these (sc. pleasures) are touch and taste' (1118a26). In the case of intemperate people taste is of little or no importance, the pleasures not only of sex but also of food and drink being ascribed to the sense of touch. Taste is important for the discrimination of flavours, but the intemperate are not at all interested in flavour, but merely in the tactile sensation of swallowing; hence the greedy man who wished that his gullet were longer than a crane's 'since he enjoyed the touch' (1118a26-b1). It is possible that in this passage Aristotle characterizes not merely intemperate enjoyment, but all enjoyment of food, drink and sex as pleasure in bodily sensations, specifically sexual sensations and the sensation of swallowing.[14] He thinks that these are particularly discreditable forms of enjoyment because they

---

[13] All the manuscripts agree in reading 'the pleasures of thought differ in kind from those of perception'. Following these words they vary between 'and themselves from one another', 'and these from one another' and 'and these themselves from one another'. On the first reading pleasures of thought are referred to, on the second and third pleasures of perception. The best sense would be 'and pleasures of either kind from one another', which may be what Aristotle meant, but which is not confirmed by any manuscript.

[14] He does say that all enjoyment of food, drink and sex arises from touch, but he is discussing the enjoyments of the intemperate person, and it is possible that the force of 'all' is 'in all such cases' (i.e. all cases of intemperate enjoyment), rather than 'in all cases whatever' (1118a29-32).

are common to humans and other animals (1118b2-3); this point, which applies to every case, not merely to that of the intemperate, may suggest that the account of these pleasures as pleasures in bodily sensations is also general. Whatever is the truth on that particular point, the main interest of the chapter as a whole for our present discussion is in its confirmation of the thesis that Aristotle regards the fundamental classification of human pleasures as that of pleasure in or of thought on the one hand and in or of the exercise of the senses on the other.

The application of this analysis to the four possible accounts of the enjoyment of food listed above yields the result that Aristotle definitely rejects (1) and (2), and accepts either (3) or (4), or an undifferentiated thesis covering both. In the particular case of food, the tactile sensation account suggested in III.10 favours thesis (3); Aristotle looks to be saying that what we enjoy is having certain tactile sensations, the having of which is itself an exercise of the sense of touch. Yet it does not follow that what we enjoy is not eating, but just a sort of perception. Rather, what is enjoyable about eating, on this (bizarre) view, is the sensation of swallowing; to put it another way, the way we enjoy eating, according to Aristotle, is by enjoying the sensation of swallowing.[15]

If we generalize this result to the problematic cases of enjoyment of activities like building, we arrive at a reductive account, not of enjoyment itself, but of its object; enjoyment of building is just enjoyment of perception of and thought about building, as sketched in the quotation from Bostock given above. But Bostock takes the upshot to be that pleasure is in these thoughts and perceptions, not in the actual process of building, on the ground that Aristotle thinks that pleasure takes place in the mind, whereas building does not. But he produces no evidence that Aristotle thinks that pleasure is 'in the mind' in a sense which is inconsistent with one's literally enjoying building. Of course pleasure is not in the body, as Aristotle points out (1173b9-11), but then neither is building in the body. Building is something which an embodied agent does, and sensory pleasure is also an attribute of an embodied agent. Rather than accept Bostock's contention that pleasure is in the builder's thoughts and sensations and not in the process of building itself, we should say that the pleasure which is in the builder's thoughts and sensations is the builder's pleasure in the process of building itself. After all, what else could pleasure in the actual process of building be, than the pleasure that is in the builder's thoughts and perceptions?

But now we are confronted by the crucial ambiguity of the expression 'pleasure in the builder's thoughts and perceptions'. This may be construed as 'enjoyment of the builder's thoughts and perceptions'. On that construal, the notion of enjoyment remains primitive, and the account of pleasure consists in the reductive account of its object; enjoyment of building just is enjoyment of the builder's thoughts and perceptions. But the expression can also be understood as 'enjoyment consisting in the builder's thoughts and perceptions'. On this construal, unlike the other, we are

---

[15] For a fuller discussion of this point see my article 'Urmson on Aristotle on Pleasure', in J. Dancy, J.M.E. Moravcsik and C.C.W. Taylor (eds.), *Human Agency: Language, Duty, and Value. Philosophical Essays in Honor of J.O. Urmson* (Stanford: Stanford University Press, 1988), 120-32.

given an account of what enjoyment itself is, viz. certain kinds of thought and perception. For the builder to enjoy building is for him to see the wall going up straight and cleanly, to feel his muscles moving effortlessly, to think of all this as something worth doing, etc. We may recall how Aristotle moves in *NE* III.10 from speaking of enjoying the objects of sight and hearing (*chairontes tois dia tês opseôs, tois peri tên akoên*) to the statement that the pleasures with which *sôphrosunê* is concerned are touch and taste. That might of course be understood as the claim that they are the pleasures of touch and taste, but equally it can be understood literally as the claim that those enjoyments are exercises of those senses. And we should also recall that the discussion of X.4, which is to make it clearer what pleasure is, starts by explaining that seeing, unlike a process, is complete at every moment of its existence, and goes on to show that pleasure shares that characteristic. It is certainly possible, and perhaps even natural, to take this as making a point, not about the objects of pleasure, but about pleasure itself, namely that in a crucial point it is like seeing.

The texts which favour Bostock's account, then, at least leave it open that Aristotle is attempting to provide an account of pleasure as consisting in thought and perception, or that his theory is undifferentiated between that and an account of what is enjoyed as thought and perception.[16] This issue affects the crucial question of how Aristotle's account is supposed to apply to the virtuous agent's pleasure in his or her virtuous activity, which is crucial, as we have seen, to virtue and the good life. Does Aristotle think that what the virtuous agent enjoys is being aware, in thought and/or perception, of acting virtuously, or that his or her enjoyment of virtuous action just is his or her awareness, in thought and/or perception, of acting virtuously, or is his view undifferentiated between the two?

The nearest I can come to answering this question is to offer the following tentative suggestion. Notoriously, the discussion of Book VII appears to identify pleasure with unimpeded activity, whereas that of Book X avoids that identification, preferring to describe pleasure as something which perfects activity in a special way 'as a sort of supervening perfection, like the charm of those in their prime' (1174b32-3). My suggestion is that this change may reflect an increased awareness on Aristotle's part of the distinction between an account of what is enjoyed and an account of what enjoyment is. The 'unimpeded activity' formula straddles the two, whereas if Aristotle had come to a clearer conception of pleasure in an activity as a sort of awareness of that activity, he would be reluctant to identify it with the activity itself, while yet seeking for a way of characterizing the inseparability of the awareness from the activity. An additional attraction of the idea of pleasure as awareness, divided into thought and perception, is that it is applicable to all pleasures, including cases where the object of pleasure is nothing but thought or perception itself. For Aristotle, thought and perception are self-intimating; we are aware of thought by or in thinking, and of perception by or in perceiving (*De Anima* 425b12-25, *NE* 1170a29-33), while in the case of other activities thought and perception are

---

[16] Bostock himself explicitly leaves these questions open at the conclusion of his paper ('Pleasure and Activity in Aristotle's *Ethics*', 272).

the means by which we are aware of doing them.[17] I suggest, then, that the virtuous agent is aware in thought of what the content of his or her good *proairesis* is, and in perception that the description of the action fits the content of that *proairesis*,[18] and that those thoughts are inseparable from the agent's enjoyment of virtuous activity. But whether they are that enjoyment, or its object, or undifferentiated between the two I am unable to determine.

This suggestion has an obvious affinity with G.E.L. Owen's celebrated thesis,[19] but is not a mere restatement of it. Owen sees the discussions of Books VII and X as simply directed to different questions, the former to the question of what is really enjoyed or enjoyable, the latter to the question of what enjoyment is. Moreover, the methods of the two discussions are different; the former proceeds by looking for some feature common to everything which is enjoyed, the latter by reviewing the logical characteristics of pleasure-verbs. On the alleged difference of method, I adhere to the criticism of Owen's view in GT.[20] On the content of the two discussions I agree with Owen in detecting a shift, but identify the shift differently. For Owen the two discussions are directed to quite different questions, and it is then puzzling why those questions are expressed in the same words 'What is pleasure?'. I see the two discussions as stages in the articulation of a single enquiry. In each case Aristotle is

---

[17] According to GT the distinction between Books VII and X is terminological only. Both share the same substantive view of pleasure as the unimpeded, i.e. perfect, actualization of capacity, but whereas that view is expressed in VII as 'pleasure is unimpeded activity', the thought in X is that pleasure is the perfection in virtue of which the unimpeded activity is perfect, or in other words the formal cause of its perfect actualization (249). That suggestion now seems to me less plausible. If Aristotle's point is one which requires to be expressed by means of his own terminology of kinds of cause, and specifically via the notion of a formal cause, it is mysterious why he does not employ that terminology. The 'charm of those in their prime' appears to be a simile intended to elucidate a relation (between pleasure and the activities enjoyed) which eludes literal exposition in standard terminology.

In rendering Aristotle's *tois akmaiois hê hôra* as 'the charm of those in their prime' I revert to the traditional understanding of this expression as referring to the visible aspect of the perfection of those in the prime of life, normally translated 'the bloom on the cheek of youth'. GT, pointing out that that sense of *hôra* is secondary to its primary sense of 'season', which is then extended to that of the right season, the springtime of life, render, in conformity with their interpretation of pleasure as the formal cause of perfect activity, 'the springtime of youth for those in their prime' (212). As the Greek phrase may bear either sense, the rendering must be determined by one's overall interpretation of the context.

[18] For instance, the agent is aware in thought that his/her *proairesis* is to eat a portion of chicken qua healthy food, and via perception that this food on the plate is a portion of chicken (*NE* 1147a3-7, b9-17). The agent's knowledge of what he or she is doing thus combines direct awareness of his or her intention with perceptual knowledge of whether and how that intention is realized.

[19] 'Aristotelian Pleasures', *Proceedings of the Aristotelian Society* 72 (1971-2), 135-52; reprinted in J. Barnes, M. Schofield and R. Sorabji (eds.), *Articles on Aristotle 2. Ethics and Politics* (London: Duckworth, 1977), 92-103, and in G.E.L. Owen, *Logic, Science and Dialectic: Collected Papers in Greek Philosophy*, M. Nussbaum (ed.), (London: Duckworth, 1986), 334-46.

[20] See ch. 11.3.

addressing the question 'What is pleasure?', because the answer to that question is a precondition of the correct evaluation of pleasure. But Aristotle's question is itself ambiguous between 'What do we enjoy?' and 'What is enjoyment?', and my suggestion is that the discussion of Book X shows some indication, absent from Book VII, that Aristotle had moved towards separating those questions. If that is correct, it favours the prevalent (though not universal) view that the discussion in Book VII is the earlier.

Reply to C.C.W. Taylor

Sarah Broadie

Christopher Taylor's paper provides a very clear and full discussion of Aristotle's account or accounts of pleasure, with attention to the context of Academic debate. I shall confine my remarks to just a small number – three, in fact – of the many interesting issues he covers, together with a fourth which he does not deal with here.

(1) He begins by observing that, while Aristotle is interested in both the nature of pleasure and its value, the question of value predominates. The evidence for this seems to be twofold. First there is the fact, to which Taylor draws attention at the outset, that Aristotle discusses pleasure only in his works on ethics, not in his treatises of theoretical psychology. This strongly suggests that Aristotle is interested in pleasure as a phenomenon having a certain nature only to the extent that grasping this nature leads to a correct understanding of pleasure's place in ethical life. Secondly, there is the fact, which Taylor brings out well, that even if we allow for developments and changes of emphasis and possibly of doctrine in Aristotle's views about pleasure, the views turn out, to our eye, strangely vague and unfinished by analytic standards. This encourages one to suspect that Aristotle may not even be trying to be as philosophically scientific about pleasure as we might have wished – a failure which might be explained by supposing that for him the only worthwhile questions about pleasure are the ethical ones. The most striking defect of his approach is the failure to formulate a distinction between a pleasure as something – some activity, perhaps – which we enjoy, and pleasure in the sense of our enjoyment of it. Almost equally striking is the failure to be clear on how cognition enters in: is what I enjoy the activity of perceiving something or thinking about something, or is it rather that I enjoy all sorts of things that are not my cognition or thought, such as someone else's joke or some mountain scenery? In Aristotle's defence it might be said that the lack of these distinctions does not stand in the way of his doing what he is concerned to do, i.e. find a *via media* between ethical enmity towards pleasure and ethical hedonism. What is more, his efforts in this direction are strongly shaped by the particularity of actual dialectic already on the table. His results are original, but are reached within a framework set by others. Hence his failure to register certain rather elementary distinctions may simply be due to the fact that, in addition to his not needing them to pursue his ethical agenda, no one else had made them in the debate so far. And that may have been simply accidental. One can imagine a piece of dialogue going like this:

What kinds of things do you call pleasures (*hêdonai*) then?

Oh, things that I enjoy (*hêdonai*), like hunting, shooting, fishing, listening to music and talking philosophy.

But these pleasures of yours don't give pleasure to everyone; in fact, they don't always give you pleasure when you take part in them, do they?

That is so. But then other people have different pleasures, such as drinking, dicing and gossiping; these things give them pleasure, and they give me pleasure too sometimes, when other things don't.

But now consider this: hunting is sometimes a pleasure and sometimes not, but surely the pleasure you get when you do enjoy hunting is not sometimes pleasure and sometimes not?

No, of course not; how could it be?

So if hunting is (a) pleasure, it is (a) pleasure in a different way from the way the pleasure you get from hunting is (a) pleasure.

As I said, one can imagine something like this argument, which, whether completely valid and perspicuous or not, brings out the distinction between a pleasure as what one takes pleasure in, and the pleasure one takes. But such an argument seems not to have been lurking in Aristotle's background.

(2) I now want to turn to Aristotle's view that 'the sort of person who does not delight in fine actions does not even qualify as a person of excellence: no one would call a person just who failed to delight in acting justly, nor open-handed if he failed to delight in open-handed actions' (*NE* 1099a17-20, trans. Christopher Rowe). The language leaves it open whether the actions are those of the one who delights in them, or of others. But the context makes clear that it is one's own good conduct in which one is supposed, if virtuous, to delight, and throughout I shall take the point to be this. Now, as Taylor observes, it is not obvious that Aristotle gives an unbiased report of contemporary Greek usage. He may, Taylor suggests, be assuming that usage conforms (or in fact he may be telling us that it should conform) to what must hold if his own theory of the acquisition of moral excellence is correct. Aristotle could also, however, be leaning on a point made in the Academic debate on pleasure, i.e. Eudoxus' point that pleasure (*hêdonê*) added to any other good such as just or moderate conduct – these were Eudoxus' examples – makes it better (*NE* 1172b23-25). The fairly obvious assumption that no one's conduct is better than that of the virtuous person then yields the doctrine that one cannot be virtuous unless one takes pleasure in the corresponding actions. If this is where the doctrine comes from, then perhaps it was thanks to Eudoxus that Aristotle arrived at the distinction between virtue and continence. Certainly there is little sign that he was helped towards it by Plato.

But what are we to make of the claim that the virtuous person takes pleasure in good actions? If one states it using '*chairein*', it can be taken as saying that the good person acts as he does readily, unreluctantly. This is uncontroversial if it means that if A does reluctantly some kind of good thing which B does readily, *ceteris paribus*, then B more than A has earned the title 'virtuous'. And this point may be sufficient to yield the distinction between virtue and continence in connection with the kind of good action envisaged. But understood in this way, the point is consistent with the view that some kinds of good actions are such that, although human beings are regularly called upon to do them, even the virtuous agent does them reluctantly. One might now argue that where such actions are concerned, one who does them readily, *ceteris paribus*, is that very rare phenomenon, the agent of superhuman or divine virtue. (Cf. *NE* VII, 1145a18-29, although there, it must be admitted, Aristotle introduces superhuman virtue not by analogy as standing to virtue as virtue to continence, but as an extreme condition corresponding to the opposite extreme of brutishness.) But the task of Aristotle's *politikos* is to promote virtue, not superhuman virtue, as the essential basis of the happiness it makes sense for human beings to aim for; and it is the connection between non-superhuman virtue – or, rather, non-superhumanly virtuous activity – and happiness that Aristotle is trying to defend when he claims that no one would call a person virtuous who does not delight in fine actions. Aristotle is responding, of course, to the possible objection that whereas pleasure is obviously bound up with happiness, his own account of happiness seems to overlook pleasure. The response, to be effective, must imply that it is typical of good actions in general that the virtuous agent does them with pleasure.

If we take 'with pleasure' to mean 'readily, unreluctantly', then what we have is a strong condition on who is to count as a virtuous agent, given that the dictum is to apply to virtuous actions across the board. It is surely more stringent than what common sense would insist on, but perhaps we can hail this as a reasonable (and non-superhuman) ideal of virtue. Even though the courageous man registers the pain and destruction of combat for what they are, so that perhaps on some levels (that of the psycho-physical organism, and that of a basically un-bloodthirsty human being[1]) his every fibre is in revolt against these horrors, we easily grant that on another level nothing in him holds back from the actions he has to take.[2]

If, on the other hand, we take 'with pleasure' to mean that the agent enjoys what he is doing, or, as we might say, has a good time doing it, then the claim is, I believe, ethically grotesque and conceptually flawed. It, however, is what has to be true in order to constitute a sound response to the complaint that Aristotle's definition of happiness fails to provide room, in happiness, for pleasure. I have to confess that I do not see with clarity why the claim appears to me ethically grotesque, and I suppose I may come to realize that it is not (the sense of 'with pleasure' being kept constant). Let me, however, try a simple argument to show at least that it is conceptually flawed.

I suggest, first, that the question whether someone φs reluctantly or readily ('willingly', in a non-technical sense of that word) applies not only to doings or actions, but also to emotional reactions, to feeling distressed, and to enjoying something. Shame provides obvious examples. If I am ashamed of my anger, or of being pained at hearing of a decent neighbour's good luck, I may be experiencing

---

[1] Cf. *NE* 1177b9-12.

[2] The fact that we easily grant it suggests that this is not the point Aristotle labours to make at 1117a34-b6; hence that there he means that courageous action is carried out 'with pleasure' in the sense distinguished in the next paragraph.

the emotion or the distress every bit as much as someone who has it without qualms. Certainly with some kinds of anger one could conceive of measuring the intensity of particular episodes by measuring some physical effect, and it might well be that by such a measure the degree of anger is the same. Clearly, being ashamed or having some other sort of qualm about the response could result in one's trying to dampen the response, but the point being made has to do with the agent's pre-dampened state. Surely it is the same with enjoyment. I can be as we say 'unhappy with myself' at enjoying something I enjoy, perhaps because I consider it in bad taste or because enjoying it shows me that I am disloyal or malicious or no better than a lot of other people whom I affect to despise. Alternatively, I can enter into my enjoyment with complete willingness and self-approval. It would be a mistake from an Aristotelian point of view to describe this as my enjoying my enjoyment of the first order activity (such as the activity of contemplating someone else's good fortune). For, firstly, the *NE* VII account recognizes no distinction between a pleasure or enjoying and the enjoyed activity itself; hence on the suggested description willingly enjoying an activity logically collapses into simply enjoying the activity. But in that case there is no logical room for feeling qualms, e.g. of shame, at enjoying the activity and surely Aristotle ought not and probably would not wish to rule this out as impossible. Secondly, the *NE* X account puts enjoyment and what is enjoyed into different categories: the latter is an activity, the former a 'supervenient perfection' grounded in the activity (1174b31-3). This, I think, rules out going on to treat the enjoyment itself as something which is enjoyed. Therefore enjoying something unreluctantly (i.e. *chairôn*) is not the same as enjoying it. Consequently, behaving well unreluctantly may be a necessary feature of the virtuous agent, but it is a mistake to infer from that that he or she gets pleasure from behaving well.

Someone might complain that this argument, in postulating the possibility of reluctant pleasure, goes against Aristotle's linkage of pleasure with absence of impediment. I do not see that it does. The unimpededness necessary for pleasure is of the activity enjoyed. Not every factor that casts a shadow over the pleasure impedes the activity. If the activity is impeded, there is no pleasure; but in the cases relevant to the argument, there is pleasure but one wishes there were not.

(3) Taylor brings out the strengths of Aristotle's view, in particular its power to save the *endoxon* that pleasure belongs in the good life. He argues, however, that it faces major problems, the worst of them being (he suggests) one of circularity. The view is that 'pleasure is or arises from the exercise of natural capacities in good or appropriate conditions'; but Taylor doubts 'whether it is possible to identify appropriate conditions without including among them the condition that the activity is pleasant to the agent'. He concludes that unless this doubt is settled (and he argues that it cannot be), 'the analysis is viciously circular' (10). Taylor's argument is this: in some kinds of case we can identify good or appropriate conditions without presupposing that the subject takes pleasure in the relevant activity. Thus good conditions for eating consist in the combination of healthy food, healthy powers of tasting, chewing and swallowing, and a degree of appetite. Good conditions for smelling consist in working olfactory organs plus a distinctly

odorous object within range. Adverting to Kenny's manure example, Taylor points out that smelling under good conditions can be unpleasant (anyway to humans), and that eating under good conditions might simply not be pleasant: for instance, the food, though healthy, might be unpalatable, i.e. such that the subject does not enjoy it. If palatability is made one of the good conditions, then we have what Taylor sees as a problem of circularity.

It seems to me that if Aristotle's view is appealing on many grounds, then one might be justified in dismissing some of the above difficulties by arguments that would seem thin if they were offered in support of a less appealing position. For instance, in the manure case one might insist that the cognitive act, sensory in nature, of discerning the smell of manure (or, if we like, of something worse) is pleasant in itself, being a moment in the creature's active aliveness, and that what is unpleasant about it is the association with filth. If the smell as such is disgusting to us, one could insist that this shows that it is not in fact an appropriate object for the human sense of smell: that it is disruptive of the sentient organism.[3] (More on the notion of 'appropriate object' in a moment.) As for possibly not enjoying eating under good conditions which are specified without reference to pleasure in eating: surely Aristotle is not committed to holding that pleasure is inevitable under a complete such set of good conditions, but only to holding that it typically occurs when the conditions obtain and does so because they obtain. He does not after all have a theory of causation according to which an efficient causal connection between particulars x and y holds only in virtue of a universal and perhaps necessary connection of kinds under which x and y respectively fall.

One might, however, argue even in the exceptional case of failing to enjoy that there must in fact be something wrong with or missing from the supposed set of good conditions. And certainly this would be one's inference if the failure occurred more often. Now one is using lack of enjoyment as a sign that the conditions are not quite right. But this must be stated more accurately. It is assumed in the examples just used that what is at issue is the objective or in Aristotelian jargon unqualified goodness of subject and object considered in the context of a well-functioning human being considered in the abstract. On that assumption, lack of enjoyment is the sign that something is wrong without qualification. However, lack of enjoyment shows this only because it primarily indicates a lack of fit or suitability of subject and object for each other, i.e. that the subject is not right for such an object or the object for such a subject. Pleasure and the lack of it (in the theory of Book X) are indicators of fitness or lack of it between a certain subject and a certain object regardless of whether it is objectively or without qualification good to be a subject that gets/fails to get pleasure from such and such an object.

I agree with Taylor that in many cases, perhaps in most, we cannot specify fitness conditions without reference to resulting pleasure. Thus food suitable for a certain kind of eater must be palatable to him or her, i.e. such as to give some

---

[3] This argument is too thin, even if we want Aristotle to be right. For it is reasonable to hold that finding a filth-based smell unpleasant is exactly the right reaction to it, and that far from being disrupted the sense faculty is then working just as it should. This objection was made in discussion.

pleasure to that sort of person. Bagpipe skirling is suitable music only for someone with a taste for such sounds, i.e. who likes or gets pleasure from typical examples. This would introduce the vicious circle of which Taylor complains if one either analytically defines pleasure as what accompanies the activity of a mutually suitable subject and object, or holds that we cannot tell whether something is pleasant unless we first know that it is an activity relating a mutually suitable subject and object. But although Taylor several times calls Aristotle's account an analysis, there seems no reason to assume that Aristotle intends it as that, i.e. as the breakdown of a concept into elementary and more perspicuous ones.[4] Nor does there seem to be any reason why Aristotle should disagree with common sense that we usually simply tell by experience whether something is pleasant to us, and find out in the case of others by asking them or making ordinary observations.

It is perfectly true that 'Listening to bagpipes is pleasant to those and only those who are constituted so as to take pleasure in it' does not say a great deal. It is no good as a guide for discovering who those people are to whom listening to bagpipes is pleasant; but then we have other ways of discovering this. But this kind of statement has its uses. Insofar as we tend unreflectively to equate the pleasant with the objectively desirable, it can serve as a caution in a particular case, reminding an agent that an X's apparent objective desirability may say more about his own defective taste or character than about the X's goodness. Again, suppose it is impossible to state fully the nature of moral goodness without including the point (let us grant it for the sake of the present discussion) that the virtuous take pleasure in doing what is just, moderate, etc.: of course this does not enable us to identify just or moderate etc. actions, but the statement is useful in that it provides the rationale for a certain approach to moral education: an approach which, however obviously correct to us, has not always seemed so. This is the approach that tries to form good character not by threats and blows, but by getting the child practised in willingly doing good things.

(4) Finally, I would like to propose for discussion a question which Taylor leaves on one side in his paper, i.e. whether Aristotle does not in fact cut off the branch he is sitting on, in order to deal with Eudoxus. The two philosophers shared, as Aristotle acknowledges, the schematic premise 'The good (i.e. the *summum bonum*) is that which everything seeks'. Eudoxus interpreted 'everything' as 'all animals, non-rational and rational', and inferred that the good is pleasure, while Aristotle interprets 'everything' as 'every skill, inquiry, action and undertaking', and infers that the good is what the *politikos* aims to bring into being (*NE* 1094a1-28, 1172b9-15). Aristotle, in discussing the Eudoxan view, emphatically rejects any suggestion that 'what all things seek' might simply not be good (1172b34-1173a4). Here, he allows himself to share Eudoxus' understanding of 'everything';

---

[4] As C.C.W. Taylor pointed out in discussion, at *NE* X, 1174a13ff. Aristotle undertakes to explain, and explains, 'what' (*ti*) or 'what kind of thing' (*poion*) pleasure is. Perhaps his technical theory of definition requires him to answer the 'what is it?' question by an analysis, but his actual answer in *NE* X.4 seems to consist, rather, in a placing of pleasure in relation to the concepts of activity, process, perfection/completeness.

and he also agrees that what everything in the sense of 'all animals' seek is: pleasure. At this point, his only difference with Eudoxus is that Eudoxus holds that pleasure is the good, whereas Aristotle holds that pleasure is good, or a good.

Now it is often noted that at the beginning of the *NE* Aristotle fails to establish that there is just one ultimate end of 'everything' in the sense in play there. So far as we can tell from the scanty evidence, the same is true of Eudoxus, *mutatis mutandis*: while insisting that all animals seek pleasure, he omitted to show that pleasure alone is what they all seek. And Aristotle does not bring up this omission against Eudoxus: understandably, perhaps, since he is guilty himself of a corresponding one. Conceivably, Aristotle's 'Everything seeks' argument in *NE* I.1 is an imitation of the one framed by Eudoxus, and consequently simply reproduces its ungrounded assumption that there is only one thing that everything seeks. Certainly, Aristotle cannot be expected to worry about this weakness in Eudoxus' argument when he does not worry about it in his own. So it is as if Aristotle proceeds as if each of them is right: as if Eudoxus is justified in assuming that there is just one *telos* that every animal seeks, and he himself, Aristotle, is justified in assuming that there is just one *telos* that every human skill, inquiry, action and undertaking seeks. But now there seems to be another worry that Aristotle ought to have. Given that he accepts Eudoxus' premises, and holds that what everything seeks (in the Eudoxan interpretation of this phrase) is a good but not the good (cf. 1172b26-7), ought not Aristotle to worry that his own 'Everything seeks' argument establishes at most that the single (as he assumes) ultimate end of all human projects is not the good, but just a good?

Or does this not matter? For perhaps Aristotle could reply: 'Yes, I should have done more to show that everything in the sense of every human project seeks just one good. But if you allow me to help myself to that assumption, then you cannot reasonably object that all I am entitled to say is that this good is a good. True, this is all I am entitled to say if we just appeal to the logical form of my response to Eudoxus. It is also true that if one views things from a perspective that takes in the entire universe, the *telos* which every human project seeks is clearly only a good. For the highest *telos* of each species is no more than one good among many such goods if one considers the species all together. But even so, the one *telos* every human project seeks is unique among human practicables. So within the sphere of human life it is rightly called "the good".'

Chapter 2

The Irreducibility of the Ethical
in Plato and Aristotle

A.W. Price

I

To describe an agent ethically is to ascribe to him some virtue or vice; to describe an action ethically is to interpret it as somehow virtuous or vicious. Such description is higher-level in that mastery of the concepts it deploys involves some ability to cite reasons explaining when and why they apply. Thus a grasp of courage or justice is manifested by an ability to ground ascriptions by pertinent observations of the kind 'He is brave, for he is undeflected by danger', or 'That is just, for it is the keeping of a promise'. One might then expect to be able to analyze any ethical concept in terms of necessary and sufficient conditions that are not only lower-level but neutral, in the sense that attitudes play no part in detecting whether or not they obtain. For it may be supposed that the object of an attitude is only identifiable if it can be identified independently of the attitude, and that an ethical description is only determinate in content if it is equivalent to a description that is neutral. Otherwise, perhaps, we incur an unacceptable degree of indeterminacy (as in the early maps that shrouded most of the world in cloud). Explaining *what* one admires may require a language that is not the language of admiration, and a virtuous act may have to be of a virtuous kind that can be demarcated otherwise than *as* virtuous. Apparently, therefore, determinacy may demand a *reduction* of ethical to neutral concepts.

Among the lessons that Aristotle learnt from Plato is that these intuitions are illusions. A neutral language for explicating the object of an ethical attitude, or the extension of an ethical concept, would presumably need to be concrete: no term as abstract as 'just' or 'brave' could share its extension without being equally evaluative. An *analysans* might be pursued along the paths of complication and disjunction, but unpromisingly: any developed virtue is so variable in the behavioural forms it must assume if it is to match the varieties of circumstance that we cannot expect to be able fully to capture its content within any formulation in concrete terms applicable by human beings.[1] This is first intimated within the

---

[1] God could always ensure equivalence by a gerrymandered description, of an indefinite degree of complexity, that tracked the extension of the concept artificially. That is

Republic when Socrates objects to Cephalus that it is wrong to identify being just with telling the truth and returning what one has borrowed, for these acts are not always just (as when a borrower is asked to return some weapons by a lender who has gone mad, 331c1-d3). A more resilient participant than Cephalus might suppose that one has only to try again; but the objection falls within a pattern to which Socrates later alludes when he describes how the young can be corrupted by counter-examples to attempts to define the just or the fine by appeal to general laws or maxims (538c6-e4).[2]

Thus, when Laches attempted to define courage as a willingness 'to stand fast in the ranks and fight back at the enemy without running away' (*Laches* 190e5-6), Socrates objected by reminding him how varied the tactics are that have proved successful; also that he was not just asking about soldiers, let alone hoplites (190e-191e). Equally, it transpires, temperance cannot be identified with a quiet or gentle manner (*Charmides* 159b1-160d3), nor with shame (160e3-161b2), nor courage with endurance (*Laches* 192b9-d9). We need to add that the endurance is wise – but in what sphere of operation (192d10-193a2)? One way out is by a special kind of vagueness: perhaps justice is giving all men their due (*Republic* 331e1-4), and temperance is doing one's own things (*Charmides* 161b3-6). But such paraphrases remain within a moral circle, and do nothing to satisfy the expectations with which we began. Thrasymachus will have no truck with glosses on 'justice' that simply equate it with 'the right', or 'beneficial' or 'advantageous'; instead, he demands that Socrates speak 'clearly and precisely' (*Republic* 336c6-d3). Yet it appears to be in the nature of the case that attempts at definition are Dædalian, running away and refusing to stay put (*Euthyphro* 11b9-c4).

We may call this feature of the virtues *uncodifiability*. In some places, Plato sees this as a source of *contestability*, which may be practical, or notional. The *Euthyphro* proposes a bold contrast between ethical judgements and others (7b6-8a2). Some questions, as about the relative sizes of numbers or weights, can be settled definitively by measurement; others, about what things are just or unjust, beautiful or base, good or evil, do not lend themselves to 'a satisfactory decision' (or 'discrimination', 7d4), and so are disputed. The distinction is best interpreted as turning not on particular judgements, but on the very concepts that they deploy. *These* are 'essentially contested' (in a well-known phrase of W. B. Gallie's)[3] in that they turn, by their very nature, upon attitudes whose interconnections, and significance in life, constantly provoke reflection, dissension, and revision. Yet in

---

uninteresting. An interesting success would produce an equivalent that was *projectible* from old instances to new ones, and held together as an intelligible or explanatory *unity* within some neutral perspective.

[2] I have learnt here from Terence Irwin, *Plato's Moral Theory* (Oxford: Clarendon Press, 1977), 43-46. Note that this falls for Plato within a still wider pattern of argument. Just as it cannot be that what makes an action just may be either that it is the returning of a loan or that it is not, so it cannot be that what makes things two may be either addition or division (*Phaedo* 97a2-b3).

[3] See Gallie, 'Essentially Contested Concepts', *Proceedings of the Aristotelian Society* 56 (1955/6), 167-98.

identifying the upshot as indignation, faction, and hostility (7c11-12, e3, 8a1-2), Socrates shows that he here has in mind not just contradiction in applying or withholding a concept, but conflict in deciding upon action. Elsewhere, he opens up a debate rather notional than practical. In the *Laches* he exploits the plasticity of the virtues by extending the sphere of courage to take in battling with desires or pleasures (191d6-e3). Yet we might well agree that such action is often right without being persuaded that it is then courageous (rather than temperate).[4] Thirty years ago, in a genuinely original essay that deserved to be seminal, Myles Burnyeat justified him as follows: 'It is typical of a virtue concept that its range should be liable to controversial extension or modification. For to state and defend criteria for collecting manifestations of a virtue is to articulate a way of grouping certain phenomena which exposes something of one's outlook on life in general'.[5]

The flexibility of values may also show up in a contrast in the *Gorgias*. Here Socrates counts health and wealth as goods, and sitting, walking, running, sailing, stones, sticks as intermediates (*ta metaxu*, 468a5) which are neither good nor evil (sc. in themselves), in that they sometimes share in the good, sometimes in the evil, sometimes in neither (467e1-468a4). When we do these we do them for the sake of good things, not wanting the things we do, but the things for the sake of which we do them (b9-c1); more exactly, we do not want to do these things 'just like that' (*haplôs houtôs*, c3), but only if they are beneficial (c2-5). One way of reading this passage is as distinguishing ends from means, but a wider application is suggested by John Ackrill's ruminations about a related passage in Aristotle's *Ethics* (*Nicomachean Ethics* 1139a35-b4).[6] Plato's contrast applies equally whether we think of walking as an instrumental means towards a goal (say, walking in order to recover one's health), or as itself a way of realizing a good (say, walking when one has promised to walk). And then the point is not only that the relation of means to end is contingent and hence variable, but also that it is variable what kind of action, from occasion to occasion, realizes some value.[7]

---

[4] The difference is not between Greek and English. For a similar extension, cf. a passage in chapter 5 of Conrad's *Lord Jim* (1900):

> [By the instinct of courage] I don't mean military courage, or civil courage, or any special kind of courage. I mean just that inborn ability to look temptations straight in the face, – a readiness unintellectual enough, goodness knows, but without a pose, – a power of resistance, don't you see, ungracious if you like, but priceless – an unthinking and blessed stiffness before the outward and inward terrors, before the might of nature and the seductive corruption of men – backed by a faith invulnerable to the strength of facts, to the contagion of example, to the solicitation of ideas.

[5] 'Virtues in Action', in G. Vlastos (ed.), *Socrates* (London: Macmillan, 1971), 209-34 at 212. However, in section II we shall find Plato later aspiring to resolve all practical indeterminacies – by measurement.

[6] 'Aristotle on Action', *Mind* 87 (1978), 595-601; also in A.O. Rorty (ed.), *Essays on Aristotle's Ethics* (Berkeley: University of California Press, 1980), 93-101.

[7] This is particularly plausible given Socrates' conception that it is acting well or badly, and not any *consequence* of action, that is supremely beneficial or harmful (see, e.g., *Crito* 30c7-10).

This thought is recurrent in Plato's mature writings. It was surely one provocative of a conception of Forms as transcending concrete properties.[8] In a famous passage of the *Republic*, Socrates asks whether there is any of 'the many beautiful things' (*ta polla kala*) that will not also appear ugly, or of 'the just things' (*ta dikaia*) that will not also appear unjust (479a5-7). It is debated whether he is thinking of types or tokens, and it can indeed be said of the individual Helen that she was a beautiful *for a woman*, but not in comparison with the gods (see *Hippias Major* 289a9-b3). Yet that fails to apply to justice (on occasion, walking can be simply just); and a later remark that 'the many opinions of the many' concerning beauty (*kalon*) and the rest roll around between being and not being (479d3-5) relates as much, if not more, to types than to tokens. Thus the thought is again present that evaluative generalizations fail. The lover of sights and sounds who cannot accept 'that the beautiful is one and the just one' (a3-5) is best understood not as denying a piece of Platonic metaphysics of which he is unlikely to have heard, but as rejecting the unity of a class of phenomena which, viewed concretely, is indeed a medley.

Thus Plato excludes a reduction of ethical description to description that is neutral and concrete. And yet there appeared initially to be reason to suppose such reduction requisite for a determinacy of content sufficient for there to *be* a content. Let us first ask how *we* might question the expectation. After that, we may consider the reasons for disappointing it that are evident in Plato, and still evidenced in Aristotle.

A general distinction that we are likely to draw between the kinds of relation in which attitudes may stand to their objects is the following. The objects of certain attitudes can be captured by descriptions that are neutral and *attitude-independent*. Such attitudes may well colour terms that are pejorative or meliorative. Thus it appears that the Greeks permitted themselves a mildly denigratory attitude towards all non-Greeks. This attitude was expressed by the term *barbaros*, whose extension was fixed by the phrase 'not Greek', but which possessed a tone or colouring (Frege's *Farbe*) uncongenial to anyone who lacked the attitude. That Persians were *barbaroi* was as much a fact, for it was the same fact, as that they were non-Greek – though only Greeks can have been happy to use the expressions *barbaros* and 'non-Greek' interchangeably. However, the objects of other attitudes can only be captured by descriptions that are *attitude-dependent*. Thus the concepts of *fear* and of *danger* are made for each other. An ability to identify what is dangerous goes with a capacity to entertain fear oneself, and to empathize with the fears of others. Of course there is a normative aspect to the concept of danger: to identify a real danger is to define a *proper* object of fear. But the proper objects of fear are apparent not to some extraneous faculty (say, an intuitive sense of the fitting), but to a capacity for fear that has been educated and refined. We can start to list

---

[8] As John McDowell wrote in 'Virtue and Reason' (1979), 'It seems plausible that Plato's ethical Forms are, in part, at least, a response to uncodifiability: if one cannot formulate what someone has come to know when he cottons on to a practice, say one of concept-application, it is natural to say that he has seen something'; *Mind, Value, and Reality* (Cambridge MA: Harvard University Press, 1998), 50-73, at 72-3.

varieties of danger in neutral language, but this exercise is governed by a sense of danger, and is not an alternative to it. Thus, when Socrates is casting doubt on any concrete paraphrase of what it is to be brave, he proceeds from imminent danger as the enemy advances across the battlefield, to other forms of attack, to danger at sea, to illness, to poverty, to danger in public life, and even to appetites and pleasures (*Laches* 191a1-e2). Here he is extending the range of the concept of danger within a quality-space within which distances are measured not neutrally but ethically. As I cited Burnyeat, he is articulating 'a way of grouping certain phenomena which exposes something of one's outlook on life in general'. Socrates' sense of danger is educated partly by attitudes that he shares with his interlocutors, and partly by an ethic of his own that is governed by Democritus' maxim (that it is worse to do than to suffer wrong). A neutral survey of his list of dangers would be multiply at a loss, unable either to detect any unity, or to identify central cases, or to assess marginal cases. Thus, *even if* the total list had a finite and surveyable limit, falling short of the marginal cases, so that it could be memorized by someone who (like the young Siegfried) didn't know what fear was, a neutral grasp of it could only be incomplete.

Such is the story that *we* are likely to tell, from the point of view of current ethical theory, to justify Plato's rejection of any reduction of ethical to non-ethical description. However, Plato's own ground is more specific, and it is one that he bequeathed to Aristotle. The justification of his position that I have just sketched goes with the conception of a class of descriptive predicates as *evaluative*, in that they have senses, determining their extension, that are attitude-dependent.[9] Plato's own focus is less general: it is upon virtue-terms (such as 'brave' and 'just'), and within the perspective of a distinctive and philosophical view of the virtues. An argument in the *Charmides* may be condensed as follows: temperance is a good since it makes men good; hence modesty (*aidôs*), which is not a virtue in everyone, cannot be temperance (160e6-161b2). If, as I take it, the term 'makes' (*poiei*, 161a8) here connotes not a causal relation but a direct and logical one,[10] this indicates that the possession of any single virtue suffices for making any man good and virtuous. It follows that every virtue is identical to every other (for it is *by* the presence of each virtue that a man counts as being virtuous in general), and that to act temperately is to act well and virtuously. This also entails a special reading of Socrates' correction of Cephalus. His point might have been that, although it is generally just to return what one has borrowed, in certain contexts returning what one has borrowed lacks that value. To which Cephalus might have replied that irresponsible action (such as entrusting an axe to a lunatic) can still have the value of justice if it involves giving something back – though the Greek term *dikaios* may well have a slightly wider sense than our 'just'. But Socrates' thought is rather the simpler one that, since it is not advisable to hand a lunatic an axe, it cannot be

---

[9] Thus David Wiggins has written of 'non-natural predicates with a distinctive sentiment-involving kind of sense'; 'Ayer's Ethical Theory: Emotivism or Subjectivism?', in A. Phillips Griffiths (ed.), *A.J. Ayer: Memorial Essays* (Cambridge: Cambridge University Press, 1991), 181-96, at 190.

[10] Sarah Broadie points out to me that *poiei* is plainly so used at *NE* 1106a19-20.

just either. On this conception, calling a practical option 'just' is not only an ethical evaluation, but a practical judgement that has prescriptive force in identifying it as *the thing to do*. Given the variability of advisable action in different circumstances, it is then transparent that the term 'just', and all virtue-terms, escape concrete paraphrase.

I call this view distinctive and philosophical. It is not plausible of *our* usage of virtue-terms, and is unlikely to be any truer to Greek usage. Gregory Vlastos adduces from Sophocles' *Philoctetes* one indicative text among many.[11] Neoptolemus, urged by Odysseus to prevail over Philoctetes by trickery, remarks of a more honest mode of proceeding that, if it is just, it is better than prudent (*all' ei dikaia, tôn sophôn kreissô tade*, line 1216). Socrates' view, by contrast, is that any act that is just is also prudent. And we can infer from the passage just referred to from the *Charmides* (160e6-161b2) why he is likely to have held this. He takes a virtue – *aretê*, after all, signifying a good state – to be an unqualified good, and not variably good and bad; hence he cannot allow that, on occasion, a soldier might act inadvisably out of courage.[12] So the assessment of an option as 'brave' or 'just' entails a recommendation. Ethical evaluations of possible acts that invoke a virtue or a vice are indeed equivalent to practical judgements.

Consequently, the failure of generalizations about how best to act in a situation of a certain kind carries over into a failure of generalizations about how to apply the language of the virtues.[13] A much later statement of the deficiency of rules comes in the *Statesman* (294a10-b6):

> Law could never accurately embrace what is best and most just for all at the same time, and so prescribe what is best; for the dissimilarities between human beings and their actions, and the fact that practically nothing in human affairs ever remains stable, prevent any kind of expertise whatever from making any absolute decision in any sphere that covers all cases and will last for all time (trans. Rowe).

---

[11] *Socrates: Ironist and Moral Philosopher* (Cambridge: Cambridge University Press, 1991), 211. There is further evidence in Thucydides. In the debate about the fate of Mytilene, Diodotus supposes, 'Whereas Cleon claims that this punishment combines justice and expediency (*to auto dikaion kai sumphoron*), it appears that in such a policy the two cannot be combined' (3.47). And, during the Melian Dialogue, the Athenians convey that it is a *fault* in the Spartans' conduct of foreign affairs that they 'consider what is pleasant to be fine, and what is expedient just' (5.105). See also, for evidence that what is just may yet be shameful, and may not be equitable (*epieikês*), passages cited by K.J. Dover, *Greek Popular Morality* (Oxford: Basil Blackwell, 1974), 190-91.

[12] Suppose, instead, that sensitivity to some other consideration sometimes leads an agent not to the brave action but to something better. Then it would appear that the virtue, or desirable state, is not courage alone, but courage as qualified by that sensitivity. (To which it might be replied that courage takes in all desirable attitudes towards danger, but not all attitudes to considerations that may arise within circumstances of danger.)

[13] Universalization, as R.M. Hare has taught us, is another matter: what ought to be done *here and now* is also what ought to be done *in any situation precisely like the present one*. Yet to specify the situation type one may need to cite a situation token, using the term 'like' to universalize but not to generalize.

It equally follows, on Plato's conception, that there can be no unexceptionable generalizations about which concrete acts constitute acting bravely, or otherwise virtuously. Virtue in action is protean.

Of course much changed in Plato's ethics between the *Charmides* and the *Statesman*. A less rationalistic psychology than Socrates', intimated in the *Gorgias* and *Phaedo* and elaborated in the *Republic*, was to leave wisdom a central directive role, while distinguishing it and other virtues (notably courage, temperance, and justice) by their relations to the multiple 'parts' of a composite, incarnate, distinctively human soul. To our present point, however, this development made little difference. Socrates' *identity* of the virtues is replaced by Plato's *unity* of the virtues: various virtues are distinguished by their roles within a composite psychology, but the presence of any one entails the presence of the others.[14] On this more complex conception, for agents to possess one virtue is for them to possess all the virtues. The same will not hold of actions themselves: a virtuous action within a context free of danger (even in an extended sense) cannot be an exercise of courage. It remains true that an act cannot be brave but unwise: predicating a virtue-term of a practical option (say by saying 'That would be brave') retains the force of a practical judgement (for it still follows, 'That is the thing to do').

Thus there emerges from Plato this line of argument: the virtues relate as a unity if not as an identity; hence a brave man, say, is also unqualifiedly a good man, and a brave action is unqualifiedly a good action; the application of a virtue-term to a practical option constitutes a practical judgement; consequently, given the variations of circumstance, the extension of a virtue-term can never be captured in concrete and neutral terms. The present relevance of this train of thought is obvious: Aristotle takes it over. Spelling this out would be describing very familiar territory. In brief, Aristotle clusters the virtues around practical wisdom much as Plato around wisdom simple. In both, wisdom, courage, and temperance are the central virtues of three divisions of the soul (for Aristotle, see *NE* 1117b18-19). Aristotle could be replying to Thrasymachus on Plato's behalf when he rejects any demand for precision (*akribeia*) in practical contexts as the mark of a lack of education (see *NE* I.3, especially 1094b12-13, 23-5). He accepts a few negative rules apparently without exception (against adultery, theft, and murder, *NE*

---

[14] Within the *Republic*, this is clearer in the case of the philosophers, who are wise, than of the auxiliaries and artisans, who are hardly wise and yet need to be just, and brave or temperate. However, I have tried to argue elsewhere that 'the unity of the virtues proper is reflected in a unity of popular virtue'; 'Plato: Ethics and Politics', in C.C.W. Taylor (ed.), *Routledge History of Philosophy Volume I: From the Beginning to Plato* (London: Routledge, 1997), 394-424 at 402-3. It is true that, within the *Statesman* itself (306a8-308b9), courage may appear to be separated from temperance, and even opposed to it. However, John Cooper may well be right to suggest that the Visitor is not talking of actual or full virtues, but of natural orientations. See 'The Unity of Virtue', in his *Reason and Emotion: Essays on Ancient Moral Psychology and Ethical Theory* (Princeton: Princeton University Press, 1999), 114-16. True virtue may require true and constant opinion about 'things fine, just and good' (309c5-7), that is, a fully reliable practical judgement.

1107a11-12), but perhaps only because the application of the terms ('adultery', 'theft', and 'murder') is contestable at the margin. He can accept positive concrete principles only with the qualification 'for the most part' (*epi to polu*). He gives a chapter within his book on justice to a virtue of 'equity' (*epieikeia*), requisite when rules are lacking or imperfect (*NE* V.10), that he takes over from Plato.[15] An act is brave if the circumstances are appropriate (*NE* 1115a28-b6), and it is such as a brave man would do (see *NE* 1105b5-7). The brave man is the one 'who faces and who fears the right things and from the right motive, in the right way, and at the right time'; for he 'feels and acts according to the merits of the case and in whatever way the *logos* directs' (*NE* 1115b17-20).[16] The brave thing to do turns out to be the right, recommendable thing to do, all things considered, in circumstances of non-commonplace danger.[17]

Of course, there are many differences as well, to some of which we must proceed. But it should stand out, within a true perspective, that there is a kernel common to the ethics of Plato and Aristotle that is in part a core of common sense (uncongenial to many other philosophers), and in part a creation of philosophy (intelligibly if contentiously correcting common sense).

II

So far, one may complain, so negative. Grant that the sense of a term for a virtue or a vice cannot be explicated in concrete and neutral terms. What then makes it correct or incorrect to apply the term in some ways and not in others? Certain broad correlations restrict areas of application: courage is shown in situations of danger, temperance in situations of sensual temptation, and so on. But what constitutes its being the case, though at times contestably, that, of two acts performed or performable in some context, *this* act is brave or temperate, and *that* is not?

Plato had, of course, a general metaphysical answer: a brave act or agent partakes of the Form of Courage, a temperate one of the Form of Temperance, and so on. Such pronouncements, however often reiterated, are not themselves more than promissory. To flesh out a theory (if that was his ambition), he needed to clarify two points.

---

[15] See *Laws* VI, 757e1-2, and, more fully, *Statesman* 294a6-295e2.

[16] 'Direct' is supplied by W.D. Ross, as it often needs to be. When he is explicit, Aristotle variably uses the verbs *tassein* or *prostassein* (see, e.g., *NE* 1114b30, 1125b35), which indicate prescriptive force.

[17] It remains a substantial issue for us whether there is a virtue of practical wisdom by which 'the right, recommendable thing to do, all things considered' can be identified. If there is, we should not resist a revisionary conception of the ethical virtues proper as a unity. For virtues can then be reconceived as dispositions to do the right thing in different contexts, each implying and implied by practical wisdom, and so each implying every other. If there is no such state, then our common conception is right to be less ambitious.

The first is the relation of such description to other, lower, levels of description. We may call this the problem of *supervenience*. We must not overstate the upshot of section I. It is indeed a mistake to try to reduce the justice of an act to its being, say, an instance of returning a loan. And yet it may well be true, in an appropriate context, that an act is just *through* being an act of returning a loan. Plato is implicitly sensitive to this. When Socrates tells us, in the *Phaedo*, that it is beauty that makes things beautiful, and not a blooming colour, or shape, or anything of that kind (100c4-d6), he reveals an awareness of relevance: we are not to give anything but Beauty itself as *the* explanation of physical beauty, and yet it may be true that Helen would have ceased to be beautiful if she had lost her complexion, or damaged her profile. Again, in the *Symposium*, when Socrates (pretending to report Diotima) assures his hearers that Beauty itself is pure and unmixed, not 'full of' human flesh and colouring and other such trash (211e1-3), he is preferring the Form to particulars whose beauty, by implicit contrast, *is* 'full of' such things. It would seem that an understanding of why one face is beautiful, and another is not, would not take participation in Beauty as a brute fact (in Elizabeth Anscombe's phrase), but would need to explain, without false generalization, how, say, one face would lose its beauty by a change of colour, when nothing else changed, another by a change of shape.

More frequently rehearsed by Platonists is the problem of *self-predication*. Socrates pronounces in the *Phaedo*, 'If anything else is beautiful besides the beautiful itself, it is beautiful for no reason at all other than that it participates in that beautiful' (100c4-6). Apparent here is that Beauty itself is beautiful, but not through partaking of itself (a reflexive relation that I think Plato would have rejected as nonsense). Yet what is the beauty of Beauty itself if it is not participation in Beauty? Perhaps there is nothing to be said beyond that it is that in virtue of which anything that partakes of the Form will be beautiful.[18] Yet such an answer surely disappoints (much like, in scientific explanation, the ascription of a disposition without any categorical base). And there is clear evidence that Plato would not stop there. For he is willing to infer, from the premise that 'soul, whatever it occupies, always comes to that thing bringing life' (105d3-4), that the soul is itself alive, and essentially so, and in a way that does not differentiate it categorially from living persons. On departing this life, it may display either 'a state of desire for this body' (108a7-8), or 'purity and moderation' (c3); so Socrates can imply that *he is* his soul (115d3-4). In the case of beauty, Plato's assumption is surely that the beauty of the Form is contagious just because the Form is so beautiful itself (rather like a fire that is so hot that it communicates heat to *anything* in its vicinity).[19] For a full appreciation of the Form, Socrates urges us to turn our minds to *it itself*, and our eyes away from *its workings* (*Symposium* 211d3-e4). What distinguishes the beauty of the Form of Beauty from that of its participants is not that it is a power, but that it is not supervenient: there is nothing

---

[18] Gail Fine calls this 'broad self-predication', in contrast to 'narrow' (*On Ideas: Aristotle's Criticism of Plato's Theory of Forms* (Oxford: Clarendon Press, 1993), 62).

[19] Compare Jonathan Barnes' 'Synonymy Principle of Causation', *The Presocratic Philosophers*, revised edn. (London: Routledge & Kegan Paul, 1982), 119.

subjacent *in virtue of which* the Form is beautiful. However, yet other problems arise with other Forms, not least with ethical ones. Take justice. It is argued that a city is just in virtue of each of its classes 'doing its own thing' (if we may make unidiomatic use of a phrase literally close to *to heautou prattein*), a soul in virtue of each of its parts doing its own thing (*Republic* 441d8-e2). We need not infer a problem for the justice of a soul-part (which lacks further parts); for the passage ends with an equation between 'being just' and 'doing one's own thing', which applies to soul-parts. Plato is implicitly contrasting the justice of a complex, which is derivative, and the justice of an element, which is primitive. However, it is unclear how the Form of Justice could 'do its own thing', derivatively or primitively; for Forms are not agents. When Socrates once remarks that Forms neither wrong nor are wronged by one another (500c3-4), he either overlooks that, or subtly brings it to our attention through the very looseness of the metaphor. What, then, is the intrinsic nature of the Form to partake of which is to be just?

I believe that Plato may have a single line of answer to both these objections. We must remember that the Socrates of the *Republic* differs no more from the Socrates of the early and so-called 'Socratic dialogues' than he does from the *Republic*'s ideal of a philosopher fully schooled in dialectic and competent to rule with authority.[20] The Socrates who was Plato's teacher was unable to move from the virtues as he knew them to the Forms; the Socrates of the *Republic* is unable, perhaps, to move from the Forms of virtues (as when he speaks at 520c5-6 of 'the true things concerning the beautiful, the just and the good' – an habitual trio, cf. 484d2) to the Forms as they really are. The true Forms are indeed paradigms of rational order, displaying *kosmos* according to *logos* (500c4-5, an implicit but immediate gloss upon c3-4), but hardly of anything more anthropomorphic. It is nothing less than the Form of the Good itself that 'is indeed the cause for all things of everything right (*orthos*) and beautiful' (517b8-c2, cf. 505a2-4). Man's distinctive mission is to manifest order within human life, our outward life that is social and our inner life that is psychological; but order itself, like the ideal Beauty of the *Symposium*, is not full of soul and city, but 'pure, clean, unmixed' (211e1). A city or soul can imitate that order through achieving internal justice; but the structure to which internal justice approximates can also be realized purely and abstractly. Plato's conception is not easy to grasp. On the one hand, the studies short of dialectic that put us in a position to begin to master it are not ethics or psychology, but mathematics and geometry. The true theoretical *principia ethica* are *principia mathematica*.[21] On the other hand, dialectic also requires a grounding

---

[20] See my 'Plato: Ethics and Politics', 417.

[21] As F. M. Cornford argued already in 1932, 'The mathematical and moral Ideas are not so sharply distinct in Plato's mind as in ours' ('Mathematics and Dialectic in the *Republic*', in R.E. Allen (ed.), *Studies in Plato's Metaphysics* (London: Routledge & Kegan Paul, 1965), 61-95, at 92). This has been more fully explored recently in an invaluable essay by Myles Burnyeat, 'Plato on Why Mathematics is Good for the Soul', in T. Smiley (ed.), *Mathematics and Necessity in the History of Philosophy* (Oxford: Oxford University Press, 2000), 1-81. Note that 'the fundamental concepts of mathematics', which he takes also to be

in practical experience. As I shall argue below, dialectical knowledge is a close relation of practical knowledge. We must suppose that, for a knower who is also an agent, a grasp of the Forms cannot be purely theoretical, but must engage with his own mode of agency.[22] If we can coherently conceive both that the Forms are not themselves inherently ethical, and yet that a human grasp of them must have an ethical aspect, we can hope to dissolve both our worries. Self-predication can become literal if the true Forms are Forms only of properties that are appropriate properties of Forms. And supervenience may become explicable once the world of Forms is revealed to contain structures that a particular object or action may imitate in one way or another either internally or in relation to its visual or practical setting. The beauty of Helen's face was not a brute fact somehow accompanying other brute facts, such as the shape of her nose, but was constituted by the proportions between the dimensions of her nose and of the rest of her face – proportions also present, but there more open to sober analysis, within geometry. And the same may be true, though more obscurely, of the appropriateness of some act to its practical context.

Aristotle concedes more credibility to such correspondences than we might expect. Early in the *Metaphysics* he insists that, since goods as ends explain action, and so change, they have no explanatory role in mathematics; 'nor is there any demonstration of this kind, "because it is better, or worse", but the mathematical sciences take no account of goods and evils' (*Meta.* 996a21-b1). And yet he later concedes that, since they demonstrate 'order and proportion and definiteness', they implicitly tell us things about the beautiful, perhaps even about the good (*Meta.* 1078a31-b2).[23] However, he insists that familiar human goods enjoy a human reality, and are to be understood in their own terms (*Eudemian Ethics* 1218a15-24):[24]

> They ought in fact to demonstrate the Good itself in the opposite way to the way they do it now. At present, they begin with things that are not agreed to be goods. For example, starting from numbers they show that justice and health are goods, on the grounds that justice and health are types of order and numbers, while numbers and units possess goodness because unity is the Good itself. They ought rather to start from agreed goods like health, strength, temperance, and argue that the beautiful is present even more in unchanging things, which are all examples of order and stability. Then, if the former are goods, a fortiori the latter must be goods, because they have order and stability to a greater degree.

But then, of course, Aristotle faces the questions that opened this section. What can he say positively about the reality of ethical values when he rejects both a

---

'the fundamental concepts of ethics and aesthetics as well', are 'concord, proportion, and order', and nothing so specifically ethical as justice or temperance (*ibid.*, 76).

[22] This holds even of Plato's gods; see, on *Phaedrus* 246a6-b3, my *Mental Conflict* (London: Routledge, 1995), 74-5.

[23] See Burnyeat, 'Plato on Why Mathematics is Good for the Soul', 79-80.

[24] The translation is from Burnyeat, *ibid.*, 78.

reduction to the neutral and concrete, and an ascent to the abstract and in some way numerical?

It would seem that both Plato and Aristotle find the notion of *the good* itself elusive, but seek to clarify it by moving in opposite directions. Plato ascends to a realm of transcendent value towards which we advance through geometry and mathematics as well as practical experience. Aristotle descends from the *thin* term 'good' to *thick* terms (in Bernard Williams's terminology). Parallel passages in the *Eudemian* and *Nicomachean Ethics* are over-concise, and have been interpreted variably (*EE* 1217b25-34, *NE* 1096a23-9; cf. *EE* 1236a7-9, *Topics* 107a3-12). *Post* and *propter* Ackrill,[25] I read these together as follows. An intuitive point is that, as Ackrill puts it in modern jargon, 'the criteria for commending different things as good are diverse and fall into different categories'.[26] Thus one thing may count as good because it is God or *nous*, another because it is just, another because it is moderate, and so on. An action may be good in that it is brave (that is *what it is* for it to be good); and we may then say that its goodness, or value, consists of courage. When the thin predication '*x* is good' is to be glossed by the thick one '*x* is brave', we can say that the goodness of *x* is identical to courage.[27]

So Aristotle holds, against Plato, that there is not, *in rerum natura*, any such single property as *being good*. This leaves him with a semantic problem: 'But what then do we mean by *the good*? It is surely not like the things that only chance to have the same name' (*NE* 1096b26-7). His response is indicative but evasive (*NE* 1096b27-31, trans. Ross):

> Are goods one, then, by being derived from one good or by all contributing to one good, or are they rather one by analogy? Certainly as sight is in the body, so is reason in the soul, and so on in other cases. But perhaps these subjects had better be dismissed for the present; for perfect precision about them would be more appropriate to another branch of philosophy.

From here and elsewhere (compare *NE* 1097a15-24, *EE* 1218a30-32), we can supply the following analogies, within two broad classes. There is (a) the good relative to an object: sight to eye, health to body, reason to soul. Then there is (b) the good relative to an activity: health to medicine, victory to strategy, house to building. Within (a), we would seem to have only analogies. Within (b), there is the possibility of an ultimate or overarching end: 'If there is an end for all that we do, this will be the good achievable by action' (*NE* 1097a22-3). Of course, (a) and

---

[25] 'Aristotle on "Good" and the Categories', in J. Barnes, M. Schofield, R. Sorabji (eds.), *Articles on Aristotle 2. Ethics and Politics* (London: Duckworth, 1977), 17-24.

[26] *Ibid.*, 21.

[27] Note that the thought is not, more abstractly, that goodness may be good substance, or good quality, and so on – which would provoke Ackrill's query whether 'the differentia of an item in one category cannot be the differentia of an item in another' (*ibid.*, 18). Within the category of quality, it makes a difference here that Aristotle accepts the unity, but rejects an identity, of the virtues. For 'good' within that category, the *Eudemian Ethics* offers 'just' as a gloss (1217b31), the *Nicomachean Ethics* 'the virtues' (1096a25). Thus the goodness of an act, or agent, consists not just in *virtue* (singular), but in (e.g.) *courage*.

(b) can intersect. Plato had counted 'harmless pleasures' (*hai hêdonai hosai ablabeis*) among things desirable in themselves, and 'thinking and seeing' (*to phronein kai to horan*) among things desirable both in themselves and for their consequences (*Republic* 357b7, c2). In a verbal allusion to that, Aristotle lists 'thinking and seeing and certain pleasures' (*to phronein kai horan kai hêdonai tines*) among things good in themselves (*NE* 1096b17-18), but objects to Plato's understanding of what that involves that 'just in respect of their goodness, the accounts are distinct and diverse' (b24-5). Viewed as effects, thinking exercises reason, which is a good of the soul, seeing sight, which is a good of the body. Viewed as causes, thinking and seeing are activities preliminary to deliberate action serving an ultimate end. For Aristotle, (a) and (b) have crucially in common that they both invite teleological explanation. Use of 'good' is in place when we can identify a final end. Thus, after mentioning other kinds of cause, Aristotle writes in the *Metaphysics*, 'The remainder are causes as the *end* and the good of the other things; for that, for the sake of which other things are, is naturally the best and the end of the other things' (1013b25-7, trans. Ross; cf. 983a31-2, *NE* 1094a5-6). Within action, this conception is most easily applied (as within *NE* I.1) to productive activities. In the case of action that itself is an end (see 1139b3-4 on *eupraxia*), we appear to have a complex teleology that alternates between the good (*to agathon*) and the fine (*to kalon*). A man acts in a certain way, say staying put as the enemy advances, in order to act well, that is in the context, bravely. And why does he act bravely? 'For the sake of the fine; for this is the end of virtue' (1115b12-13). It is *good* to stay put in the face of danger if, in the circumstances, it is *brave*; and an agent who acts bravely, or indeed otherwise virtuously, acquires the *fine* for himself (see 1168b25-7, 1169a21-2).[28] And then it is further supposed (as I shall discuss in section III) that acquiring the fine by *eupraxia* subserves the good of the agent, which is a *eudaimonia* achievable only 'in a complete life' (1098a16-20).

For their conceptions of ethical practice Plato's and Aristotle's rejection of any reduction of ethical to concrete properties matters as much as their different construals of the good. Good conduct depends not upon subservience to general principles, but upon sensitivity to particular situations. Aristotle conveys this in the doctrine of the mean. Ethical peaks are to be scaled not through blind heroism (like that celebrated in Longfellow's 'Excelsior'), but through the minute observance of a mean between excess and defect in respect of all the variables relevant to the assessment of action. Acting rightly involves acting, in some general way itself neutral (e.g., giving or spending money), 'to the right person, to the right extent, at the right time, with the right aim, and in the right way' (*hôi kai hoson kai hote kai hou heneka kai hôs*, *NE* 1109a27-8). Here he broadly follows Plato. Expert statesmen, like all practical experts, we read in the *Statesman*, must be able to measure excess and deficiency in relation not only to each other, but 'to the attainment of due measure' (*to metrion*, 284b9-c3). And due measure is subject to

---

[28] Though the term *kalos* has, of course, a wider meaning, it appears here to indicate a distinctively moral motivation (whence Ross's rendering 'noble').

multiple assessment: it is 'the moderate, the fitting, the timely, the necessary, and all else that falls into the mean between extremes' (284e6-8).[29] Yet there are differences, at least in aspiration. More seriously, I would suppose, than when writing the *Protagoras*,[30] Plato hopes for the precision of a technique of measuring, a precision that would presumably abolish the contestability (at least when it matters in practice) that the *Euthyphro* associated with our present lack of ethical measurement. When the *Philebus* contrasts 'arithmetic, measurement, and weighing' with 'guessing, by constant use and experiences training one's senses and then using one's capacities for estimating – capacities that develop their power with laborious practice' (55e1-56a1, trans. Gosling), it could be deprecating in anticipation Aristotle's less ambitious verdict that 'discrimination lies in perception' (*NE* 1109b23; cf. 1126b4). And the contrast is recurrent in Plato. Thus, in the *Laws*, he contrasts doctors of two kinds, empirical and scientific, to the advantage of the second: the former 'gain their professional knowledge by watching their masters and obeying their directions in empirical fashion', whereas the latter learn their art 'in a scientific way' and 'teach it to their pupils' (720b2-5, cf. 857c6-e1).

Not that Plato isolates theory from practice. The *Republic* links abstract knowledge to practical experience, entrusting legislation inspired by philosophy to 'those who have learned to know the ideal reality of things and who do not fall short of the others in experience and are not second to them in any part of virtue' (484d5-7, trans. Shorey), on the ground that 'the combination of qualities that we seek belongs to the same persons' (485a6-7), since good proportion (*emmetria*) in a mind is a precondition both of good character and of cognitive capacity (486d4-487a6). After an initial five years of dialectic, philosophers are sent down again into the Cave and compelled 'to hold commands in war and the other offices suitable to the young, so that they may not fall short of the other type in experience either' (539e4-5). Indeed, this fieldwork is to occupy no less than fifteen years. Why should it last so long? And why should it *precede* their final ascent towards the Good (540a4-8)? Surely not simply so that they may learn how to devise means to ends – in which case it would better come afterwards. Rather, experience must be needed, together with training in mathematics, to prepare for a dialectic whose origin, for human beings, is in part human. There is an attitude-dependence to our grasp of the ideal as of the ethical world, though in a different way: it is attitudinatively that we are receptive both of the ethical affinities of things that are concretely disparate, and of the austerer values that, in an abstract form, may each already hang together as an object of geometrical analysis. Pure proportion may enjoy a unity that perceptible proportions lack; and yet an unimpassioned apprehension of it – which could not be an appreciation of it *as a Form* – can only be partial and preliminary.[31] Forms display numerical structure; yet they have to be

---

[29] Other passages in Plato invoking the mean can be found in *Republic* 619a5-6, *Laws* 691c1-d5, 792c8-d2, and, above all, in the *Philebus*, e.g. 66a5-b3.

[30] See my *Mental Conflict*, 26-7.

[31] Thus mathematical studies stand to dialectic as 'helpers and co-operators' (533d3). One may recall how, in the *Symposium*, love stands to virtue as a 'co-worker' (212b4), and the

understood as determinations of the Good, and *therefore* meet to be copied.[32] Such an understanding must at last transcend and direct (540a8-b1), but at first build upon, distinguishing their best approximations within the personal and political spheres of practical engagement. It is thus that we may comprehend how civic activity 'augments' (*auxanein*) not only Form (as Plato writes, 540e3) but also philosopher (as he also writes, 497a4): to propagate Justice is to advance in understanding. It is true that on re-entering the Cave the philosopher will initially have difficulty seeing in the dark; but once he is rehabituated he will discern even 'the obscure things there' incomparably better than its denizens (520c2-5). Anyone who has mastered the theory will require only a little re-immersion in the world of action to be able to put it into practice; dialectical knowledge is *virtually* practical (which implies a view of practical knowledge very different from Aristotle's). It is far from a truism, but for Plato is a truth, that a good philosopher who rules is a good philosopher-ruler, and the only danger of the ivory tower is that he may be disinclined to leave it. Ethics is what dialectic becomes within the world of practice, and ethical theory needs to be grounded upon a wider theory of values. Yet, although ethics connects with mathematics through dialectic, an ethical education is only partly mathematical; for we need practical experience both to pursue dialectic, and to apply it ethically.

III

Aristotle takes from Plato not only the unity of the virtues, but an egocentric (though not vulgarly egoistic) eudaimonism.[33] There is a salient exchange in the *Symposium* (204e2-205a3):

> 'Come on, Socrates: the person who loves, loves good things; why does he love them?'
> 'To possess them for himself', I said.
> 'And what will the person who possesses good things get by possessing them?'
> '... He'll be happy.'
> 'Yes', she said, 'because those who are happy are happy by virtue of possessing good things, and one no longer needs to go on to ask "And what reason does the person who wishes to be happy have for wishing it?" Your answer seems to be complete' (trans. Rowe).

---

parallel is indicative: mathematics is a largely neutral prelude to dialectic rather as Platonic love is an affective re-orientation preliminary to philosophy.

[32] See D. Wiggins, 'Teleology and the Good in Plato's *Phaedo*', *Oxford Studies in Ancient Philosophy* 4 (1986), 1-18 especially 12-13, 17-18. At this level of understanding, the 'concord, proportion, and order' that were previously subject to mathematical analysis (see n. 21) are apprehended not only *as* values (which was anticipated within the idealized harmonic theory of 531c2-4), but even as imperative of action that subserves them (cf. 540e2-3). It is indeed an aesthetic numerology that approaches closest, within mathematics, to dialectic.

[33] See Burnyeat, 'Virtues in Action', 203.

This appears both to take an omnium gatherum view of *eudaimonia* (human goods are identifiable as good independently of *eudaimonia*, but then all contribute towards it), and to make 'for the sake of *eudaimonia*' the final and alone finally satisfying answer to the question 'why?' asked, on behalf of the agent, about any action or option – two claims that stand in apparent tension. It is unspecified what kind of 'possession' of what kinds of 'good things' is intended.

Perhaps a passage in the *Euthydemus* is clarificatory. This takes it as obvious that we all wish *eu prattein* (278e3-279a2), that is, to be *eudaimôn* (280b6, 282a2, cf. *Charmides* 174b12-c1). As in the *Symposium*, being *eudaimôn* is first equated with possessing many goods (280b5-6). This seems a popular conception set out more fully in Aristotle's *Rhetoric*, which gives a long and miscellaneous list of the many 'parts' (*merê*) of *eudaimonia*, such as being well born and having a good old age, wealth, having many and good friends and children; also enjoying honour, and the virtues of body and soul (1360b19ff.). The *Euthydemus* links *eu prattein* to enjoying *eutuchia*, which conveys that its primary meaning is *fare well*. Yet the effect of the argument is to change that: being happy involves *using* good things (280d4-7), and rightly (*orthôs*, e3-4); so *eupragia* depends upon *epistêmê* (281b2-4); so wisdom makes other things good (d8-e1), if indeed it is not that wisdom alone is good (e3-5). The upshot is that to be happy is to *act well*, that is, wisely and virtuously, with an apparent assurance that success will follow. This anticipates a shift in Aristotle: he takes everyone to equate being happy with living and faring (or doing) well (*NE* 1095a18-20), but then glosses that as acting 'in accordance with *aretê*', that is, with virtue or the best virtue (1098a16-18). Whether the conception of *eudaimonia* in Aristotle and early Plato thereby becomes entirely ethical or intellectual, so that external and other goods are, except as means or instruments, either dismissed as unreal, or admitted as real but relegated outside *eudaimonia*, is debated. Aristotle takes the two features of the good from which he argues its identity with *eudaimonia* in *Nicomachean Ethics* I.7, viz. finality and self-sufficiency, from the *Philebus* (20d1-5). Here Plato relates self-sufficiency to lacking or needing nothing (*prosdeisthai* or *prosdein*, 20e6, 21a11). This may suggest a selective conception of happiness as the object of all a man's needs, but not of all his desires. However, in the *Symposium* (200a5-b2) lacking something (being *endeês* of it) is both a precondition and a provocative of desiring it: one desires what, and only what, one lacks. So it remains open whether anything that a man desires falls within *eudaimonia* as he himself conceives it. Which need not entail that he must fail to be *eudaimôn* if he has to go without it; for *eudaimonia* may have a threshold, or come in degrees.

Comparison is difficult when interpretation is so disputed. However, an apparent and intelligible contrast is this. In Plato, *eudaimonia* may be the final end of action, but the ultimate source of value is, of course, the Good, which is a Form, and not an achievable end. As Aristotle reports, 'They [the Platonists] say that the good-itself is the best thing of all, and the good-itself is that to which it belongs to be both first among goods, and the cause by its presence, for other things, of their being good' (*EE* 1217b2-5, trans. Woods). Here we may take the 'and's to be epexegetic: the Good is best *because* it is first among goods, and the cause of the goodness of other things. Now it seems that Aristotle, who rejects Forms but aspires to the objectivity and unity of values that Plato associated with Forms, wishes to ascribe to *eudaimonia* the same focal role that Plato attached to the Good. Thus he writes, 'It is evident that happiness also must be set down as best among things realizable by human beings' (*EE* I.7, 1217a39-40), and explains this as follows (*EE* 1218b7-13):

> It is clear, then, that neither the Form of the good nor the common good is the good-itself that we are seeking, as the first is unchanging and not realizable, the second changing, yet still not realizable. But that-for-the-sake-of-which, as it is an end, is best, and cause of the things falling under it, and first among all goods. This, therefore, is what the good-itself, the end of things realizable by man, must be.

There is nothing equally indicative in the parallel chapter of the *Nicomachean Ethics* (I.6). However, a claim later in Book I that *eudaimonia* is 'the source (*archê*) and cause (*aition*) of good things' (1102a3-4) may be supposed to have the same ancestry. We probably find the same focality ascribed to *eudaimonia* early in Plato, *if* the *prôton philon* of the *Lysis*, which is the first object of love and the final end of all desire, is indeed *eudaimonia* (see 219c5-d2, 220b6-7). Forms are absent from the *Lysis*, as from Aristotle's *Ethics*; and we may surmise that it is in their absence that *eudaimonia* assumes an objectifying and unifying role that, we may think, it must have trouble sustaining. It may be that a brave act will always subserve the agent's *eudaimonia* (see *NE* 1169a16-26); yet how can its value *as brave* derive from that?[34]

In the *Republic* Plato internalizes his conception of the virtues in order to argue, in effect, that they are necessary and sufficient for the enjoyment of a *eudaimonia* connected to good external action, but identified with an inner state of harmony and unity (see 443c9-444a2). This internalization, which perhaps leaves a trace in Aristotle's thesis that ethical virtue governs passions as well as actions (*NE* 1106b16-17, 1109b30), risks an objection: is just conduct, which Glaucon wished to be justified for its own sake as well as for its consequences, really justified only as cause and effect of what truly constitutes *eudaimonia*? We may regret that Plato's picture of the soul as lying *inside* the body (like an oyster within its shell, *Phaedrus* 250c5-6) blinds him to the possibility that psychic harmony may be present or absent as much in external action as in internal states and happenings. But what I want finally to consider is how differently Plato and Aristotle stand to any justification of morality. John McDowell has been influential in arguing, in a

---

[34] Despite the evidence that I have now cited, a more modest and less unified possibility really coheres better with Aristotle's pluralistic view of the good as I gave it in section I. Situational appreciation, informed by practical wisdom, might identify how the agent must act here and now in order to act *well*, e.g. bravely. The egocentric long-term question (inescapable though usually implicit) how this will be not just good *of* him, but good *for* him, would then be answered by reference to his *eudaimonia*.

series of papers, that Aristotle is not concerned to justify morality from outside.[35] His intended audience is already morally educated; for to Plato's 'men who are uneducated and inexperienced in truth' (*Republic* 519b8) he has nothing that he wishes to say (cf. *NE* 1095a2-11). By contrast, it is often supposed that Plato aims a justification of justice at the immoralists instanced by the real Thrasymachus and the fictional Gyges. For he is taken to be appealing to common conceptions and experiences of happiness and unhappiness in order to persuade *everyone* to rank one way of living, the ethical way, over others.

In fact, it may be no accident that Socrates' prime interlocutors – who ask him to justify justice *to them* (*Republic* 358c8-d3, 367d5-e3) – are Glaucon and Adeimantus, people represented as already committed to morality, but unable to justify it as they would prefer (both intrinsically and consequentially, and not as a second best created by a social contract). A passing hope of persuading even Thrasymachus politely presumes that he has lived better than he has thought.[36] Again and again, in his presentation of a utopia, Socrates stresses the importance of character-training in advance of theoretical education.[37] It might still be that the value of morality can be appreciated vulgarly, though too often ineffectually. So we need to reconsider whether he is resting his case upon familiar values, of inner peace and harmony, as they are commonly conceived and experienced. For what do we find when we turn to the moralized characterology of Books VIII and IX? Most striking, and least easily reconcilable with such a reading, are the apparent charms that Socrates is willing to attribute to the life and character of the democratic man. He indeed objects, 'There is no order (*taxis*) or necessity (*anankê*) in his existence' (561d5-6). As Dominic Scott describes him, 'He is someone who has desires for many different things: parties, exercise, money, victory and discovery. But he just "goes for" these different things; they capture his fancy, nothing more; he pursues them all merely because he happens to enjoy them'; in contrast to the oligarch, who has a 'surrogate for rational order' in the compulsion or necessity (*anankê*, 554d2) that he imposes upon his unnecessary appetites, the democrat leads a life that has become 'a jumble of desires'.[38] What is less explicit is the point of view that makes this feature a devastating defect. For it does not condemn him to discontentment or regret: after listing the variety of his avocations (which is much like that of the average Londoner), and complaining that they lack order and necessity, Socrates admits, 'He calls this life of his the life of pleasure and freedom and happiness and cleaves to it to the end' (561d5-7). Thus, although he enjoys different things at different times, he resembles Aristotle's good and stable man in being free of regret (cf. *NE* 1166a27-9). Indeed, it is candidly

---

[35] See the papers numbered 1, 2, 3, and 9 in McDowell's *Mind, Value, and Reality.*

[36] Compare *Republic* 498c9-d4 with 619c6-d1. (I owe these references to Myles Burnyeat.)

[37] For a discussion of difficulties arising, see Christopher Gill, 'Plato and the Education of Character', *Archiv für Geschichte der Philosophie* 67 (1985), 1-26.

[38] 'Plato's Critique of the Democratic Character', *Phronesis* 45 (2000), 19-37, at 26-7. It is irrelevant to the present issue whether his tastes fall all if not only within his appetite (as I had supposed, *Mental Conflict*, 62-63), or are divided between the parts of his soul (as Scott argues).

conceded that both democratic man and city seem ideal to a vulgar view: 'Like that city he is the fair and many-coloured one whom many a man and woman would count fortunate in his life, as containing within himself the greatest number of patterns of constitutions and qualities' (561e4-7). It thus emerges that the disvalue that Socrates ascribes to democratic disorder and contingency is not an evident one surfacing in subjective discontent, but a subtle one perhaps visible only to the reader or interlocutor who has been reoriented by a vision of Plato's utopia, and demonstrable only by the philosopher who has escaped from the complacencies of the Cave into an austerer world of value.[39]

Socrates is less concessive about the tyrant, and we might expect at least to find *him* pictured as a paradigm of vulgar unhappiness. There is indeed some contrast. The 'travail and pain' (574a3-4) to which he is said to be liable is likely (though not certain) to be self-ascribed since it explains some of his actions. Yet we may wonder how readily Socrates would expect *him* to agree that his soul is 'needy and unsatisfied' (578a1), or 'maddened by its desires and passions' (a11). Might he not rather experience a passionately desirous life as a life that is at last *alive*? Socrates remarks that 'the many have many opinions' (576c3-4), and that some do not share his view that the actual tyrant is worse off than the tyrant *manqué* (579d9-e6). His conclusion is strikingly moralistic and a priori: '*He must needs be, and, by reason of his rule, come to be still more than he was*, envious, faithless, unjust, friendless, impious, a vessel and nurse of all iniquity, and *so in consequence* be himself most unhappy and make all about him so' (580a2-7, my italics). It may well be that Plato's strategy is not consistent, but adapted to its differing targets. It remains true that Socrates' appeal is most often, and unapologetically, to the phenomena as they show up (Thrasymachus may think distortedly) from Plato's own philosophical point of view.

If this is broadly correct, we can indeed understand how nothing less than the *conversion* vividly conveyed in the simile of the Cave is sufficient to enlighten a man about the true costs or benefits of justice or injustice. The 'self-mastery', 'beautiful order', 'unity' and 'unison' that Socrates hymns (in Shorey's translation of 443d4-e2) are not, as he means them, familiar psychological *data* and *desirabilia*, but values to which we may be introduced by a reading of the dialogue, but into which we could only be fully initiated by the actual education that it sketches. In this respect, the cameos that he offers of the various imperfect characters of Books VIII and IX rest, like the ensuing distinction between real and unreal pleasures, not upon subjective experience, but objective reality. Socrates is preaching, if not to the converted, at least to potential converts.

How does Aristotle compare? McDowell's conception of him as unconcerned to ground morality from outside is generally well based in some things he does say (notably in *NE* I.3), and a great deal he refrains from saying. However, there is one

---

[39] David Wiggins puts to me that re-evaluation can also come of novel experience. A period of military service, say, may lead certain people to perceive their previous lives as undisciplined. However, such changes of heart rather display a propensity latent in the individual than prove the validity of a critical revaluation.

chapter that contains the seeds of an external justification of morality.[40] *Nicomachean Ethics* IX.4 is in fact *less* interpretable than *Republic* Books VIII and IX as commending the ethical life from a point of view that is already distinctively evaluative. Consider such straightforwardly falsifiable claims, on the face of it, as these: 'Those who have done many terrible deeds ... even shrink from life and destroy themselves ... And wicked men ... shun themselves ... And having nothing lovable in them they have no feeling of love for themselves' (1166b11-18). Here the terms 'terrible' and 'wicked' are of course ethical; but the phrases 'shrink from life', 'destroy themselves', 'shun themselves', and 'have no feeling of love for themselves' seem ethically unloaded. It is true that Aristotle is unconcerned to separate such observations from other complaints resting on philosophical premises, such as that 'the element that thinks would seem to be the individual man' (1166a22-3), which is a theoretical ground for limiting genuine self-love to those who act as reason dictates (cf. 1168b28ff.). Yet it appears that, despite his lack of concern to advance such an argument, he is willing to supply the materials for a vulgar justification of morality of the kind that interpreters may have misascribed to Plato.

If this is a real divergence, what may explain it? I find illuminating an observation by Burnyeat upon a passage already cited from the *Eudemian Ethics* (1218a15-24): 'Aristotle's point, I take it, is that the value of unity and harmony in their psychic and social realizations is made intelligible from below, as it were.'[41] When Aristotle ascribes disunity and disharmony to the bad man, he offers his complaint as a piece of common observation. When Plato employs a similar language, he is generally writing within a distinctively Platonic perspective. It is from an eminence achieved by a long ascent through mathematics, practical experience, and dialectic that the philosopher perceives lives of ethical as well as intellectual virtue as alone approximating, in the impure worlds of cities and souls, to ideal order and harmony. In short, it seems that Raphael's contrast got it right.[42]

---

[40] This is not *NE* I.7, on which see Alfonso Gomez-Lobo's salutary article 'The Ergon Inference', *Phronesis* 34 (1989), 170-84.

[41] 'Plato on Why Mathematics is Good for the Soul', 79.

[42] This paper has benefited from the kindly acuity of its respondent.

Reply to A.W. Price

Sarah Broadie

No theme, surely, is more central to ethical philosophy than the 'irreducibility of the ethical', to quote from Anthony Price's title, and none has been more seminal in the historical development of the subject. Thus a study of it in the ethics of the two most seminal philosophers of all time gives us plenty to think about – all the more so when the study is as thoughtful and acute as the one Anthony Price has offered us. Perhaps, therefore, a commentator has even more excuse than usual for being rather selective, and leaving out of her current consideration many of the important questions Price has raised in his paper.

I should like to begin with some familiar points about different kinds of reasons why conduct expressive of personal excellence cannot be adequately summarized in rules, that is, substantial, non-empty, rules which if followed would give guidance. Three reasons come to mind, although there may be more.

Firstly, the relevant situations are frequently not run of the mill. That is, they have one or another feature which is rare or which it is reasonable not to be able to predict in advance, but which, in combination with others that are present, calls for or justifies an action that breaches any rule or set of rules by which one might have hoped to define good or right conduct. Not returning a borrowed axe to an insane person is an obvious example. It illustrates the way in which a rare fact, someone's insanity, activates an extremely common, indeed all but universal concern, namely concern for life and limb, in an area, such as lending and borrowing, where we are normally in a position to place that concern on hold.

Secondly, the relevant situations may be ones where different principles apply but cannot be simultaneously satisfied. This particularly tends to happen where what is called for is the just response, or the response of a quality in some ways like, if it is not a species of, justice, namely piety. One has obligations to this person and to that person. One has reason, when distributing goods, to favour the neediest and to favour the most deserving. One owes pious respect to the gods of the city and to one's father.

Thus decent conduct cannot be summed up in a practicable rule or set of rules, because the rules may direct one to opposite actions, so may not be collectively practicable. It is perhaps typical of this kind of conflict that agents who have no trouble in seeing, and in agreeing with each other on what to do in the first type of case (where it is a question of whether to return an axe to madman) are sometimes indecisive within themselves and sometimes in disagreement with each other. In the latter case we are inclined to say that they share the same values, but (in this situation, at least) accord them different priorities.

Here we are beginning to verge on the idea that ethical concepts are, with respect to their application, essentially controversial or 'contested'. It seems to me that this is not true of the first type of case considered above. There is nothing controversial about not handing a maniac's weapon back to him. What is shown by such a case is that we have to use intelligence to decide what to do, and we have to be ready to be thoughtful. This suggests a reply to Hume's objection to rationalist ethics, that moral judgements cannot be deduced from relations of ideas or from universal laws of cause and effect. The reply is that if they could be, they could be mechanically extracted from a code of rules formed in accordance with relations of ideas and causal laws. The result would be that we could reach, perhaps fairly easily, a point where we did not have to think what to do in particular situations; which might well suggest to some of us that reason now has no part to play in forming particular practical judgments. The very set-up which for Hume would vindicate reason's claim to be at work in forming moral judgements would, to some of us (perhaps to common sense), render reason jobless.

However, uncodifiability[1] is one thing, and contestability is another. In the second type of case sketched above, the dilemma kind, it is reasonable to think that the application of phrases such as 'the just thing to do', 'the pious thing to do' might turn out to be insolubly controversial. (These phrases with the definite article indicate that even if it is uncontroversial that some alternative action is just or pious too, it is not what is just or pious to do (anyway, in this situation).) But it is not, I find, clear that this essential contestability is a feature of virtue-concepts as such (as Burnyeat appears to claim in a passage which Price cites approvingly), as distinct from being a feature of concepts where the virtue in question has to do with giving people (including gods, if necessary) their due. In other words, contestability as sketched so far might be closely linked to the double fact that 'someone's due' (a) can be sensibly interpreted in different ways, and (b) is often an issue with respect to competing claimants. It is not clear, in short, that similar dilemmas can be constructed with regard to 'the courageous thing to do', 'the temperate thing to do', or (to take one of Aristotle's 'conversational' virtues) 'the witty (*eutrapelos*) thing to say', if one focuses on these qualities themselves, as distinct from questions about justice. One might be happy to say, in the spirit of Plato and Aristotle, that an action inferior in terms of justice cannot count as the courageous thing to do; and one might therefore have a dilemma about what is the courageous thing to do. For example, one might have a case where (a) each of two alternative actions could neatly count as courageous provided it were just, but (b) it is not at all obvious under the circumstances which is just. Here it would be only incidentally if at all that the application of 'the courageous thing to do' is essentially contested or contestable.

The third kind of reason for holding that non-empty rules cannot summarize good conduct or the qualities expressive of it, comes to mind if one considers that there is a sense of words such as 'rational' and 'sensible' such that different subjects can both be rational and sensible, yet see the same situation as calling for

---

[1] McDowell's word; cf. the reference in Price, note 8.

opposite kinds of action. To borrow from Thucydides and R.M. Hare, one man sees a proposed action as brutal and outrageous, while another sees rejection of it as utterly stupid or as cowardly. I am imagining this so that, unlike the case of the dilemma, neither party goes from side to side between his own and the other's position, and neither allows that the other would be right except that there is a superior principle at stake. Each detests and despises what the other stands for. This, I think, is the sort of disagreement Aristotle has in mind when he says that e.g. the coward looks on the courageous man as rash, while the rash person looks on the courageous man as cowardly (*NE* II.8, 1108b11ff.). According to Aristotle, this point about radically different moral perspectives is a general one: the possibility of such disagreement arises out of the nature of the moral dispositions. This point, then, unlike (if I am right) the one about dilemmas, by no means loses its force once it ceases to be restricted to predicates of justice and justice-like qualities such as piety. In fact, since Aristotle's understanding of this deeper kind of disagreement is grounded in the view that the moral dispositions come in triads whose members represent positions of intermediacy, excess and deficiency within the same general area, he ought to conclude that it cannot arise in the case of justice, given the notorious fact that the virtue of justice is not 'flanked' by distinct vices of excess and deficiency.

In this last kind of case, then, the reason (if it really is one) for holding that courage or justice, and the corresponding conduct, and the use of the corresponding terms, cannot be summarized in rules, is that, setting aside the problem that no ethical rule could be exceptionless, there can exist no rule acceptable by all supposedly rational and sensible subjects. For presumably a rule is meant to apply to everybody to whom it can apply; for example, a rule for use of a word like 'courageous' should, like other rules for use of some word in the language, apply to everyone who speaks that language, setting a norm for all of them. But clearly this is what cannot happen between parties to the kind of disagreement sketched above.

There are, then, these three different ways in which ethical matters generate conflict and evade capture by rules. But in Plato's and Aristotle's way of looking at things, there is a huge difference between the first two and the third. In the first case, the 'conflict', such as it is, is between a rule and a valid exception; in the second it is between contending claims of justice and the like; in the third it is between contrary moral outlooks. According to the two great philosophers, we as reflective observers ought to be on both sides in the first two cases. In the first, the rule represents the good habit typical of the well-brought-up person: he internalized the rule in simple situations to which it clearly applied, and he thereby internalized respect not just for the property of others but for those others themselves, hence for their wellbeing. In correctly recognizing the exception he is both exercising his existing ethical nature and developing it by going beyond the initial simplicities. We are or should be with him in feeling the force of both rule suspended and the reason for suspending it; and we should also be with him in unhesitatingly siding with the latter. In the second kind of case, discussed more by Aristotle than by Plato, it is right to be torn. But as for the third kind, the two philosophers are definite that we, and in general, the decent person cannot identify with both sides of the conflict; this despite the fact that we have a great deal in common with the person on the opposing side: we belong to the same species, and therefore we have the same basic psychology, the same basic propensities to feel pleasure, pain and emotions, the same basic needs, the same basic desire to have a good life rather than a bad one. We also (in the kind of example that concerns Plato and Aristotle) belong to the same society, share a language, and have a great deal of knowledge and understanding in common.

I turn now to some of Price's specific reflections on the *Republic*. Price's discussion of irreducibility brings out very clearly the dilemma that came to light through the inquiries of Socrates as Plato portrays them. Our very best efforts to answer a question such as 'What is courage?' will end either in a statement that is (to use Price's word) determinate or substantial, but false in some cases, or in one that is universally true but truistic. The question now arises: what, then, can philosophy contribute to ethical life? It is perfectly true that philosophy in the form of the Socratic elenchus cannot lose its power to bring to light inconsistencies in belief-sets answerers hold; and that this removes (at least for a while) one obstacle to improvement, namely the placidity of complete self-satisfaction about grasp of the values in question. It seems to me, however, that a Socrates or a Plato cannot honestly pursue the elenchus just as a kind of therapy, however honest the kind. That is to say, even while it remains true that the negative effect of elenchus is genuinely beneficial,[2] one cannot honestly engage someone in a line of questioning under a heading such as 'What is courage?' if one is convinced that no satisfactory answer will ever be forthcoming. It will also continue to be true that the conduct of such a line of questioning shows the world that the answerer, who might be any one of us, somehow commands a power of understanding (even if it emerges only in seeing flaws in what he previously believed) which no amount of sensory input could explain. But, again, one cannot honestly engage someone in an erotetically futile line of questioning simply because one can thereby demonstrate a truth. The answerer must believe that a satisfactory answer is possible; and Socrates must believe this too, or they are not in it together – as Plato often has Socrates insist that they should be.

So if philosophy is to contribute to ethical life, it must take a different form from the Socratic elenchus. The elenchus, however, suggests a way philosophy should go. For what makes sense of the actual experience of the elenchus is the assumption that there is indeed (to continue our example) a Form of courage, which the mind somehow grasps from within itself, which guides us in questioning and answering, which enables us to see when, and why, answers fail, and perhaps even in the end why none can succeed, yet which, for all its closeness to us in controlling our steps along the path of negative criticism, cannot be brought under control by us in a satisfactory definition. Since the criticism is beneficial (it brings us closer to true belief, at least), and this is helpful for practice, one great ethical

---

[2] If it fails in this respect in some cases, that is because of the recalcitrance of the person being examined, not because of any defect in the intellectual and perhaps moral correction that the examination would deliver if it could.

task of philosophy now is to work out an answer to the following question: how would human affairs have to be arranged so that how we live is maximally determined by the intellectual light of the uncodifiable ethical Forms?

Leaving aside the question of the desirability, even in pursuit of a solid ideal, of any radical re-arrangement of imperfect but non-chaotic actual institutions, Plato's answer in the *Republic* seems on several broad counts obviously right. It seems obvious that wisdom should govern, and that wisdom in the relevant sense means a combination of moral integrity with penetrating, searching, critical intellectuality both about ultimate aims and about detailed arrangements. It seems obvious too that this intellectuality must be developed by deliberate, systematic, education. But where this part of Plato's answer fails to convince is in its emphasis on abstract mathematical learning. No doubt many factors explain the bias. One may have been the natural assumption that the currently most highly developed branch of knowledge is the uniquely suitable tool for forming the intellect; another, the belief that the soul and all reality is structured by mathematizable relationships; another, perhaps, the assumption, surely not unreasonable and borne out by experience of mathematical activity, that life is full of objective non-obvious relationships of balance, imbalance, contrariety, analogy, fit and misfit, which will not reveal themselves except to minds trained and eager to look for them. Yet another, perhaps, was the thought that unless rulers come to power firmly addicted to the beauty of something purely theoretical, and buoyed by the hope of returning to it within a finite number of years, they will addict themselves to power instead.

It is extraordinary, really, that nowhere in the *Ethics* or *Politics* does Aristotle say what he thinks of the amount of mathematics in the education of rulers in the *Republic*. Perhaps he thought it was a good idea up to a point: witness his own enthusiastically mathematical analyses of distributive and corrective justice. We cannot but feel that he would have done a better job on corrective justice had he not been wedded to seeing it as a matter of splitting the difference between two lengths and adding the result to the shorter. It is presumably in the treatment of particular justice that Aristotle comes closest to abandoning 'irreducibility'. That is, he comes closest to laying down non-vacuous a priori accounts of what the virtuous actions would look like.[3] Price's discussion makes us see it as no accident that justice, unlike any other virtue, does at one point get treated as not issuing in the right or appropriate action; it is because this can happen that there is need for the virtue of *epieikeia*, 'equity' or 'reasonableness'.[4]

Let me end by commenting on the interesting turn at the end of Price's paper. It is often thought that the purpose of the *Republic* is meant to justify morality as against the immoralism of Thrasymachus and Callicles, whereas Aristotle is not concerned to justify morality. Price draws attention to often overlooked points in the *Republic* and in Aristotle's *Ethics* which may suggest that this contrast is too stark, in both directions. In the stark contrast, it is assumed that Plato means to

---

[3] The accounts of actions typical of other virtues are vacuous to the extent that they rely, as they do, heavily, on phrases like 'as he should', 'when he should', 'to whom he should', etc.

[4] At *NE* V.10, 1137a31-1138a3, *epieikeia* is the corrective to justice as law; at V.9, 1136b20-1, it is the quality of not insisting on all of one's fair share in a distribution.

offer what many philosophers would love to have, namely a defence of morality capable of rationally persuading those who do not embrace it to embrace it after all. Such a defence would lead Thrasymachus and Callicles (in a cool hour) to abandon their principles and adopt those of morality; or it would lead a genuinely morally neutral mind (whatever that would be like) to affirm morality and deny immoralism. By contrast, the fact that Aristotle's chosen audience or readership consists of well-brought-up people (*NE* I.4, 1095b2-6) is often regarded as decisive evidence that, as Price and others put it, Aristotle is not trying to justify morality from outside. ('From outside' means, of course, 'to outsiders'.) Now this reasoning from Aristotle's text should lead us to expect that, if the stark contrast is correct, Plato in the *Republic* is addressing either Thrasymachus or someone who begins as morally neutral. This is not the place to get involved in fine-tuning a response to the fact that while the dialogue called the *Republic* is addressed to Plato's readers, whoever they are – and he never says what sort of readership he would like to have – most of the discourse within the dialogue is addressed by Socrates to Glaucon and Adeimantus. For now I am going to take it as obvious that the argument of the *Republic* is for people like Glaucon and Adeimantus. And the fact about them which Price highlights is that they are presented as already committed to morality, but as wanting to see how a philosophical defence of it would go. It is a case of '*fides quaerens intellectum*'. Price also observes that in the *Republic* the state of the just and therefore happy soul is not such that a contrary state is necessarily felt by its owner as disturbed and miserable. For the soul of the democratic man is in a definitely unhealthy and therefore unhappy state (the worst bar one); yet the democratic man is presented as pleased with his life and himself. Thus perhaps we are to infer that no argument, not even the argument of the *Republic*, could lead the democratic man to hate his own ways and embrace Platonic justice. Only to the extent that one already adheres to justice will one hate the democratic state of soul. What Plato offers is not a proof to convert the unconverted into believers in morality, but what we might call a philosophy of morality, the phrase being used as in 'philosophy of science' or 'philosophy of logic'. And he thereby refutes any suggestion that morality is an outlook only for the backward, the inarticulate, the intellectually timorous.

Price then casts doubt on the stark contrast as it applies to Aristotle, by bringing forward the passage in *NE* IX.4 (1166a1-b29) where Aristotle says quite generally and categorically that bad people are full of regret (1166b24-5). Aristotle ends the passage by warning: 'So if being like this is too miserable a condition, one must strenuously shun badness and try for decency; for in this way one will both have a friendly disposition towards oneself and become friends with another person' (1166b26-9, trans. Christopher Rowe). One might moralize like this to well-brought-up people if one doubted whether they were all completely committed to the values in which they were nurtured. Aristotle, like many a preacher to a decent congregation, may have reasonably entertained this concern; but it surfaces nowhere else in the *Ethics*, as far as I know. Even here, his main point, I think, is not to motivate people towards morality by brandishing the prospect of internal sanctions for sinners. Rather, he is driven by a sort of logic or pseudo-logic that says: 'The bad person is his own worst enemy, and X's enemy (whoever the enemy may be) is, by definition, someone X flees from (1166b13-14) and hates'.

Chapter 3

Socrates and Aristotle on Happiness and Virtue

Roger Crisp

This Keeling volume concerns Plato's influence on Aristotle. I trust that it will be acceptable for me to speak not directly of Plato, but of the literary character, Socrates – 'the Socrates', as Aristotle calls him.[1] I shall assume that it makes sense to ascribe views to this character, and to identify him as the same person in different dialogues.[2] The main claim of my paper is that Socrates' views on the relation of virtue and happiness led to tensions in his position and intimations of a rejection of eudaimonism, and that Aristotle can be read as attempting to continue the eudaimonistic project.[3] What I mean by 'eudaimonism', and other pieces of jargon, should become clearer as I proceed.

Socratic eudaimonisms

Consider the following view:

> *Psychological Eudaimonism*: Each person, when acting rationally, pursues her own perceived greatest happiness.[4]

This thesis is descriptive. A close prescriptive analogue is:[5]

---

[1] See W. Fitzgerald, *Selections from the Nicomachean Ethics of Aristotle* (Dublin: Hodges and Smith, 1853), 163; T.H. Irwin, *Plato's Ethics* (New York: Oxford University Press, 1995), 8, 355, n. 12.

[2] I shall thus avoid the debate over whether the earlier dialogues represent the views of the real Socrates, and the later those of Plato. But of course my claims about the views of what might be thought to be the later Socrates could be translated into claims about the views of Plato. The fact that Plato used the character of Socrates throughout his career may be taken to suggest that he himself would not have objected to the strategy I adopt.

[3] In this respect, then, my view is the opposite of Irwin's, that 'it would not be a gross exaggeration to describe Aristotle's ethical theory as a systematic defence of the theory that Plato develops in opposition to [the real] Socrates' (*Plato's Ethics*, 9).

[4] Cf. Irwin, *Plato's Ethics*, 2.

[5] I say 'close' primarily because Rational Eudaimonism concerns happiness, not perceived happiness.

Rational Eudaimonism: Each person has strongest reason to pursue her own greatest happiness.[6]

Socrates appears to hold both of these views. In the *Protagoras*, Socrates seeks to explain what is happening in cases that the majority calls 'being overcome by pleasure' (352d8-e1). He ascribes to the majority the view that pleasure is the only good, and pain the only 'evil' (353e5-354a1, 354b5-c2), and suggests (354c3-5) that they act on this view. Thus they seem to accept a hedonistic version of Rational Eudaimonism, and their actions are consistent with a hedonistic version of Psychological Eudaimonism.[7]

Whether we should believe that Socrates himself accepts this view depends on how we should interpret Socrates' question about bodily pleasures to the majority at 353e5-354a1:[8] 'Don't you think, gentlemen, that, as Protagoras and I claim, these things are bad for no other reason than that they lead to pains and deprive one of other pleasures?'. The straightforward reading of 'as Protagoras and I claim', as Taylor points out,[9] has Socrates here associating himself with some of the views of the majority. It has to be admitted that it may be read as: 'as Protagoras and I claim [that you think *or* on your behalf]'. But, again as Taylor notes, this reading seems less plausible, 'since in his presentation of the imaginary dialogue with the many Socrates has so far represented himself as concerned to elicit their views by questions, and not as anticipating their replies in such a direct fashion'. Socrates also introduced the topic of hedonism sympathetically, saying: '*As I myself put it*, in so far as things are pleasant, are they not to that extent good?' (351c4-5). The alternative reading also seems quite unnatural, requiring too much of the reader to make it plausible. Why does Socrates ascribe this position to Protagoras as well as himself? That, surely, is a rhetorical device, one already used at 353c4, and again below, at 357b7 and 358a2.

At *Euthydemus* 278e3-5, Socrates asks: 'Don't all of us human beings want to do well? Or is this one of the questions I was afraid were absurd, since it is no doubt silly even to ask such things?'.[10] That by 'doing well' here, Socrates has in mind the acquiring of goods for oneself is made clear at 279a2-3, the first examples mentioned being wealth, health, good looks, good birth, powers, and honours

---

[6] One might wish to add the prefix 'expected' to 'happiness' in either of these formulations of eudaimonism; cf. *Protagoras* 356b2.

[7] C.C.W. Taylor (*Protagoras*, trans. and annot. (Oxford: Clarendon Press, 1976), 175) notes that most of the examples used by Socrates suggest he has in mind egoistic rather than non-egoistic hedonism. This, the natural interpretation, is borne out also by the description of the good as 'living a pleasant life without pains' (*Prot.* 355a2-3).

[8] For further defence of the attribution of hedonism to Socrates, see Irwin, *Plato's Ethics*, 86-94.

[9] Taylor, *Protagoras*, 176.

[10] Cf. *Meno* 77c1-2: 'Don't you think that everyone desires good things?'. The mention of bad things as causing *harm* at 77e5-78a3 suggests that Socrates sees 'good things' as things which are 'good for' those who desire them. See n. 11 below.

(279a7-b2).[11] And at 280b5-8, we learn that, once we have these good things, we do well and are happy, and are happy through their benefiting us. Further, possessing and using these good things are necessary and sufficient for happiness (280d4-e3). What we have here sounds very much like a commitment to Psychological Eudaimonism, if we assume that human beings act on their desires, and there are no countervailing desires in the offing. A later passage advocates an intellectualist version of Rational Eudaimonism: 'Since we all desire to be happy, and we have been shown to become such by using things and using them rightly, and rightness and good fortune were provided by knowledge, it is necessary, so it seems, that every man in every way take steps to be as wise as he can' (282a1-6).

The *Gorgias* also provides evidence of Socrates' acceptance of both Psychological and Rational Eudaimonism. Socrates obtains Polus' agreement to the thesis that certain things – such as wisdom, health, and wealth – are good, while others are mere means to such goods. He goes on: 'So it is in pursuit of the good that we both walk when we walk, thinking it is better, and on the other hand stand still when we stand still, for the sake of the same thing, the good' (468b1-4).[12] One might find a commitment implied here to Rational as well as to Psychological Eudaimonism, but it anyway emerges quite explicitly at 499e6-500a1, where Socrates asks Callicles:

> For we thought that everything should be done for the sake of goods, if you remember – Polus and I. So do you agree with us as well that the good is the end of all actions, and that we should do all other actions for the sake of the good, not the good for the sake of them?

What reasons might Socrates have for accepting the two forms of eudaimonism we have been discussing? In the case of Psychological Eudaimonism, one answer is suggested at *Phaedo* 99a5-b2. Socrates is criticizing Anaxagoras' attempt to provide materialistic explanations of human action:

> If someone were to say that without having such bones and sinews and whatever else I have I should not be able to do what I thought best, he would speak the truth. But to say that it is because of them that I do what I do, and not through choice of what is best – even though my mind is involved in my action – would be an exceedingly heedless way to talk.

Psychological Eudaimonism, then, is based on the power of explanations of human action as aimed at the agent's own perceived good. And that explanatory

---

[11] Examples such as this suggest that Socrates is, other things being equal, to be understood as seeing an agent's good as equivalent to what is good for an agent, and the good pursued by an agent to be equivalent to that agent's happiness. See n. 12 below. It has to be admitted, of course, that Socrates may be understood to be using stock examples to illustrate points independent of any particular conception of the good. But I submit that my more straightforward interpretations are not unreasonable.

[12] As G. Vlastos notes (*Socrates* (Cambridge: Cambridge University Press, 1991), 203, n. 14), Socrates 'shifts, *without argument*', from 'better' at b2 to 'better for us' at b6.

power itself rests on the notion that, to each human being, her own good appears as worth pursuing. Since Socrates is speaking with other human beings, he perhaps thought it unnecessary to provide any explicit justification for Rational Eudaimonism. At *Symposium* 205a2-3, Diotima and Socrates agree that 'there is no need to ask further why someone should want to be happy'.

Now it is of course true that at least a good deal of human action can be explained and justified by reference to the agent's own good, perceived or actual. But one important and obvious question remains: are there non-egoistic explanations and justifications available, which may throw doubt on both forms of eudaimonism? Before answering this question, and enquiring into what appears to be evidence of Socrates' adopting a more ambivalent attitude towards eudaimonism, let me first examine his views on the relation of virtue and happiness. For, I shall suggest, it is not implausible to claim that it is recognition of some of the implications of these views that leads Socrates to question eudaimonism.

Happiness and virtue

In the *Apology*, Socrates says that he knows that doing wrong is an evil, as opposed to a good (29b6-7; cf. *Gorgias* 469b8-9, *Republic* 444e7-445b4). Further, no greater good could have befallen his fellow citizens than his encouraging them to put virtue first (*Apology* 30a6-b4). For, we learn elsewhere, virtue guarantees happiness, whereas vice guarantees unhappiness (*Charmides* 175e6-176a1, *Gorgias* 507b8-c5; cf. *Republic* 444d13-e1, 521a2-4).[13]

Does Socrates think that virtue is merely instrumental to happiness?[14] No: if doing wrong itself constitutes an evil, Socrates is most plausibly understood to be

---

[13] This is to say something stronger than that virtue guarantees one some happiness. One might have some happiness in one's life, and yet not a sufficient degree to merit the description 'happy'.

[14] See Irwin, *Plato's Ethics*, 67, which attributes to Socrates the 'instrumental principle' that if we choose *x* for the sake of *y*, then we cannot also choose *x* for itself, which makes virtue instrumental if happiness is desired for its own sake and everything else for it (cf. e.g. *Euthydemus* 282a1-2). I agree with Vlastos (*Socrates*, 306-7) that the primary text cited by Irwin in support of the attribution of the instrumental principle – *Lysis* 220a7-b5 – need not be taken to refer to the good of virtue. For further argument against Irwin's interpretation of the *Lysis* passage, see D. Zeyl, 'Socratic Virtue and Happiness', *Archiv für Geschichte der Philosophie* 64 (1982), 225-38, at 234-5; C.D.C. Reeve (*Socrates in the Apology* (Indianapolis: Hackett, 1989), 131, n. 29). See also Vlastos' discussion of *Gorgias* 468b-c (*Socrates*, 303-4). Irwin's response to Vlastos' citation of 468c2-5 is to modify his reading of 476d6-e1 so that it implies that things wanted for the sake of something else are not wanted for their own sake. Once again, I would prefer to take the scope of those passages more narrowly than Irwin, to concern only 'the intermediates' – genuinely instrumental goods – and not non-instrumental goods which may also be constituents of some more final non-instrumental good. All the examples offered are of intermediates. And Socrates allows that health and wealth are goods, and wanted for their own sake. Since he would,

claiming that doing right constitutes a good, and so is a constituent of happiness. This gives us:

Moralism: Virtue is a constituent of happiness.[15]

Is virtue the only constituent? According to Vlastos, several passages suggest that it is, in particular (*Crito* 48b4-10):

> Do we still hold, or do we not, that we should attach highest value not to living, but to living well?
> We do.
> And that to live well is the same as to live honourably and justly: do we hold that too, or not?
> We do. (trans. Vlastos)

Vlastos suggests that the natural reading of this passage is that:

> the happy and virtuous forms of living are identical, that is to say, that the form of life we call 'happiness' when viewing it under desirability criteria (as the most deeply and durably satisfying kind of life) is *the same form of life* we call 'virtue' when viewing it as meeting moral criteria (as the just, brave, temperate, pious, wise way to live).[16]

This is what Vlastos calls the 'Identity Thesis of the relation of virtue to happiness'. Vlastos himself goes on to read the passage as claiming an entailment between virtue and happiness, but I confess that he seems to me to be making rather heavy weather of it. As I read the passage, it is implying merely a sameness of reference of the phrases 'the happy life' and 'the virtuous life'. The happy life, that is to say, will be the life of the virtuous person. But there is no implication that happiness can be constituted by nothing other than virtue.[17]

---

presumably, allow such goods to be constituents of happiness and hence desired for the sake of happiness (they are 'the good', 468b1), it is plausible to assume that his claim at 468b8-c1 is restricted to purely instrumental goods. Indeed, Irwin's division of goods into two – those desired for the sake of another, and those (or that) desired for their (or its) own sake – goes against the tenor of the tripartite distinction here in the *Gorgias* between instrumental goods, goods, and the good. Cf. the distinction in *Republic* 357b-d between goods desired for their own sake, goods desired for their own sake and for their consequences, and goods desired solely for the sake of other goods. Irwin (*Plato's Ethics*, 364, n. 8) says that L. Versenyi's appeal to this passage ('Plato's *Lysis*', *Phronesis* 20 (1975), 185-98, at 175) to interpret the *Lysis* is illegitimate. But the claim of illegitimacy seems to rest merely on Irwin's own interpretation of the *Lysis*: see *Plato's Ethics*, 198.

[15] I am placing no weight on any distinction between virtue and its exercise, since I do not see Socrates doing so. Cf. Vlastos' criticism of Brickhouse and Smith (*Socrates*, 232, n. 103).

[16] *Socrates*, 214.

[17] I find Vlastos' interpretations of two other passages that might suggest the Identity Thesis – *Gorgias* 470e4-11 and 507d6-e1 – more plausible.

What else, then, might be constituents of happiness? We have already come across some of them: wealth, health, good looks, good birth, powers, and honours (*Euthydemus* 279a7-b2; cf. *Crito* 54b2-5, *Lysis* 218e5-219a1, *Gorgias* 467e4-5, *Meno* 87e6-7). It is also worth considering the account of the lives of the guardians in the *Republic*. Their happiness is of course partly constituted by their virtue. But this good brings others (465d5-e2):

> [The Olympian victors] are accounted happy on the basis of only a fraction of what the guardians have. For the guardians' victory is even finer, and their public support more complete. The victory they win is the preservation of the whole city, and their crown is support and everything else necessary for life for themselves and their children. They receive prizes from their city while they are alive, and when they die a worthy burial.

Victory, then, or perhaps rather accomplishment (497a1-5), and its recognition, are among the constituents of the guardians' happiness. And it is generally true of just people, Socrates claims near the end of the *Republic*, that 'towards the end of each action and association and life they enjoy a high reputation and bear off the prizes from their fellow men' (613c4-6). Further, they have power and decide whom they will marry, whereas the unjust person is ridiculed, insulted, and physically punished (613c8-e4).[18] These are the 'prizes, payments, and gifts that a just person receives from both gods and human beings while he is alive, in addition to those goods which justice itself provides' (613e6-614a3), and they are 'nothing in number or extent compared to those which await just and unjust people on their deaths' (613e6-614a6). And, of course, pleasure also plays an important role in the happiness of the guardians (580c9-588a11).

Now all these goods may quite clearly be worth having, but there are two significant further features of them to be noted. First, they are good only for the virtuous (*Charmides* 174c3-d1):[19]

> Critias, if you wish to take away this science [concerning good and evil] from the others, won't medicine nonetheless make people healthy, shoemaking make them shod, weaving clothed, navigation prevent their dying at sea and generalship dying in war?
>
> They will nonetheless.
>
> But, my dear Critias, each of these will not be well or beneficially done if this science is absent (cf. *Apology* 30b3-4,[20] *Gorgias* 511e6-512b2, *Menexenus* 246d8-247a2, *Meno* 88c4-d2; also *Laws* 661a4-d4, 727e3-728a5).

---

[18] At *Gorgias* 477a2-3, Socrates claims that just punishment actually benefits the unjust person.

[19] See T. Brickhouse and N. Smith, 'Socrates on Goods, Virtue, and Happiness', *Oxford Studies in Ancient Philosophy* 5 (1987), 1-27, at 4-12; *Plato's Socrates* (New York: Oxford University Press, 1994), 106-12; G. Santas, 'Socratic Goods and Socratic Happiness', *Apeiron* 26 (1993), 37-52.

[20] Taking *agatha* as predicative: see J. Burnet, *Euthyphro, Apology of Socrates, Crito*, ed. and annot. (Oxford: Clarendon Press, 1924), n. *ad loc.*; also Reeve, *Socrates in the Apology*,

Second, their contribution to happiness, in comparison with that of virtue, is trivial (*Apology* 29d9-30a3):

> Are you not ashamed that you give your attention to acquiring as much money as possible, as much reputation and honour, and give no attention or thought to truth or to how your soul might be as good as possible? And if any of you disagrees and says he does give attention to these things ... and if I think he hasn't acquired virtue, but just says he has, I shall reprove him for putting least weight on what matters most, and more weight on rather paltry things (cf. *Crito* 47d8-48a4).

Virtue is sufficient for happiness,[21] but goods other than virtue can increase the happiness of the virtuous person. That is, Socrates accepts:

Pluralism: Happiness is constituted by more than virtue alone.

There are of course some famous passages in which Socrates appears to be claiming that nothing bad can happen to a good person: 'Neither Meletus nor Anytus could do me any harm. He couldn't. For I think it is forbidden by divine providence that a better person be harmed by a worse' (*Apology* 30c9-d1);

124-25, n. 2; Vlastos, *Socrates*, 219-20, n. 73. For a different view, see Irwin (*Plato's Ethics*, 363, n. 22) who prefers the traditional 'wealth and the other goods come from virtue' on the ground that it balances better with the preceding clause. But Irwin does not provide a response to Burnet's dry remark: 'As Socrates was now *en penia(i) muria(i)* (23b9), he could hardly recommend virtue as a good investment'. Brickhouse and Smith (*Plato's Socrates*, 20, n. 33, 108 and n. 11) deny the very availability of Burnet's translation. But they provide no argument. In fact, as Margaret Howatson has pointed out to me, such an ellipse of the third singular copulative is quite common in Greek, and the Greek of the *Apology* is very loose. Also, after *ho allos* an adjective or participle used substantivally usually requires the article; cf. e.g. *Apology* 22d7.

[21] See Irwin, *Plato's Ethics*, 59 and refs.; Vlastos, *Socrates*, 224-31; G. Rudebusch *Socrates, Pleasure, and Value* (New York: Oxford University Press, 1999), 119-22. Irwin (*Plato's Ethics*, 199-200, 249) notes that in *Republic* II Socrates sets out to prove only that the just person is happier than the unjust. But this does not imply that he has given up the sufficiency thesis. Irwin claims that Plato 'never suggests in the *Republic* that the just person is happy despite all the possible misfortunes that Glaucon and Adeimantus describe' (249). But Irwin, like Vlastos, ignores 612e-613b, which I discuss below. Passages such as *Crito* 47e3-5, in which Socrates says that 'life is not worth living for us with a body in poor condition and diseased', should be read on the assumption that such bodily conditions can themselves affect one's very capacity for virtue; see Vlastos, *Socrates*, 218 n. 69; Reeve, *Socrates in the Apology*, 141-2. For different views, see Brickhouse and Smith, 'Socrates on Goods, Virtue, and Happiness', 16; *Plato's Socrates* 111-12, 119 and n. 30; Rudebusch, *Socrates, Pleasure, and Value*, 115-17. Brickhouse and Smith (*Plato's Socrates*, 119, n. 30) note that at *Gorgias* 512a2-5 Socrates implies that someone with a serious and incurable illness is wretched for not having died, rather than merely not happy. But if we assume that the person can no longer benefit from virtue, and therefore from other goods, the suffering caused by his illness will be enough to make his life worse than nothing. For arguments against the sufficiency thesis, see Brickhouse and Smith, *Socrates on Trial* (Princeton: Princeton University Press, 1989), 163-7, 262-7.

'Gentlemen of the jury, you must … focus on this single truth: that there is nothing bad for a good person in life or in death' (*Apology* 41c8-d3).

Vlastos understands Socrates to be saying not that no harm can come to a good person, but that any harm that comes may be only trivial, as in the usage of negation in the following exchange:

> You ask, 'Might I trouble you to post this letter for me?' and I reply, 'It would be no trouble – none at all', though I know and you know that the errand would take me several blocks out of my way. You understand me to say 'no trouble' and mean 'a mini-trouble – too trivial to be worth mentioning'.[22]

This interpretation, however, does not resonate with the emphatic form of the statements made by Socrates. Nor is it clear why, if this is what he meant, he did not say it more directly. To support a more straightforward interpretation, let me cite the following (*Republic* 612e8-613b1):[23]

> Shall we not agree, then, that everything whatsoever that comes from the gods to someone beloved by the gods is the best possible …? … Then we must assume the same is true of a just person, if he falls into poverty, disease, or some other apparent evil – that these things will end in something good for him, during his life or in death. For he who wishes to strive to become just and who by caring for virtue makes himself as divine as a human being can, is never neglected by the gods.

As Burnet says in his note, this passage echoes *Apology* 41c-d: there is the same reference to life and death, and *amelein* is used for what the gods do not do – ignore the good person or his fortunes.[24] The exact meaning of the passage is not

---

[22] Vlastos, *Socrates*, 219; cf. Reeve, *Socrates in the Apology*, 151; Brickhouse and Smith, *Socrates on Trial*, 162-3.

[23] Cited also by Burnet, *Euthyphro, Apology of Socrates, Crito*, 251, n. 41d. Adam makes the reference back to the *Apology* (citing Morgenstern) in J. Adam, *The Republic of Plato*, ed. and annot. (Cambridge: Cambridge University Press, 1921), *ad loc*. It is described by De Strycker and Slings as an 'authorized commentary' on *Apology* 41d (E. de Strycker, *Plato's Apology of Socrates: A Literary and Philosophical Study with Running Commentary*, S.R. Slings (ed.), *Mnemosune* suppl. 137 (Leiden: Brill, 1994), *ad loc*). Such apparently intentional cross-references by Plato may count against interpreting the earlier dialogues as representing the views of the real Socrates, and the later those of Plato.

[24] Vlastos (*Socrates*, 221) does not mention that the *Apology* passage continues: 'nor are his fortunes ignored by the gods' (41d2-3). Further, he translates '*themiton*' at *Apology* 30d1 merely as 'permitted', as if equivalent to some form of *eaô* (*ibid.*, 219). H. Tredennick prefers 'the law of God permits' (in *Plato: The Collected Dialogues*, eds. E. Hamilton and H. Cairns, (Princeton: Princeton University Press, 1961)), Allen and Stokes 'in accord with divine law' (R.E. Allen, *The Dialogues of Plato* (New Haven: Yale University Press, 1984); M. Stokes, *Apology* (Warminster: Aris and Phillips, 1997)), while Griffith has 'god allows' (T. Griffith, *Symposium and the Death of Socrates* (Ware: Wordsworth, 1997)). Burnet also suggests 'permitted', but gives '*fas*' as an equivalent. 'Forbidden by divine providence' for *ou themiton* was suggested to me by Margaret Howatson. For a discussion of Socrates'

entirely clear, but I assume that the idea is that something *pro tanto* bad, such as an illness, is not an overall evil, if one is virtuous, since it will lead to some kind of compensation in the form of something *pro tanto* good, the overall result, combining both the bad and the good, being either neutral or good overall.[25] In other words, what Socrates is claiming is that, though health, wealth and so on are genuine goods for a virtuous person, depriving him of them will not be a genuine harm, in the sense of an overall loss: for the gods will take care of it that he is compensated, either now or later.[26] And in case it may be thought irresponsible to interpret claims made by the 'non-republican' Socrates by reference to claims of the republican, let me note further that, though Socrates in the *Apology* says he is not sure of the nature of death (29a5-6, 40c6-41c7), he does think it will be good, that is, good for him (40b8-c2, c5-6).[27] Indeed, when he says that death may be like a dreamless sleep (40c10-d1), we would do well to listen again to Burnet: ' We are not to suppose that Socrates has any real doubt on the matter'.[28]

Socrates' view on happiness and virtue, then, can be summarized as follows. Happiness is constituted largely by virtue, but also – as long as one is virtuous – can include other goods, such as health or wealth. And if something apparently bad overall happens to a virtuous person, whether through human agency or otherwise, the gods will take care to ensure that this bad thing is compensated for by something good, either in this life or the afterlife. Choosing virtue, then, will always be best for one, and the apparent dangers of virtue, in circumstances prejudicial to its continued existence or its exercise, turn out not to be real.

---

views on divine providence, see N. Gulley, *The Philosophy of Socrates* (London: Macmillan, 1968), 179-92. Elsewhere in Plato, *themiton* appears always to be used in divine contexts: *Gorgias* 497c4, *Phaedo* 61c10ff., 67b2, *Phaedrus* 256d3; see also *Epinomis* 992a6. Reeve suggests that *themiton* here, as at *Phaedrus* 256d3, carries the implication that what is contrary to it is impossible (*Socrates in the Apology*, 151).

[25] I have been helped here by discussion with David Wiggins.

[26] At *Gorgias* 469b12-c1, Socrates is asked whether he would wish to suffer injustice rather than do it. He says that he would wish for neither, but if he had to choose would go for suffering rather than doing. Vlastos (*Socrates*, 227) understands him to be preferring that he not suffer injustice, but in fact all he says here is that he would not wish for it. In other words, suffering injustice may be something Socrates does not wish for because it is neither good nor bad for him. Cf. Irwin, *Plato's Ethics*, 119. Brickhouse and Smith (*Socrates on Trial*, 162) note that Socrates accepts (37b5-e2) that certain penalties would be harmful to him: prison and banishment. But, as they themselves note (219), Socrates has to do what he can to obey the oracle, and he realizes he would not be able to do that either in prison or in exile. And if he were not to do his best to obey, he would have seen no reason to think that the gods would compensate him for any loss.

[27] Note that Socrates claims not that he knows nothing of death, only that his knowledge is insufficient (29b5). It has to be admitted, however, that Socrates' cheerful attitude to death might well be said to rest on exactly the same error of which he here charges those who fear death; see C. Rowe, *An Introduction to Greek Ethics* (London: Hutchinson, 1976), 36; and D. Roochnik, '*Apology* 40c4-41e7: Is Death Really a Gain?', *Classical Journal* 80 (1985), 212-20, at 214. Something has to give here, and I am more tempted to find some irony in 29a-b than in the positive claims about the nature of death.

[28] Burnet, *Euthyphro, Apology of Socrates, Crito*, 246, n. 40c5.

Reasons for action

So far, we have seen that Socrates appears to accept that human beings act to further their own perceived greatest happiness, that one's strongest reason for action lies in advancing one's happiness, that happiness consists in virtue and other goods, and that choosing the path of virtue guarantees one the greatest possible happiness. In this section of the paper, I wish to examine how this set of views might relate to Socrates' position on justifying (grounding, normative, or prescriptive) reasons for action.[29]

Let me first draw a distinction between derivative, and non-derivative or ultimate, reasons. Consider this famous passage from Hume:

> Ask a man, *why he uses exercise*; he will answer, *because he desires to keep his health.* If you then enquire, *why he desires health*, he will readily reply, *because sickness is painful.* If you push your enquiries farther, and desire a reason, *why he hates pain*, it is impossible he can ever give any. This is an ultimate end, and is never referred to any other object (*An Enquiry concerning the Principles of Morals*, app. 1.18.).

So I have derivative reasons to find my trainers, open the front door, and start running. Ultimate reasons explain why I have such derivative reasons. According to Hume, since I have an ultimate reason to seek the greatest balance of pleasure over pain for myself, this gives me reason to take exercise.

Recall now:

> *Rational Eudaimonism*: Each person has strongest reason to pursue her own greatest happiness.

If we allow that, if I have a single reason in some situation, then that is my strongest reason, Rational Eudaimonism is neutral on whether there may be reasons other than those issuing from my own happiness. According to:

> *Monistic Rational Eudaimonism*: Each person has ultimate reason only to pursue her greatest happiness.

Socrates, Plato, and Aristotle are, I suspect, often understood, by those who understand them as eudaimonists, to be Monistic Rational Eudaimonists.[30] But it is important to distinguish that position from:

> *Pluralistic Rational Eudaimonism*: Each person has an ultimate reason to pursue her greatest happiness, alongside at least one other ultimate reason.

---

[29] Here I am wishing primarily to distinguish such reasons from explanatory or motivating reasons. See e.g. M. Smith, 'The Humean Theory of Motivation', *Mind* 96 (1987), 36-61, at 37-41.

[30] See e.g. Vlastos, *Socrates*, 203.

Monistic Rational Eudaimonism is, by default, egoistic. Pluralistic Rational Eudaimonism does not require that eudaimonistic reasons – those grounded in the advancing of my own happiness – conflict with non-eudaimonistic.[31] For example, on some occasion it may be that I have reason to promote my own happiness, and am required by morality to show gratitude, and that both reasons speak in favour of the same course of action. But Pluralistic Rational Eudaimonism does allow for the possiblity of such conflict.

Socrates appears to accept that there are non-eudaimonistic reasons. In the *Apology*, he allows that the obvious interpretation of a divine sign may be mistaken (21b1-8), but again and again insists that his constant questioning of his fellow citizens is a religious duty:[32]

> After that I went to people one after another, afraid and distressed to recognize that I was hated for it. But I thought it necessary to put the god first (21e2-4).

> So that's why I still go around enquiring and searching, in accordance with the god (23b4-5).

> So in truth do things stand, men of Athens. Where somebody has taken a position where he thinks it's best, *or is positioned by his commander*, there, as it seems to me, he must stay and face the danger, taking thought neither for death nor anything else before what is shameful (28d5-9).[33]

---

[31] For a helpful discussion of different forms of egoism, see R. Kraut, *Aristotle on the Human Good* (Princeton: Princeton University Press, 1989), 78-86.

[32] A. Nehamas points out that Socrates interprets the oracle as an order only *after* he has tested it ('Socratic Intellectualism', in *Virtues of Authenticity* (Princeton: Princeton University Press, 1999), 27-58, at 44). But the 'test' is not of the oracle's veracity: he knows it is not 'lawful' (*themis*) for the oracle to lie (21b6-7). Socrates is inquiring into what the god *means, so that* he can obey. He seeks to test or refute (21c1) the oracle not because he questions the god's authority, but because he wants to find out just what it is that the god wants him to do. He finds out – and goes on doing it 'in accordance with the god' (*kata ton theon*) (23b5). He is not, *pace* Nehamas (*ibid.*), testing the wisdom of the god. Cf. Brickhouse and Smith, *Socrates on Trial*, 96; Reeve, *Socrates in the Apology*, 22-3.

[33] Cf. Kraut: 'Socrates has been commanded by the god, just as a soldier is commanded by a captain' ('Plato's *Apology* and *Crito*: Two Recent Studies', *Ethics* 91 (1981), 651-64, at 659); cf. 28e4-5. The second disjunct in the text here (which I have italicized) speaks against Nehamas' claim that 'the whole notion of obedience and submission ... is deeply unimportant to Socrates ... There is, in my opinion, not a trace of voluntarism in Socrates' "obedience" to the god; on the contrary, he only does, as he always has done, what he thinks is, on independent grounds, the best thing' ('Socratic Intellectualism', 44). Nehamas says of this second disjunct that 'it depends on Socrates' obeying his commanders in a particular case having already agreed, on rational grounds, to obey them in general' (*ibid.*, 57, n. 53). But no evidence is offered other than a general reference to Kraut's book *Socrates and the State*. And if the idea of its being best to obey is to be understood in the background to the second disjunct, why, given that the first disjunct has already mentioned what is best as a reason, should Socrates mention the case of obedience to superiors at all? Cf. also Brickhouse and Smith: 'There is no trace of pure duties in the Kantian sense in Socratic thought. What is good is good simply in virtue of its contribution to one's happiness'

That being unjust and disobeying one's superior, whether god or man, is bad and shameful I know (29b6-7).[34]

I shall obey the god rather than you (29d3).

This is what the god commands (30a5; cf. 33c4-7, 37e6-7).

So one may 'take a position' where one thinks it is best; but one may also be positioned – commanded – by a superior, and this is how Socrates sees his own case: he has a duty not to leave his post (28d9-29a2). Leaving his post would be shameful, so we see that Socrates allows for at least two sources of ultimate non-eudaimonistic reasons: divine command, and morality (cf. 32d2-4, 35c8-d1).[35] But these sources appear not to conflict with one another or with the agent's happiness, since obeying the god is pious, hence virtuous, and hence morally required (cf. 35d1), and the god, Socrates suggests, directs him in the direction of his greatest good (40b7-c4; cf. 41d4-6). So Socrates is not just a pluralist about the components of happiness. He is also a pluralist about reasons, though there is no conflict between them. Virtue provides its own reasons, as do the gods, but these reasons are perfectly consistent with reasons grounded in the advancement of one's own happiness.

('Socrates on Goods, Virtue and Happiness', 3; *Plato's Socrates*, 103); though note their recognition ('Socrates on Goods, Virtue and Happiness', 18; *Plato's Socrates*, 116) that Socrates saw himself as divinely commanded.

[34] Nehamas says of this passage: 'The word Kraut translates here as "disobey" is *apeithein*, and it is, of course, clear that "obey" and "disobey" are common enough senses of the verbs *peithesthai* and *apeithein* … But the etymological connection between *peithô* and its cognates and the notion of persuasion is never, I think, far from the surface in the use of the terms' ('Socratic Intellectualism', 44). But Nehamas provides no evidence in support of this claim, and – *pace* Nehamas (47) – *apeithein* cannot to my knowledge mean anything other than 'disobey' (broadly construed). Cf. Burnet (*Euthyphro, Apology of Socrates, Crito*, 201, n. 29a3): 'The verb *apeithein* is a solemn one, and is generally used of disobedience to God or the State'. Nehamas suggests that Socrates 'goes on to imagine that, not having been *convinced (ou peisometha)* by Anytus' call for the death penalty, they will spare him on condition that he no longer engage in philosophy' (44). Nehamas may well be right to choose this translation rather than the more common 'not having obeyed'. But it shows nothing about *apeithein* at 29b6.

[35] Reeve prefers to see the reason to obey the god as itself grounded on an independent ethical reason, making apt reference to 29b6-7 (*Socrates in the Apology*, 62-66). I shall not pursue the issue further here, since what matters for my argument is that Socrates allows for at least one source of non-eudaimonistic reason. For a good statement of Socrates' religious attitude, see Brickhouse and Smith (*Plato's Socrates*, 188-89, 201).

Morality and self-sacrifice

In response to an egoist such as Thrasymachus, who agrees with Socrates that it is rational to pursue one's own happiness, but sees happiness as consisting only in goods such as wealth, pleasure, and honour, and not in virtue, Socrates has a two-pronged response. The first is his commitment to both Moralism and Pluralism about happiness, the latter of which – plausibly enough – allows that Thrasymachus is half-right. The goods Thrasymachus has identified are indeed worth having. But he has failed to recognize the towering importance of virtue in happiness, in so far as it is sufficient for happiness and without it nothing is good. Secondly, Socrates may claim, there are non-eudaimonistic reasons, grounded in divine command or morality, which support the life of virtue.

But here we need to note some possible hostages to fortune in Socrates' position. Thrasymachus may allow that virtue is a good, but put so much weight on non-moral goods such as the avoidance of severe suffering, or huge power and wealth, that he can make a reasonably strong case that in certain cases happiness is best served by immorality. Further, it will be tempting for a defender of Socrates' position, in these cases, to appeal to non-eudaimonistic reasons in favour of virtue. But these will be reasons in favour of self-sacrifice, against which Thrasymachus can wield the plausibility of Rational Eudaimonism.

I now wish to suggest that we can see these tensions in Socrates' own position. First, however, let me offer a clear example of how they might be avoided. At *Phaedo* 61d-62c, Socrates explains to Cebes how it can be forbidden by divine law to commit suicide and yet a philosopher be willing to follow someone who has died. He considers those cases in which it would be better for the person concerned to be dead (62a5), and one might think that Socrates is here ready to allow that a non-eudaimonistic, moral reason can trump the eudaimonistic reason to promote one's own happiness. Morality, that is, might seem to be requiring one not to kill oneself, though it would be better to do so. But it becomes clear that when Socrates says that death would be better for such people, he means a non-suicidal death. For his reason against suicide is that the suicide will be punished by the gods for his crime: 'So if one of your possessions were to kill itself, without your signalling that you wanted it to die, wouldn't you be angry with it, and punish it, if you had some punishment available?' (62c1-4).[36] There is no opportunity for one to sacrifice oneself for the sake of virtue: the virtuous action is the best for one. Virtue – 'the ordinary virtue of a citizen' – will guarantee one happiness in Hades (82a11-b2).

But now consider the famous passage in the *Republic* at the end of the account of the cave, in which the philosophers are required to descend again into the cave.[37]

---

[36] This is of course the other side of the divine compensation scheme we have already seen operating in favour of the virtuous.

[37] As Nicholas White puts it: '[T]he existence, not to mention the importance, of this case suffices to show that he does not think that the only possible or reasonable motive for acting justly is to increase one's own happiness' (*A Companion to Plato's Republic* (Indianapolis:

Socrates says that it is the job of him and his interlocutors, as founders of the city, not to allow the philosophers to remain contemplating the good, once they have seen enough of it. Glaucon asks: 'Are we to do them an injustice, then, and make them live a worse life when they could live a better one?' (519d8-9).

Now we might expect Socrates to say several things in response. He might say that, because it is just for the philosophers to descend, they would be worse off remaining outside the cave, for virtue is a necessary condition for happiness,[38] and if they do gain some good from the contemplation, the gods will anyway punish them sufficiently on their deaths that they will lose overall. Or he might claim that they have no choice, since they themselves will be worse off overall if they allow others to govern in the cave.[39] What Socrates in fact says is that 'it is not the concern of the law to bring it about that any one class in the city does especially well' (519e1-3; cf. 420b5-c4, 421b3-c6), thus appearing to accept that it is a loss for the philosophers to descend.

Socrates goes on to claim that the demand being made of the philosophers is a just one, since they owe a debt of gratitude to the city and should recognize that

---

Hackett, 1979), 44; see also 23-24, 43-60, 189-96). The 'sacrificial' interpretation is also offered by P. Shorey, *What Plato Said* (Chicago: Chicago University Press, 1935), 235; M. Foster, 'Some Implications of a Passage in Plato's *Republic*', *Philosophy* 11 (1936), 301-8, at 301; H. Prichard, *Moral Obligation* (Oxford: Clarendon Press, 1949), 108; A. Adkins, *Moral Responsibility* (Oxford: Clarendon Press, 1960), 290-91; S. Aronson, 'The Happy Philosopher – A Counterexample to Plato's Proof', *Journal of the History of Philosophy* 10 (1972), 383-98, at 393-6; R. Kraut, 'Egoism, Love, and Political Office in Plato', *Philosophical Review* 82 (1973), 330-44, at 331-3; J. Annas, *An Introduction to Plato's Republic* (Oxford: Clarendon Press, 1981), 266-71; N. White, 'The Ruler's Choice', *Archiv für Geschichte der Philosophie* 68 (1986), 22-46; N. Pappas, *Plato and the* Republic (London: Routledge, 1995), 119; J. Yu, 'Justice in the *Republic*: An Evolving Paradox', *History of Philosophy Quarterly* 17 (2000), 121-41, at 130-31.

[38] See R. Kraut, 'Return to the Cave: *Republic* 519-521', *Proceedings of the Boston Area Colloquium in Ancient Philosophy* 7 (Lanham: University Press of America, 1991), 43-62, at 47-50. It might be claimed that the philosophers *must* be better off descending, if this is what they have strongest reason to do, since continuing to contemplate would lead to disharmony in their souls. In fact, however, the motivation to contemplate itself emerges from reason, so the conflict here is contained within one part of the soul (White, 'The Ruler's Choice', 28).

[39] C.D.C. Reeve (*Philosopher-Kings: The Argument of Plato's Republic* (Princeton: Princeton University Press, 1988), 202) reads the passage as if it were saying just this. But even if this is the correct reading, it is about what the philosophers as a group would be better off doing. It will still be the case that any individual philosopher would be better off free-riding: see Aronson ('The Happy Philosopher', 397); (Aronson also points out that this interpretation leaves justice as merely instrumentally good); Kraut, 'Egoism, Love, and Political Office in Plato', 332-3. In a city of virtuous people, after all, there will be competition not to rule (347d2-4, cited by White ('The Ruler's Choice', 30)). Kraut also notes that the Reeve position leaves Socrates' case resting on a quite contingent empirical calculation, and makes the whole point of the moral argument here mysterious ('Return to the Cave', 50-51).

they are best suited to governing the city, taking it in turns to do so (520a6-d4).[40] So here it seems that we have a case of moral self-sacrifice, in which the philosophers, who would have a better life were they to remain in the light of the sun, are required by justice to do what is worse for themselves.[41]

It might nevertheless be thought that they have no choice, and that therefore the apparently better option is not available to them. Here we should note again that Socrates never denies Glaucon's suggestion that life for the philosophers would be better were they to remain outside the cave. But what of the fact that they will be 'compelled' to descend (520a8; cf. 519c8-9, 519e4, 520e2, 521b7, 540b5)? Well, what will compel them? It would be absurd to imagine that the auxiliaries might be empowered somehow to leave the cave and drag the philosophers down. They cannot leave, trapped by their own intellectual limits. What will compel the philosophers will be the claims of justice itself,[42] instantiated in the law underlying *Kallipolis* (519e1) or in the speech made to them by Socrates. Socrates puts the argument from justice in the form of words spoken directly to the philosophers, introducing it as follows: "'Note, Glaucon", I said, "that we shall not be doing an injustice to our philosophers, but will say just things to them, compelling them to care for and protect the others'" (520a7-9).[43]

---

[40] The argument from gratitude is of course one of 'vulgar' as opposed to 'Platonic' justice (see D. Sachs, 'A Fallacy in Plato's *Republic*', in G. Vlastos (ed.), *Plato: A Collection of Critical Essays, II* (Notre Dame: University of Notre Dame Press, 1978), 35-51, at 35-45). I take it that Socrates, in the *Republic* as in the *Apology*, believes there to be self-standing moral reasons, and that if reason is to govern one's soul it will have to take these reasons into account (cf. Kraut, 'Return to the Cave', 57). Thus the 'vulgar' conception is, properly understood, as Platonic as the 'Platonic'. There is always *a* reason to be grateful – to demonstrate one's gratitude, to act. Principles requiring one to act virtuously are not susceptible to the kinds of counter-example used by Socrates against principles requiring certain non-virtuous acts (such as to return items one has borrowed); so it is a mistake to see the *Republic* as advocating an 'agent-centred' conception of justice as opposed to an 'act-centred' conception (see e.g. Annas, *An Introduction to Plato's Republic*, 157-69). Justice requires that one do certain actions – just ones. For further criticism of such distinctions in general, see my 'Particularizing Particularism', in B. Hooker and M. Little (eds.), *Moral Particularism* (Oxford: Clarendon Press, 2000), 23-47. Recognizing non-eudaimonistic moral reasons also enables one to fend off the charge that ancient ethics, in postulating virtue as a constituent of the good, is circular (see H. Sidgwick, *The Methods of Ethics* (London: Macmillan, 1907), 375-7).

[41] For the view that the implications of the passage for eudaimonism are indeterminate, see Irwin ('The Monism of Practical Reason', unpub. ts., 7).

[42] See White ('The Ruler's Choice', 24, n. 4); T. Mahoney, 'Do Plato's Philosopher-rulers Sacrifice Self-interest to Justice?', *Phronesis* 37 (1992), 265-82, at 271; Irwin, *Plato's Ethics*, 299. Mahoney (*ibid.*) suggests that the philosophers, given their education, have no need to be told. But it could be that they have understood only general ethical principles, and have not learned to whom these principles apply. This would explain the necessity for the law to be involved; it will constitute the medium through which the philosophers learn of their obligation, rather than a source of sanction in cases of possible disobedience.

[43] This translation is quite close to the Greek, in which *prosanankazontes* immediately follows *eroumen*. It is common among translators to leave more open the possibility of

When Socrates asks Glaucon whether the philosophers will disobey, once they have heard this argument, he replies not that they will not because they will be coerced, say, physically to obey, but that disobedience is impossible, because 'we are giving just commands to just people' (520e1).[44] But it is not as if they have lost sight of their own happiness, as if understanding the Form of the Good 'requires that I abstract completely from my own interests'.[45] They are 'least keen to rule' (520d2), seeing government as something 'compulsory' (520e2; cf. 540b4-5) to be 'despised' (521b2).[46] They understand their loss, but, because they have seen the

---

compulsion independent of the argument from justice itself: 'we can justify our action when we constrain them to take charge' (P. Shorey (Hamilton and Cairns (eds.) (1961))); 'what we'll say to them, when we compel them to guard and care for the others, will be just' (G. Grube, *Republic*, rev. C.D.C. Reeve (Indianapolis: Hackett, 1992)); 'shall be quite fair in what we say when we compel them' (D. Lee, *Republic* (Harmondsworth: Penguin, 1974)). *Prosanankazein* is standardly used of legal compulsion (*Symposium* 181e5, *Laws* 779c1 (cf. *Republic* 391d3)) and of being compelled by argument (*Symposium* 217d5, 223d3, *Philebus* 13b3, *Statesman* 284b7, 284b10, *Sophist* 260a2), or of non-physical compulsion (*Protagoras* 346b4, *Republic* 401b2, 526b1). *Anankazein* is used in conjunction with *peithein* at 421c1, but even here it is conceivable that the *kai* is epexegetic. In the case of the other classes, of course, the form of compulsion is unlikely to be mere persuasion.

[44] Note again the language of commands (here, *epitattein*) as in the *Apology*.

[45] Annas, *An Introduction to Plato's Republic*, 269.

[46] This attitude of the philosophers is a stumbling-block for several attempts to provide a non-sacrificial interpretation of the descent. As Aronson says, 'One must take seriously the reluctance to return' ('The Happy Philosopher', 394). See, for example, S. Waterlow, 'The Good of Others in Plato's *Republic*', *Proceedings of the Aristotelian Society* 73 (1972-73), 19-36, at 33; Mahoney, 'Do Plato's Philosopher-rulers Sacrifice Self-interest to Justice?', 273-4. Kraut claims that the philosopher who descends will most effectively imitate the Forms and so lead the best life, and that the philosophers' dislike for ruling might well sit alongside a love of justice ('Return to the Cave', 54-5); cf. R. Kraut, 'The Defense of Justice in Plato's *Republic*', in R. Kraut (ed.), *The Cambridge Companion to Plato's Republic* (Cambridge: Cambridge University Press, 1992), 311-37, at 328. But there is no textual support for this suggestion at 519-21, and at 540b4 we are told that the philosophers return to ruling 'not as if it were something fine'. The problem might appear to arise also for John Cooper's claim: 'if the degree of one's *eudaimonia* is measured by how close one comes to realizing one's ultimate end, such a philosopher [one who fails to descend] would be less *eudaimôn* than he would have been by living the mixed political and intellectual life ... any philosopher would always *prefer* the mixed life' ('The Psychology of Justice in Plato', in *Reason and Emotion* (Princeton: Princeton University Press, 1999), 138-49, at 147). But I fail to understand the import of this claim, since on the same page Cooper notes that the philosophers 'deliberately and freely (520d6-7) choose a life for themselves that is less good than a more singlemindedly intellectual life, of which however they are individually capable'. He later (147-8) goes on to suggest that the fact that the philosophers living the mixed life would be the happiest men there could be 'shows beyond any reasonable doubt that Plato's just man is no egoist', and that he never does anything out of concern for his own good, acting purely for the sake of the Good itself. But if the mixed life really is the happiest, why should the philosophers not be choosing it out of concern for themselves? And if they are concerned only for the Good itself, why do they regret the necessity for descent? Finally, let me note that I take Irwin's non-sacrificial interpretation (*Plato's Ethics*,

Form of the Good, understand also the rational force of *nomos* – the moral law.[47] One might wonder why the philosophers are not more sanguine: for they, like Socrates, must surely know that the gods will compensate them for any loss they experience during their life in the service of virtue. But, of course, the best the gods can provide for them will be philosophical contemplation in the afterlife, and they might have hoped for that anyway.[48] It is Socrates' unwillingness to place anything above philosophy as a constituent of happiness that forces him to allow that morality can require self-sacrifice.[49]

Eudaimonism in the *Rhetoric*

In the *Rhetoric*, Aristotle's view about the relation of virtue and happiness seems to have been somewhat undecided:

> Let happiness be doing well combined with virtue, or self-sufficiency of life, or security of the most pleasant life, or good condition of possessions and body, together with the power of protecting and using them. That happiness is one or more of these nearly everyone agrees (*Rhetoric* 1360b14-18).[50]

But, from what Aristotle goes on immediately to say, it seems that, in some sense, he accepts both Moralism and Pluralism about happiness (1360b19-23):

> So if happiness is such, its constituent parts must be good birth, lots of friends, good friends, wealth, good children, lots of children, a happy old age; also bodily

---

ch. 18), based on an analysis of *eros* in the *Symposium* and the *Phaedrus*, to be reconstruction rather than exegesis (as does C. Gill, 'Greek Ethics', *Philosophical Books* 39 (1998), 1-8).

[47] See Foster, 'Some Implications of a Passage in Plato's *Republic*', 304.

[48] It might be said that, since the soul is immortal, whether the philosopher is deprived of philosophy on earth will make no difference, since he or she will have overall an infinite amount of it. But it is not implausible to think that, of two infinite series of goods, that with the higher average is to be preferred. (For an excellent discussion of this issue, see P. Vallentyne and S. Kagan, 'Infinite Value and Finitely Additive Value Theory', *Journal of Philosophy* 94 (1997), 5-27.) Or it may be that the philosophers are just keen to get going on permanent contemplation, if patience is not one of their traits.

[49] As White points out ('The Ruler's Choice', 41), because the philosophers are the sole exception, the account of their descent may be said not completely to undercut the purpose of the *Republic* as a whole. It is still going to be in most people's interest to be just. But the dialectical importance of the exception is noted by Aronson ('The Happy Philosopher', 393), who says that by it 'Plato has opened a Pandora's box of obstacles to any attempt at refuting Thrasymachus'. Foster says of the passage: 'It is remarkable because it contains the conception, expressed, to my knowledge, nowhere else in Greek [i.e. Athenian] philosophy, of moral Obligation, or Duty' ('Some Implications of a Passage in Plato's *Republic*', 301). I cannot go along with this, but I do think the passage unique in both Plato and Aristotle in its recommendation of moral self-sacrifice.

[50] The indecision may be a sign of this part of the *Rhetoric*'s being early.

excellences (such as health, beauty, strength, size, athletic power), reputation, honour, good luck, virtue.

It is clear that by 'virtue' Aristotle has in mind the moral virtues (perhaps among others): the examples he goes on in this chapter to give include temperance and courage (1361a3), and in chapter 9 he lists the excellences as justice, courage, temperance, magnificence, magnanimity, generosity, gentleness, practical wisdom, and wisdom (1366b1-3). In the first passage quoted above in this section, Aristotle seems to allow that hedonism might be correct. In a sense, hedonism is neither moralistic nor pluralistic, since, according to hedonism, the constituent parts of happiness could make their contribution to happiness only by contributing to the pleasantness of the happy person's life. But, as Mill explains, we can still speak of virtue and even wealth as part of happiness even on a hedonistic account.[51] So, as far as the *Rhetoric* is concerned, we may indeed ascribe both Moralism and Pluralism to Aristotle.

It is natural to think of morality as somehow importantly involving the interests of others, and of certain moral reasons as themselves being grounded on these interests.[52] That understanding of morality lies behind the descent into the cave: the moral law that requires the philosophers to descend is concerned not with the happiness of any particular class alone, but with the happiness of all. In the *Rhetoric*, Aristotle appears to have gone along with this conception of morality. In the chapter in which he sets out to discuss virtue, he says (1366a36-1367a5):

> Virtue, it is thought, is a capacity for providing and protecting good things, and a capacity for conferring many great benefits, of all kinds and in every circumstance ... If virtue is a capacity for beneficence, then the greatest virtues must be those which are of the greatest use to others ... [Noble] are those [actions] done for things worth choosing and not for the sake of the agent, and actions good without qualification, such as those someone does for his country without thinking of himself, and actions good by nature, and those which are good not for the agent, since actions good for the agent are done for his own sake ... [Noble] also [are] actions done for the sake of others, since these are done for the agent's own sake to a lesser degree than others; and all good deeds concerned with others and not oneself.[53]

---

[51] J.S. Mill, *Utilitarianism*, ed. R. Crisp (Oxford: Oxford University Press, 1998), ch. 4, paras. 5-6.

[52] See T. Irwin, 'Aristotle's Conception of Morality', *Proceedings of the Boston Area Colloquium on Ancient Philosophy* 1 (Lanham: University Press of America, 1985), 115-43, at 116.

[53] K. Rogers ('Aristotle's Conception of *to kalon*', *Ancient Philosophy* 13 (1993), 355-71, at 362-4) argues that there is no reason to think Aristotle himself believed these claims in the *Rhetoric*. Some of her arguments assume that inconsistency with the *Ethics* counts against their being genuinely Aristotelian; I prefer to believe that Aristotle's views differ between the two works – and indeed, if the relevant parts of the *Rhetoric* are earlier than the *Nicomachean Ethics*, that they developed (see below). She is right to say that Aristotle wishes to proceed by using illustrations, and is mainly concerned with persuasion. But why should Aristotle not prefer to use 'real' illustrations, and to base persuasion itself on his

So we can see that Aristotle's position on virtue and happiness in the *Rhetoric* is in certain respects close to that of Socrates. He accepts Moralism and Pluralism about happiness, and seems inclined to accept non-eudaimonistic reasons for action, grounded in the interests of others – that is, Pluralistic Rational Eudaimonism, given that Aristotle also favoured both Psychological Eudaimonism and Rational Eudaimonism (*Rhetoric* 1360b4-13, 1362b10-12).[54] Aristotle does not appear explicitly to allow for the possibility or rationality of self-sacrifice,[55] but the non-moral constituents of happiness, along with non-eudaimonistic reasons for action, both make more plausible the idea that morality might require agents to perform actions which damage their happiness overall.

As we saw, in the case of Socrates, these aspects of his account can be seen to lead in the *Republic* to his surrendering the notion that virtue can always be justified on egoistic eudaimonistic terms. I shall now suggest that in his *Ethics* Aristotle went in quite the opposite direction, continuing the project of the eudaimonistic Socrates, and removing the potential for the position of Socrates in the *Republic* – for the moral law that conflicts with happiness – to develop.

Eudaimonism in the *Ethics*

Aristotle does not deny either Psychological Eudaimonism or Rational Eudaimonism in the *Nicomachean Ethics*. He begins the work with the claim that 'every action and rational choice is thought to aim at some good' (1094a1-2), and he takes the claim that happiness is the chief good – the good which includes all others worth aiming at (1097b14-21) – to be a platitude (1097b22-3).

Now what will Aristotle say to a rational eudaimonist, such as Thrasymachus, who claims that vice will further the agent's own happiness? The core of Socrates' response was Moralism, combined with a weighting in favour of virtue within his account of Pluralism. As we saw, the non-moral elements of Socrates' pluralistic conception of happiness came into conflict with non-eudaimonistic moral reasons in the thought of Socrates in the *Republic*. Aristotle retains Moralism, but denies Pluralism. According to the conclusion of the 'function argument', 'the human good turns out to be activity of the soul in accordance with virtue' (1098a16-17).[56]

---

conception of the way things are – assuming that others are likely to converge on the same truth?

[54] I am assuming that we should interpret Aristotle's claims in these passages as egoistic.

[55] *Pace* Irwin, 'Aristotle's Conception of Morality', 132-4, who appears to believe that the emphasis on the good of others in the *Rhetoric* implies that their interests can rationally trump those of the agent.

[56] I have tried to show in 'Aristotle's Inclusivism' (*Oxford Studies in Ancient Philosophy* 12 (1994), 111-36) how this monistic Moralistic interpretation of Aristotle is quite consistent with inclusivism, the view that Aristotelian happiness includes all non-instrumental, non-conditional, non-derivative, or ultimate goods, and how Aristotle seeks to answer possible 'more-is-bettter' objections by claiming that virtuous activity itself includes goods such as pleasure or friendship which might be used as examples in such objections.

On this view, one can never lose *anything* by acting virtuously.[57] Virtue – or rather its exercise – is not the greatest good; it is the only good. This prevents any risk of a Thrasymachean challenge to virtue grounded on non-moral goods.

But what of philosophy, and its part in happiness? What might be the Aristotelian line on the descent into the cave? In that single case, Socrates appears to accept both that a non-moral component of happiness can have greater eudaimonic weight than virtue, and that virtue requires self-sacrifice. The implications of Aristotle's view on this case seem to me indeterminate. He does emphasize that philosophical contemplation is itself the exercise of a virtue, and so to be counted as a 'moral' component of a Moralistic conception of happiness. This move might allow him to argue that the philosophers could remain outside the cave without going against the demands of morality. In a sense, of course, this move was available to Socrates, since he could have argued that, on the Platonic conception of justice, justice required, or at least permitted, the philosophers to remain outside the cave. If pushed, I would suggest that Aristotle would have thought any philosopher's strongest reason would have been to remain outside the cave, since only thus could he make himself as immortal as possible (*NE* 1177b33). But this position would be quite compatible with his claiming that in the real world, as opposed to the fictional world of the cave, the mixed life is the happiest (as indeed Socrates could have claimed, thus decreasing yet further the practical significance of the descent into the cave). There is no reason to believe that Aristotle held the exercise of the intellectual virtues to be incommensurably better for a (real) person than the exercise of the practical virtues.[58]

Happiness, for Aristotle, consists in the exercise of the virtues, and philosophy and politics both involve such exercise. Socrates, in the descent into the cave, allowed for the rationality of moral self-sacrifice. Aristotle makes such sacrifice conceptually impossible, since there is nothing for virtue to conflict with. Thus his

---

Of course, he may be said to fail to provide an acceptable response to the objection that non-virtuous pleasure or non-virtuous friendship can increase a person's happiness. Given the topic of this Keeling Colloquium, it might be worth noting that elements of Aristotle's position are clearly foreshadowed in Plato. Aristotle himself refers to the 'more-is-better' argument in *Philebus* 20e-21d at *NE* 1172b26-34. Compare also, for example, the claim that the good person is self-sufficient and lacking in nothing (*Lysis* 215a6-8; cf. *Republic* 387d11-e1) to *NE* 1097b14-16. And note – in addition to *Republic* 580c-588a, mentioned above – the claim at *Laws* 662b2-663d4 that the just life is the most pleasant; cf. *NE* 1099a7-21.

[57] I have elsewhere attempted to explain various cases in which Aristotle might mistakenly be thought to be both allowing for and advocating self-sacrifice ('Kraut on Aristotle on Happiness', *Polis* 10 (1991), 129-61, at 144-52).

[58] *Pace* J.L. Ackrill ('Aristotle on *Eudaimonia*', in A.O Rorty (ed.), *Essays on Aristotle's Ethics* (Berkeley: University of California Press, 1980), 15-33, at 32-33). See my paper, 'Aristotle's Inclusivism'. This, then, is how Aristotle deals with the threat to practical virtue from philosophy. When it comes to the other goods which Socrates saw as part of happiness, and which may also pose a threat to virtue, Aristotle's strategy will be to claim that the happy life, on his account, will include such goods, or that the alleged good is not a good in itself, perhaps being merely instrumental. See n. 56 above.

position provides the resources to defend the rationality of virtue to a Rational Egoist such as Thrasymachus, who might have been tempted by Socratic Pluralism about happiness into playing down the importance of virtue in happiness, and by the descent into the cave into seeing virtue as, at least on occasion, overriding the agent's happiness.

Socrates accepted non-eudaimonistic reasons, as we have seen, and did indeed allow them, in the *Republic*, to override eudaimonistic reasons. But as long as Aristotle nowhere allows for non-eudaimonistic reasons that are not themselves grounded in virtue, he can accept such reasons without giving up on Rational Eudaimonism or the claim that virtue is always the best choice. As far as I can tell, he does not allow for such non-virtue-based reasons. In other words, in some case where one (ultimate) reason I have to ϕ is that it will advance my own happiness, Aristotle can accept that there may be other ultimate reasons to ϕ – in particular, that the action in question will be virtuous.[59] So, though his view of happiness differs from that of Socrates, in being monistic, he may well be understood to retain Pluralistic Rational Eudaimonism.

We can understand what led Aristotle to take this strict line on the relation of virtue and happiness: it would give the critic of virtue absolutely no ground on which to stand. Nothing good (literally – not merely nothing good overall) can come from vice, only harm. But what are his arguments? The central one, of course, is the function argument itself, and others have already done a good deal to make it plausible that this argument rests on an equivocation between what is good and what is good for a person.[60] It does seem to me that the argument will work only on the assumptions that (a) reason requires virtue, and (b) it is always better for a rational agent to do what is required by reason.

But I would like to end by considering another strand in Aristotle's thought which has been less discussed, that concerning 'the noble'.[61] As we saw, in the *Rhetoric*, Aristotle spoke of the noble, and tied it closely to benefiting others: '[Noble] also [are] actions done for the sake of others, since these are done for the agent's own sake to a lesser degree than others'.[62] Though he says nothing explicit, it is tempting to read these passages as a straightforward appeal to the idea that benefiting others is noble, and that an action's being noble in itself is a reason to do it.

---

[59] See Irwin, 'Aristotle's Conception of Morality', 130-31.

[60] See especially P. Glassen, 'A Fallacy in Aristotle's Argument about the Good', *Philosophical Quarterly* 7 (1957), 319-22.

[61] There has nevertheless been some very useful discussion. In addition to Rogers, 'Aristotle's Conception of *to kalon*', see D.J. Allan, 'The Fine and the Good in the *Eudemian Ethics*', in P. Moraux and D. Harlfinger (eds.), *Untersuchungen zur Eudemischen Ethik* (Berlin: De Gruyter, 1971), 63-71; J. Owens, 'The KALON in the Aristotelian *Ethics*', in D. O'Meara (ed.), *Studies in Aristotle* (Washington DC: Catholic University of America Press, 1981), 261-77; Irwin, 'Aristotle's Conception of Morality', especially 120-38.

[62] See Irwin (*Plato's Ethics*, 34), which includes useful references to other relevant passages in the *Rhetoric*.

The idea of benefiting others is also present in the *Nicomachean Ethics*. Aristotle says, for example, that generous people tend more towards giving than towards taking, since (1120a11-15):

> it is more characteristic of virtue to do good than to receive it, and to do noble actions than not to do shameful ones; and it is pretty clear that giving implies doing good and doing noble actions, while taking implies receiving good or not doing what is shameful.[63]

What seems new in the *Ethics*, however, is the idea that in the very performance of noble actions to benefit others, the agent will also benefit himself (*NE* 1169a8-11).[64] There will be no good deeds that benefit others and do not benefit oneself (*NE* 1169a18-1169b1):

> It is true also of the good person that he does a great deal for his friends and his country, and will die for them if he must; he will sacrifice money, honours, and in general the goods for which people compete, procuring for himself what is noble … They will also sacrifice money on the condition that their friends gain more; while the friend gets money, he gets what is noble, and therefore assigns himself the greater good … In all praiseworthy actions, then, the good person is seen to assign himself the larger share of what is noble.[65]

---

[63] Cited by Irwin, along with several other significant passages, in 'Aristotle's Conception of Morality', 129-34.

[64] Cf Irwin, 'Aristotle's Conception of Morality', 132, point (3). Irwin sees a change from emphasis on the good of others in the *Rhetoric* to that on the common good in the *Ethics* (*ibid.*). I prefer to see the change in emphasis as one from the good of others to the good of the agent. See *NE* 1168a10-11: 'For the benefactor, what relates to his action is noble, so that he finds enjoyment in the person who is its object', cited by Rogers, 'Aristotle's Conception of *to kalon*', 365. (For further argument against Irwin, see 364-9.) Aristotle was not distorting the meaning of *kalos* by shifting focus in the way he did: the word was, for example, 'applied very freely indeed by the orators to any action, behaviour or achievement which evokes any kind of favourable reaction and praise … wealth and the achievements of wealth are *kalos*' (K.J. Dover, *Greek Popular Morality in the Time of Plato and Aristotle* (Oxford: Blackwell, 1974), 70).

[65] Christine Korsgaard ('From Duty and For the Sake of the Noble', in S. Engstrom and J. Whiting (eds.), *Aristotle, Kant, and the Stoics* (Cambridge: Cambridge University Press, 1996), 203-36, at 222-3) argues that Aristotle is 'more honest' at 1117a33-b20, where he 'firmly repudiates the Stoic view that virtue is sufficient for happiness', allowing that the virtuous person feels pain at the prospect of death in battle, 'for life is best worth living for such a man, and he is knowingly losing the greatest goods'. But losing (some of) 'the greatest' (or 'very great' – Aristotle does not in fact use the article) goods is consistent with one's acquiring a greater good in nobility (the 'noble in war' is chosen 'at the price of' or 'in return for' these goods (1117b14-15), and fair exchange is no loss overall, and may indeed be a gain, though one may regret what is lost and the circumstances which led to the exchange's being unavoidable).

There seems, then, a marked change in tone between the Aristotle of the *Rhetoric* and that of the *Ethics*.[66] The 'Rhetorical' Aristotle appeared happy to present beneficial actions as noble, and thereby worth doing. But the 'Ethical' Aristotle, though not denying this, seems keen to emphasize that nobility is a good for the agent who performs the noble actions themselves. Further, since virtuous action is solely for the sake of the noble, by focusing on the noble as a good for the agent, Aristotle is shifting attention away from the interests of others that might be thought to ground non-eudaimonistic reasons of a weight sufficient to override an agent's eudaimonistic reason to advance his own happiness.

The 'aesthetic' aspect of nobility of course makes this change all the easier.[67] The agent is being encouraged to attend to the beauty of his character, rather than the interests of others. The shift is most marked, perhaps, in the different views of greatness of soul, or magnanimity, taken by the Rhetorical and the Ethical Aristotle. In the *Rhetoric*, 'greatness of soul is the virtue productive of great services for others' (1366b17).[68]

In the *NE*, Aristotle's conception of the great-souled person changes radically (*NE* 1123b15-1124a5):

> If, then, he thinks himself worthy of great things – and above all the greatest – and if he is indeed so, he will be concerned with one thing in particular. Worth is spoken of with reference to external goods; and the greatest external good we should assume to be what we render to the gods, the good most aimed at by people of worth, the prize for the noblest achievements. Such is honour, since it is indeed the greatest external good ... It is primarily with honours and dishonours, then, that the great-souled person is concerned.

Now it is true that Aristotle denies that happiness consists in honour (1095b22-30), and claims also that the great-souled person 'does not even view honour as a terribly important thing' (1124a19). But the package being offered here is not mere honour, but honour for (and along with) 'the noblest achievements'. It is these achievements that the great-souled person thinks really matter, and they matter because of their nobility.

---

[66] I am not suggesting that all the work is done by the noble. There is also, for example, the important argument that virtue benefits the true or rational self, which again of course has its roots in the thought of Socrates, especially in the *Republic*. On this argument, see e.g. D. Scott, 'Aristotle on Well-being', *Proceedings of the Aristotelian Society*, suppl. vol. 73 (1999), 225-42, at 228-30.

[67] See Allan, 'The Fine and the Good in the *Eudemian Ethics*', 65, 70; Dover, *Greek Popular Morality in the Time of Plato and Aristotle*, 69; Owens, 'The KALON in the Aristotelian *Ethics*', 261-2; Rogers, 'Aristotle's Conception of *to kalon*', 355.

[68] We can see how Aristotle might be thinking of it as the 'crown of the virtues' (*NE* 1124a1-2), given that, as we saw above, he takes one common conception of virtue to be as 'a capacity for conferring many great benefits, of all kinds and in every circumstance' (*Rhetoric* 1366a38-1366b1), though, as again we saw, the examples he gives of the most honoured virtues are justice and courage.

So it is in part by appealing to the signficance of nobility and the esteem it provides from those whom we respect[69] that Aristotle attempts to persuade the rational eudaimonist that the exercise of virtue will give him everything he wants, a life 'lacking in nothing'. And his portraits of virtuous people in Books II-V of the *Ethics* can be seen as a further development of an aesthetics of character consisting in descriptions of the attractions of the noble life, and the unattractiveness of the shameful. What happened after Aristotle to this notion of the nobility of virtue as a part of happiness is a story I do not now have the time or prerogative to go into. But certainly it has now all but disappeared from contemporary philosophical ethics, though not, I suggest, from ethics as it is lived.

Let me end by noting that the idea of converting nobility from a morally loaded notion capable of providing its own reasons resting on the interests of others to an aesthetic feature of the agent's own character, the significance of which rests not so much on the interests of others but on the contribution a beautiful character can make to the agent's own happiness, is itself foreshadowed in the thinking of Socrates by the conception of the noble as a constituent of happiness. Consider his suggestion to Meno that 'noble things' are 'good things' at *Meno* 77a6-7, the following lines making it clear that 'good things' are those that are 'good for' one, or the argument at *Gorgias* 476d5-477a4, that, because the noble is good, the person who is justly punished is benefited. As so often, Plato got there first.[70]

---

[69] Rogers nicely draws connections between such esteem and self-respect ('Aristotle's Conception of *to kalon*', 359-60, 370).

[70] For comments on, and discussion of, previous drafts, I am grateful to Myles Burnyeat, Robert Heinaman, Margaret Howatson, Bob Sharples, and David Wiggins. I wish also to thank the Fellows of St Anne's College, Oxford, for a term of sabbatical leave during the writing of this paper.

Reply to Roger Crisp

Christopher Rowe

Roger Crisp's paper is a long one, and supported by a mass of footnotes, but the main thesis is clear enough. I shall restrict myself to some comments on that thesis and its parts. The thesis is not unattractive, combining a 'non-eudaimonistic' interpretation of a central passage of Plato's *Republic* with the view that, by and large, Plato's Socrates (whether earlier or later)[1] and Aristotle were eudaimonists of some sort. Eudaimonism is, as it were, the rule; it is just that a different type of view is straining to get out of the bottle, and actually escapes briefly before being put back firmly in and stoppered up by (the mature?) Aristotle.

Put briefly, the claim is

> that Socrates' [i.e. Plato's Socrates'] views on the relation of virtue and happiness led to tensions in his position and intimations of a rejection of eudaimonism, and that Aristotle can be read as attempting to continue the eudaimonistic project (Crisp, 55).

In fact, the eudaimonistic Socrates turns out to have a rather complex position:

> [So far, we have seen that] Socrates appears to accept that human beings act to further their own perceived[2] greatest happiness, that one's strongest reason for action lies in advancing one's happiness, that happiness consists in virtue and other goods, and that choosing the path of virtue guarantees one the greatest possible happiness (Crisp, 64).

Even this Socrates is a Moralist, and a Pluralist, about happiness. What about '[his] position on justifying (grounding, normative, or prescriptive) reasons for action' (*ibid.*)?

> He is also a pluralist about reasons, though there is no conflict between them. Virtue provides its own reasons, as do the gods, but these reasons are perfectly consistent with reasons grounded in the advancement of one's own happiness (Crisp, 66).

---

[1] See Crisp, n.2.

[2] I am not entirely sure what work this 'perceived' is doing; but that is one of the subjects I shall leave out in this brief response. (At any rate it might fit the *Phaedo* passage quoted by Crisp at 80.)

While other things 'can increase the happiness of the virtuous person' (Crisp, 61), virtue is sufficient for happiness, and its contribution to happiness is sufficient reason for pursuing it; but also, 'Socrates may claim, there are non-eudaimonistic reasons, grounded in divine command or morality, which support the life of virtue' (Crisp, 67).

Now it seems to me that Crisp is here going too fast. It is not at all clear to me, yet, that Socrates is encumbered, or needs to be encumbered by us, with these 'non-eudaimonistic' reasons. Crisp sees Socrates in the *Apology* as recognizing the call of 'duty', both religious and other: 'again and again [he] insists that his constant questioning of his fellow citizens is a religious duty' (Crisp, 65); and 'he has a duty [as he sees it] not to leave his post' (Crisp, 66), sc. where he has been stationed by a superior. But, apart from any general questions that might be raised about the applicability of notions like 'duty' within a fourth-century BC Greek context, Crisp's is actually not a likely reading of a passage such as *Apology* 29b6-7: *to de adikein kai apeithein tôi beltioni kai theôi kai anthrôpôi, hoti kakon kai aischron estin oida*: what Socrates knows is not 'that being unjust and disobeying one's superior, whether god or man, is [sc. morally] bad and shameful', but 'that behaving unjustly to one's better, by disobeying him, whether god or man, is bad [sc. for oneself (the agent)] and shameful'. It is things bad for the agent that he has just been talking about (death is presumably not a 'moral' evil), and will go on talking about in the sentence after 29b6-7 ('So I shall never fear, or flee from, the sorts of things of which I do not know whether they're not actually *good*, before bad things I know to be bad'). In disobeying one's better, someone 'superior' (*beltioni*) to oneself, one is failing to behave as one should towards him (betters are there to be obeyed), but also, evidently, doing what is bad for oneself. And this claim looks reasonable enough, on one reading of 'better': if you do not do what you are told to do by someone who knows more than you do – god, or your platoon-commander – it is likely to turn out badly for you. Nor will the fact that not doing what you are ordered to do by a competent authority is also *aischron* ('shameful') give Crisp what he wants, unless and until it has been shown that the force of calling something *aischron* in a case like this is not just that doing 'shameful' things is itself somehow bad for the agent – which is, after all, the most plausible reading of that familiar Socratic slogan 'no one goes wrong/does the wrong thing willingly' (familiarly attaching, that is, to Plato's Socrates too).

But this does not take me to the real core of my response. Let me agree, provisionally, that the view of the Socrates under consideration is as Crisp describes it, i.e. (minimally?) eudaimonistic: a view according to which 'a non-eudaimonistic, moral reason can [never] trump the eudaimonistic reason to promote one's own happiness' (I borrow the phrasing from Crisp, 67.)[3] But now

---

[3] The use of *Phaedo* 82a11-b2 on this page looks wrong. The most that 'the ordinary virtue of a citizen' will 'guarantee' is the best destination allotted to any of the *phauloi* – 'of these' at a10 refers to the souls 'not of the good but of the *phauloi*' (81d6-7), talked about at 81b-c. Possessors of demotic virtue will be 'happiest of these too', i.e. just as those with true, non-demotic virtue are happiest in a different context; but the 'best' destination for the demotic type turns out to be becoming bees, wasps, or some other kind of social animal. For the fate

the famous passage in the *Republic* – 519b-521b – which talks about the requirement on the philospher-rulers to go back down into the Cave turns out, on Crisp's account, to involve just such a trumping. It is in fact, on his view (Crisp, n. 49), the only passage of its kind in the whole of Plato and Aristotle:

> [T]he dialectical importance of the exception [i.e. that in this one case alone it will not be in a person's interest to be just] is noted by Aronson ..., who says that by it 'Plato has opened a Pandora's box of obstacles to any attempt at refuting Thrasymachus'. Foster says of the passage: 'It is remarkable because it contains the conception, expressed, to my knowledge, nowhere else in Greek [i.e. Athenian] philosophy, of moral Obligation, or Duty' ... I cannot go along with this, but I do think the passage unique in both Plato and Aristotle in its recommendation of self-sacrifice.

But this – so Crisp claims – expresses some real tensions already present in Socrates' position. After all, in the dispute between Socrates and Thrasymachus,

> Thrasymachus may allow that virtue is good, but put such weight on non-moral goods such as the avoidance of severe suffering, or huge power and wealth, that he can make a reasonably strong case that in certain cases happiness is best served by immorality. Further, it will be tempting for a defender of Socrates' position, in these cases, to appeal to non-eudaimonistic reasons in favour of virtue. But these will be reasons in favour of self-sacrifice, against which Thrasymachus can wield the plausibility of Rational Eudaimonism (Crisp, 67).

Since I myself think that Plato and his Socrates are thoroughgoing eudaimonists throughout, my only task need be to show that the *Republic* passage is not an exception. I shall first briefly summarize Crisp's analysis of the passage, then lay out my own rival interpretation.

A. Crisp:

(1) It is a loss for the guardians to descend back into the cave.

(2) The demand that they go down is just, 'since they owe a debt of gratitude to the city and should recognize that they are best suited to governing the city, taking it in turns to do so (520a6-d4)' (Crisp, 68-9).

Thus (3) 'here it seems that we have a case of moral self-sacrifice, in which the philosophers, who would have a better life were they to remain in the light of the sun, are required by justice to do what is worse for themselves' (Crisp, 69). Of course, it is said several times over that they are 'compelled'; but

(4) '[w]hat will compel the philosophers will be the claims of justice itself,

---

of the truly virtuous we have to turn to the myth at the end – where it also turns out that ordinary people just gather and await their next incarnation on the shores of Acheron.

instantiated in the law underlying *Kallipolis* (519e1) or in the speech made to them by Socrates. Socrates puts the argument from justice in the form of words spoken directly to the philosophers, introducing it as follows: '"Note, Glaucon', I said, 'that we shall not be doing an injustice to our philosophers, but will say just things to them, compelling them to care for and protect the others"' (520a7-9).' (Crisp, 69).

(5) It is not as if they are coerced, exactly; they comply because they are just, and in full sight of what would be in their own interests. 'They understand their loss, but, because they have seen the Form of the Good, understand also the rational force of *nomos* – the moral law' (Crisp, 70-71).

B. Rowe:

(1) The passage begins and ends with the point about *compulsion*. I paraphrase: 'our task as founders is to make sure, first, that our future rulers arrive at the highest subject of study, and then that they are not allowed the licence philosophy students presently have, i.e. to stay with their studies and refuse to come down again ...'. Then at the end of the passage: 'in a good society, the only ones who should rule are precisely the ones who do not want to do it. But who else would one compel to rule except those who (a) are qualified to do it, and (b) have a better life available to them?'

So (2) compulsion is actually a necessary part of Socrates' proposal in the passage (doubly necessary, in fact: he clearly also wants to go on maintaining that doing philosophy is the most pleasant, happiness-producing, thing in the world).

But (3) this compulsion comes from the law, and the legislators.

On the other hand, (4) the law comes with (as one might put it) a lining of persuasion, rather as in the *Laws*: in answer to Glaucon's objection that making philosophers stop philosophizing will make them live a worse life, Socrates reminds him of their principle that no part of the city should be exceptionally happy, but that each should be made to contribute according to its capacities – by means of persuasion and force (*peithoi te kai anankêi*, 519e4). The force in this case comes from the law, the persuasion from Socrates, one of the founder-legislators, explaining the law: 'Consider, then, Glaucon: neither (*oude*) will we be doing [them] any injustice', sc. in using legal compulsion on them, '... but we'll be saying just things when we compel them to look after and guard the others too (*prosanankazontes* [i.e. not just themselves])'.[4]

---

[4] The verb *prosanankazein* is often used, as I think it is here, with the sense of 'compel in addition' – of the passages cited by Crisp, *Symposium* 223d3 and *Statesman* 284d7 and 10 seem to me to be like this (see my commentaries on the two dialogues, *ad loc.*). But this does not, I think, affect the argument here. (My general approach to the *Republic* passage turns out to overlap considerably with that of Eric Brown's essay on 'Justice and

So (5) in one sense there are two kinds of *ananké* or compulsion in operation, marked by the *oude*: we will compel them in any case; but 'notice, Glaucon, that in doing so we won't be doing them any injustice, either'. But in another sense there is only one kind: the explanation Socrates gives reflects the rationality, the reasonableness, of the law itself, as it affects the addressees. We might notice more than a little resemblance to the tone of the lecture addressed to Socrates in the *Crito*, again by the law – there, of course, the laws of Athens. But actually there is at the same time a more significant difference of substance: whereas the Laws of Athens talk about the requirement on Socrates to keep his word, or his 'contract' with the city, the legislator Socrates here allows that ordinary philosophers, in ordinary cities, quite reasonably take no share in the labour of running them (*Republic* 520b2-4):

> for they grow up there spontaneously, against the wishes of the constitution in force, and it's in line with justice that something that owes its origin to itself (*autophues*), and so doesn't owe its bringing up to anyone, shouldn't be eager, either (*mēde*), to pay back the costs of its upbringing to anyone.

Callipolitan philosophers, by contrast, do have a debt to pay: it is the city that has put them in the position that they are, 'better and more completely educated than those others, and with a greater capacity for taking part in things' – i.e. both philosophy and ruling (520b6-c1). The language here, it seems to me, is simply that of fair exchange: we legislators, Socrates is saying, will not be doing any injustice to our philosophers, giving them any less than is due to them, if we make them rule; indeed *they* will be giving the city less than *its* due if they do not rule. Nothing here seems obviously inconsistent with the view that Socrates is supposed to be supporting, that justice 'pays'. Even a type who measures everything in terms of his own good, granted that he has a bit of intelligence, might be brought to see that sometimes it will be pay-back time. Or, alternatively: if an appeal is being made here to some kind of 'moral principle' that is supposed to outweigh the philosophers' desire for their own good, then the same argument will apparently have to apply, in spades, to the *Crito*. But I should prefer not to deploy that argument, since I too, like Crisp, want to claim that the Socrates of the *Crito* is a eudaminonist. (At any rate, in our *Republic* passage Socrates not only does not try to appeal to the philosophers' sense of social responsibility, duty, or whatever; he hardly even mentions other people at all. Just twice, in fact: first in that reference to the founders compelling the philosophers to 'look after and guard the others too' (520a8-9), and then in c1-3 'so each of you in turn will have to go down into the place where the others live together (*eis tēn tōn allōn sunoikēsin*) and get used to observing the things in the darkness there' – because then you will be able to sort

---

Compulsion for Plato's Philosopher-Rulers', *Ancient Philosophy* 20 (2000), 1-15, though Brown is rather less interested than I am in Plato's authorial strategy in the passage. I am grateful to Rachana Kamtekar for drawing my attention to Brown's essay, which in some important respects is more nuanced than anything I have been able to achieve in the present short piece. I hope to return to the issues on a future occasion.)

things out for the prisoners, introducing proper standards of 'the fine, the just, and the good' (c6-7). But c1-7 simply explains why they are needed to do the job they are asked to do in payment of their debt to the city. 'OK, so it's pay-back time: why do we have to do that job?' 'Because that's the one you'll do ten thousand times better than anyone else'.)

(6) The explanation Socrates gives *Glaucon*, i.e. as to why the Callipolitan philosophers must rule, is significantly different: that they are best qualified to rule, and have better things to do. That will not be enough for the philosophers themselves – yes, they do have better things to do, and the fact that they are the best qualified to do the job is not an overriding consideration for them. So at least Socrates seems to think.[5] And reasonably so, if the final consideration is supposed to be, as I think it is, what is best for the agent. (Here, one might remark, is one place where the unsatisfactoriness of the definition of justice shows up: what happens when each of two incompatible things is equally 'ours to do'? But Socrates admits anyway that the definition is merely provisional.)

(7) So then the police, the auxiliaries, do not actually have to come and get them: they are persuaded (520d6-e2) that what they are being compelled to do is the just thing, and so they will go along with it and take their turn at ruling, being just people (i.e. the sort of people who recognize a good argument when they see one: reason dominates their life in the required fashion), regarding it just as one of those necessary but annoying things one has to do (*hôs ep' anankaion autôn hekastos eisi to archein*, 520e2-3). It is not that they are unwilling to do it, it is just that they are 'least eager', *hêkista prothumoi*, 520d2; contrast the *mê ethelein* of 519d4, used of people outside Callipolis who have not had Socrates' pep-talk. There just are such things in life, like those purely biological needs that interrupt any day's study, and there is no point in trying to dream them away: that, to me, is the outcome of the passage, which looks rather far removed from any idea of '*moral* self-sacrifice'.

(8) But is it even a case of self-sacrifice at all, if the law, the city and its institutions, necessitate it? The decision is out of their hands, except to the extent that they might have waited for the police to call (but they will not do that). But in any case they only have to put up with a temporary interruption of their bliss. They have to do a bit of ruling before getting back to the real business; that is all. It is something they have to do as a condition of philosophizing (like eating enough to

---

[5] I take it, by the way, that Socrates' little speech to the philosophers stops at 520d1. He does not tell them his point about having the least willing to do the job actually doing it – at least, not in so many words: something like it is implied by the contrast he puts to them between a city ruled by experts and cities ruled by those who think ruling a great good, and something to be fought for (520c1-d1). Not much hangs on this, but it is as well to keep the two levels of discourse apart – the meta-level discourse between Socrates and Glaucon, and the first-level discourse between legislator and philosopher.

stay alive, sleeping for so many hours in every day, and so on); it comes as part of the package.

(9) There ceases, in fact, to be any real sense in which they could have had a better life, as Glaucon's objection supposes. In any other city, they could – and so much the worse for other cities, as Socrates suggests. In this one, philosophers just *are* rulers, and it would not be the city it is if they were not. This is the source of the 'compulsion' of the law; it does not, I think, come from 'morality' (I have given my reasons); 'law' is not here to be translated into 'moral law', in the way that Crisp suggests.

(10) The strength of an interpretation like Crisp's of the *Republic* passage in question (and it might be said to be the type of interpretation of the passage that is currently in the ascendant) is of course the emphasis in Plato's text on the fact that the philosopher-rulers do not want to rule, apparently get nothing out of it, and are prevented by ruling from doing other things which will benefit them. Ruling thus looks like a prime example of moral behaviour according to some classic types of modern ethical theory: doing something because it is right, and neither enjoying it nor getting anything else out of it makes it a truly moral, i.e. morally admirable, action. I can only say (a) that I find this idea wholly, indeed terminally, depressing, (b) that I hope I have provided reasons for supposing that it is not the kind of idea that Plato is operating with, and (c) that even if I have not, charity alone demands that we should go on looking for ways of acquitting him of entertaining it. And if this indeed turned out to be the only case in the whole of Plato and Aristotle where we can find it, that seems to me a cause for congratulation, not for complaint.

In short, I remain to be convinced that the *Republic* gives us any sort of exception to 'Socratic', i.e. Platonic, eudaimonism. What of the other main claim of Crisp's: that tensions in one bit of Aristotle – tensions rather like those he (Crisp) finds in Plato – were actually followed in other bits, not by any sort of break with eudaimonism,[6] but rather by a continuation of 'the project of the eudaimonistic Socrates', which 'remov[es] the potential for the position of Socrates in the *Republic* – for the moral law that conflicts with happiness – to develop' (Crisp, 97)?

First, the Aristotelian 'tensions' (Crisp, 73, drawing on selected passages from the *Rhetoric*):

> Aristotle does not appear explicitly to allow for the possibility or rationality of self-sacrifice, but the non-moral constituents of happiness, along with non-eudaimonistic reasons for action, both make more plausible the idea that morality might require agents to perform actions which damage their happiness overall.

---

[6] Or even momentary infidelity – which is what, on Crisp's account, the *Republic* passage represents (it is 'unique', as he says in n. 49, while remaining on his view a revealing testament to the underlying tensions in Socrates' position).

So Crisp. But there are grounds for scepticism here. Crisp only has the *Rhetoric* to offer as evidence for this thesis about 'tensions' in Aristotle, and most interpreters would probably now agree that it is hard to read off Aristotle's own views from the surface of this puzzling text.[7] Take even just one of Crisp's own favoured passages from the *Rhetoric* – the first (*Rhetoric* 1360b14-18):

> Let happiness be doing well combined with virtue, or self-sufficiency of life, or security of the most pleasant life, or good condition of possessions and body, together with the power of protecting and using them. That happiness is one or more of these nearly everyone agrees.

Crisp comments in a footnote 'The indecision may be a sign of this part of the *Rhetoric*'s being early' (n. 50). But I can find no 'indecision' here, only a list of what people generally say about happiness (that is, presumably, people who have articulated views on the subject). But all of this is surely of minor importance. *If* 'Socrates' surrendered to the 'tensions' in his thinking, i.e. in that one place in the *Republic*, then maybe we might expect to find the same tensions in Aristotle, because of his long and close association with 'Socrates', i.e. Plato. The striking thing, suggests Crisp, is that Aristotle eventually went the way of the eudaimonistic Socrates. Since my view in any case is that Aristotle is an out-and-out eudaimonist, I have no major quarrels with the last part of Crisp's paper ('Eudaimonism in the *Ethics*'). Apart from the precise specification of the position of 'Socrates', and the question whether that position – in any of its versions – involved 'tensions', my dispute with Crisp is over whether Plato and Aristotle in fact ever wavered in their eudaimonism. But the case for my side in that dispute, by Crisp's own criteria, will only be as good as my interpretation of that passage in *Republic* VII is defensible.[8]

---

[7] See e.g. a number of the articles in A.O. Rorty (ed.), *Essays on Aristotle's Rhetoric* (Berkeley: University of California Press, 1996). Irwin's may serve as an example: 'We will not assume that [the ethical claims presented in the *Rhetoric*] state Aristotle's own views. Nor, however, will we assume that they are simply a record of common beliefs. Aristotle is concerned with a subset of commonly held views: those that are best for leading the audience, by the appropriate rhetorical arguments, to the best conclusions that are open to them, given their starting point' ('Ethics in the *Rhetoric* and in the *Ethics*', *Essays on Aristotle's Rhetoric*, 142-74 at 147). Crisp's response in his n. 53 to the suggestion that 'Aristotle did not believe these claims in the *Rhetoric*' is surely inadequate, especially when confronted with Irwin's nuanced position. See further, briefly, below.

[8] I here assume that Crisp's discovery – nn. 50, 53 (see above) – of an early, indecisive Aristotle in the *Rhetoric* is actually a non-starter (or, if it does start, that it falls at an early fence).

Chapter 4

Glaucon's Challenge: Does Aristotle Change His Mind?

T.H. Irwin

1. Virtue and happiness

A central issue throughout Plato's dialogues concerns the relation between virtue, non-moral goods (i.e. goods other than virtue), and happiness. Socrates believes that people tend to over-estimate the relative importance of non-moral goods such as wealth, health, and honour, and to under-estimate the relative importance of virtue (*Apology* 29d-30b). This general claim is a constant theme of the dialogues, but Plato seems to explain it differently in different dialogues.

We might attribute at least these views to Plato:

> P1. *The Conditional Thesis*: Non-moral 'goods' and 'evils' are not genuine goods and evils in their own right (i.e. irrespective of whether a virtuous or a non-virtuous person possesses them). On the contrary, non-moral 'goods' become good only if they are correctly used by the virtuous person, and non-moral 'evils' are not bad for the virtuous person, since he uses them correctly. Both 'goods' and 'evils' are bad for the vicious person, since he uses them incorrectly. The goodness and badness of these non-moral goods and evils is only conditional; it depends on the way they are used.[1]

> P2. *The Sufficiency Thesis*: Virtue is necessary and sufficient for happiness.[2]

> P3. *The Non-instrumental Thesis*: Virtue is to be chosen for its own sake, not only for its consequences.

> P4. *The Stability Thesis*: One ought always to stick to virtue, no matter what it may cost in non-moral goods.

---

[1] See *Euthydemus* 280b7-d7, *Laws* 687d1-e9.
[2] See e.g. *Crito* 48b8-9, *Gorgias* 470e8-11, *Republic* 353e10-354a4, *Laws* 660e3-5.

P5. *The Comparative Thesis*: From the point of view of happiness, virtue is always to be chosen over all non-moral goods, individually and collectively.

P6. *The Composite Thesis*: The good is composite because it includes a plurality of proper parts or elements that are non-instrumental goods (i.e. each of them is to be chosen for its own sake).

P7. *The Comprehensive Thesis*: The good includes all the parts or elements that are worth choosing, so that as a whole it is complete and self-sufficient.[3]

P8. *The Dominance Thesis*: Virtue is dominant in happiness (i.e. it is always to be chosen over all proper parts of happiness, individually and collectively, that do not depend on it).

P9. *The Eudaimonist Thesis*: If I have sufficient reason to be just rather than unjust, I must be happier by being just than by being unjust.

I have ascribed all these views to Plato, simply because the Platonic Socrates maintains them somewhere in the dialogues. I believe it is reasonable, however, to attribute P1 and P2 to Socrates, and hence to the period of Plato's thought when he agreed with Socrates, and reasonable to attribute P3 and P4 to the later Plato. According to this view, the *Republic* rejects P1 and P2, but defends P3 and P4 instead.

P3-5 are the topic of 'Glaucon's Challenge' in *Republic* II.[4] First Glaucon asks Socrates to prove P3. Then he adds P4 and P5, by comparing the just person suffering from the worst non-moral evils with the unjust person possessing the highest level of non-moral goods, and asking Socrates to prove that, even in these conditions, the just person is better off. To answer Glaucon, Plato argues for P5. Though P4 and P5 are consistent with P2, they do not imply P2, and P2 has no place in the main argument of the *Republic*.[5]

A reasonable interpretation of the *Republic* takes P5-7 to underlie Plato's acceptance of P4 and his silence about P2 (in Books II-IX). But he does not actually formulate P5 in the *Republic*.[6] To formulate clearly the position that he has

---

[3] The *Philebus* ascribes these features to the good (20d1-21a2), in order to show that neither pleasure alone nor intelligence (*phronêsis*) alone can be the whole of the good, and that the good must be found in a mixed life including both.

[4] The label comes from C.A. Kirwan, 'Glaucon's Challenge', *Phronesis* 10 (1965), 162-73.

[5] I have discussed these question about the Socratic dialogues and the *Republic* in *Plato's Ethics* (Oxford: Oxford University Press, 1995). Julia Annas, *Platonic Ethics, Old and New* (Ithaca: Cornell University Press, 1999), 83-8, attributes P2 to the *Republic*.

[6] 505b-c might be taken to allude to the disputes about the good that the *Philebus* resolves by accepting P5.

in mind in the *Republic*, we must rely on the distinctions drawn in a later dialogue, the *Philebus*. Hence we might suppose that Plato's later conception of virtue and happiness is the position that we reach by combining the *Republic* with the *Philebus* and affirming P3-7 without P1-2.[7]

Whatever Aristotle takes to be Plato's own conclusion, we might expect him to find in the dialogues a source of reasonable questions for him to consider. It is surprising that, in contrast to Plato, Theophrastus, and the Stoics, he does not say much about them. Still, we can trace some significant contrasts between the treatments of them in the three ethical treatises. I will examine three sections of each treatise: (1) The general discussion of happiness. (2) The treatment of the 'mega-virtues', and especially of magnanimity. (3) The remarks on self-love.

If I am right, the same points of contrast between the three treatises can be identified in these different sections. The three treatises display different degrees of interest in Glaucon's Challenge; it is, at best, in the background in the *Magna Moralia* (*MM*) and *Eudemian Ethics* (*EE*), but it is prominent and important in the *Nicomachean Ethics* (*NE*). They also take different views about the issues raised by Glaucon's Challenge; the *NE* differs from the other two treatises in endorsing the position that Plato takes in the *Republic*.

To defend these claims about the three *Ethics*, I need to go through the relevant sections, treatise by treatise. I will have to leave many controversies to one side. Some of the controversies concern the interpretation of particular passages. Perhaps the most important controversies concern the order of the three treatises and the authenticity of the *MM*. I will assume that (1) the *EE* and *NE* are works of Aristotle; (2) the *MM* reports a course of lectures by Aristotle; and (3) the *MM*, *EE*, and *NE* should be discussed in that order. Whether these assumptions are reasonable can be decided only by detailed study and comparison of different sections of the three *Ethics*. Since this detailed study has still not gone very far (except in the case of the *NE*), it would be unwise to reach firm conclusions. But I hope the questions I discuss will contribute something to the comparative understanding of the three treatises.

---

[7] A possible objection to the view that Plato's thought develops in this direction comes from the *Laws*. I have mentioned passages where Plato still seems to maintain P2. I believe these passages do not give an accurate account of Plato's overall position in the *Laws*, and that we have good reason to attribute P4 to him rather than P2. (See *Plato's Ethics*, sect. 231.) But I do not need to argue this point here. If we are simply asking what Aristotle finds in Plato, it is useful to notice the different views that one might attribute to Plato in dialogues of all periods. 'Agreement' or 'disagreement' with Plato on virtue and happiness is not a simple matter to decide.

2. *Magna Moralia*: classification of goods

After the initial discussion of virtue, the *MM* considers types of goods. The discussion of the goods called 'capacities' covers the non-moral goods that the Platonic dialogues contrast with virtue. The good person uses them well and the bad person badly, but they are goods, no matter who uses them, because they should be assessed by the good person's use of them, not the bad person's use (1183b31-2). Aristotle therefore rejects the Conditional Thesis (P1).[8] In rejecting it, he does not necessarily mean that external goods should be chosen more often than Socrates believes they should be chosen. His point is simply to reject Socrates' suggestion that they are not goods when a non-virtuous person has them.

Happiness is the complete and best end, and therefore the best good.[9] It is best because it must be comprehensive, including all goods. The introduction of the complete and best end leads to a discussion of how 'best' is to be understood (1184a14-38). Though the details of the discussion are not clear, it points out some unwelcome consequences of treating the best good as one among a plurality of goods, not including the others.[10] In Aristotle's view, the best good, which is to be

---

[8] The next division separates goods that are ends from goods that are not, and asserts that the goods that are ends are better than those that are not. Aristotle illustrates this point by comparing health with the things for the sake of health (1184a3-7). His illustration suggests that the goods he has called 'capacities' include ends as well as means; for though he did not mention health along with other capacities, it seems to satisfy his two conditions. If this is right, he does not intend capacities to exclude non-instrumental goods.

[9] 'A complete good is one whose presence leaves us needing nothing further; an incomplete good is one whose presence leaves us needing something further; for instance, when only justice is present, we need many things further, but when happiness is present we need nothing further any more' (1184a8-12).

[10] Aristotle considers these possibilities:

1. 1184a15. Could the complete good be best by being 'counted together'? The effect of being 'counted together', in Aristotle's view, would be to make it better than itself. The absurdity of counting together is supposed to be illustrated by health and healthy things; if you take health to be the best thing, it turns out that health is better than itself. Aristotle seems to assume that 'healthy things' are healthy activities, the sorts of things that are characteristic of health. (Translators render 'healthy things', *ta hugieina*, as 'means to health', as in 1184a4ff.; but I do not see how that would fit into an argument here.) He seems to argue as follows: (1) Health (we suppose) is the best good. (2) Health plus healthy things is better than health itself. (3) Hence health plus healthy things is the best good. (4) Hence health is better than health itself. The idea is perhaps that health is supposed to be the *single* best thing; but if we confuse that with the best thing altogether (which may be a collection of good things), then we find ourselves thinking of the best good in inconsistent ways.

2. 1184a25. Should we consider the best good 'separately from itself'? Aristotle replies that, since happiness is composed of certain goods, we should not consider it in comparison with the goods that compose it. The point is that when we say happiness is best of all goods, we do not mean to say that its goodness is to be compared with the goodness of all the goods that compose it, and treated as something independent of their goodness.

identified with happiness, cannot be the single best thing, which could be combined with further good things to yield something better than the best good by itself. The best good has to include all the goods that one might try to add to produce a better good.

Aristotle therefore accepts the Comprehensive Thesis (P7). This does not by itself commit him to the Composite Thesis (P6); for if there is only one non-instrumental good, happiness is comprehensive without being composite. But if P7 is true and P1 is false, happiness includes non-moral goods; for in Aristotle's view, these are genuine goods. Hence he accepts the Composite Thesis (P6) and rejects the Sufficiency Thesis (P2).

He introduces virtue by appealing to the threefold division of goods – goods of the soul, of the body, and external goods – and claiming that the goods of the soul are best. These goods include intelligence (*phronêsis*), virtue, and pleasure (1184b1-6). Here and elsewhere he accepts the Non-instrumental Thesis (P3).

Aristotle's views about the Comparative Thesis (P5) and the Dominance Thesis (P8) appear indirectly from his use of *Republic* I. At the end of that Book Socrates argues for a connection between function, virtue, and happiness. Among the functions of the soul he lists 'taking care, ruling, deliberating, and such things', and then adds living (353d3-10). He uses this conclusion to support the Sufficiency Thesis (P2; see 353e10-354a4).

---

3. 1184a30. Should we compare happiness with other goods that are outside it? Is it the best good in the sense that it is the single good that is better than any other single good outside it? Aristotle replies that this is the wrong way to make the comparison. For prudence might be the best of goods if we mean by this 'the best single good, when goods are taken and compared one by one' (*kath'hen sunkrinomenôn*, 1184a36). But that is not the sense in which we are seeking the best good. For prudence is not complete.

This third argument suggests more clearly what the first perhaps suggests more obscurely, that happiness has to be comprehensive in some way; but in what way? If one says that happiness has to include all goods, one might mean two things: (a) If F things are goods (i.e. F things are among the sorts of things that make one's life better), and x is F, happiness includes x. (b) If a greater good results from the addition of x to our life than without x (i.e. if x makes one's life better than it would be without x), happiness includes x.

The point of distinguishing these two claims is to recognize the possibility (allowed by (b), but not by (a)) that not everything that has a good-making property necessarily contributes to the goodness of the whole that it is added to. There can be surplus goods that do not contribute to the resultant goodness of anything, but simply constitute the equivalent of butter mountains and wine lakes. When Aristotle makes his claim about wisdom and other goods, what does he mean?

To see what he means, we ought to turn back to his description of 'capacities', the third class of goods. When he says that the good person can use them well, he does not say that the good person always acquires more rather than fewer of them. In some cases, the right use of wealth and power might be to limit one's pursuit of them. If it is reasonable to include limitation in correct use, we ought not to suppose that Aristotle commits himself to the most extreme kind of comprehensiveness for happiness. It is better to suppose that he intends the more moderate kind of comprehensiveness suggested by (b).

Aristotle has this very passage in mind in his own presentation of the function argument. We can see this in a puzzling sentence that may be literally translated: 'The soul the other things also, but by the soul we live' (1184b25-6).[11] The point of the sentence is clearer in the light of Socrates' remarks on the soul in *Republic* I. In 'the other things', Aristotle alludes to Socrates' first list of functions; then he adds the crucial function of living. He follows Plato in appealing to the function of F to explain the goodness, and hence the virtue, of F.

Though Aristotle follows *Republic* I this far, he does not draw the same conclusion; for he does not affirm the Sufficiency Thesis. On this point he agrees with Plato's own implicit position in the rest of the *Republic*, which neither asserts nor defends the Sufficiency Thesis.[12]

Aristotle's silence on the Sufficiency Thesis is explained by his further comments about happiness. Living well consists in living in accordance with the virtues (1184b27-31), but he rejects the Sufficiency Thesis, by appeal to the completeness of happiness. The first implication of completeness is that happiness consists in virtuous activity, not simply in being virtuous; for the activity is better than the mere state (1184b31-1185a1).

This claim might be interpreted minimally, so as to mean that happiness requires us to do just actions (e.g.), not to be inactive. We satisfy this demand for activity if we refuse to give false evidence against an innocent person even if we are being tortured; for if we refuse, we act justly, and are not merely disposed to act justly. If this sort of virtuous activity is all that is needed for happiness, happiness is open to the just person suffering misfortune. This argument is one that the Stoics give to show that they do not deny virtuous activity to the happy person.[13] This is at most a fairly small amendment of the Socratic position.

This minimal interpretation of 'activity' may not be all that Aristotle intends. He may understand it to mean not just 'exercising virtue as much as possible in whatever circumstances we are in', but 'exercising it in the best activities possible in the best circumstances'.[14] The best activities of the virtues include not the

---

[11] 'Virtue in a given thing does well that of which it is the virtue; now the soul <does> the other things too (*hê de psuchê kai talla men*), but by soul we live; because of the virtue of the soul, therefore, we will live well' (1184b24-7). Aristotle recalls Plato: 'Has the soul got a function that you could not achieve with anything else? For instance: to superintend and rule and deliberate and all such things; will we rightly assign them to anything other than the soul ? ... And what about living? Won't we say that this is a function of the soul?' (*Republic* 353d1-9). On *kai talla men* see Susemihl's note. Dirlmeier gives the right explanation.

[12] Though Plato does not explicitly reject the argument from virtue and function to the Sufficiency Thesis, he ought not to accept it; for he accepts the connection between virtue and function (cf. 443c-444a), but does not affirm the Sufficiency Thesis.

[13] I have discussed this further in 'Virtue, Praise, and Success', *Monist* 73 (1990), 59-79.

[14] Pseudo-Alexander, among others, speaks of virtuous activity 'in the preferred conditions' (*en prohêgoumenois*; see *Supplementum Aristotelicum* II 2, 148.31 (see R.W. Sharples's note, in *Ethical Problems* (London: Duckworth, 1990), 64n). Other sources speak

widow giving her mite, but the large gifts that we cannot give unless we are magnificent people with the appropriate wealth. If this is what Aristotle means, he makes happiness depend on external circumstances, since these are needed for the best activities.

This second and more demanding interpretation of the demand for activity is supported by the following remarks on the conditions for happiness. It cannot be found in an incomplete (i.e. immature) person, but only in an adult. It can only be found in a complete time, which is the length of time that a human being lives; for common sense is right in saying that we should judge a person's happiness by the largest time of one's life (1185a1-9).[15] These temporal requirements on happiness allow room for the influence of fortune and external goods. If a virtuous person acts virtuously for a relatively short period of his adult life, but then suffers a disaster that leaves him poor, or weak, or unhealthy for the rest of his life, he cannot be happy.

Aristotle, therefore, accepts one part of Glaucon's case for the unjust person. He agrees that if just people suffer the sorts of misfortunes that Glaucon describes, they are not happy. What, then, does he think about the demand that Glaucon makes of Socrates? Does he think it is possible to show that, even in these circumstances, the virtuous person is better off than the vicious person? He does not say.

In the *Republic* and the *Laws*, the Comparative Thesis (P5) is important because Plato accepts the Eudaimonist Thesis (P9). Does Aristotle accept it? Since he affirms the Comprehensive Thesis (P7), he takes happiness to include all the ends that a rational agent might reasonably pursue. Since he also accepts the Non-instrumental Thesis (P3), happiness includes the characteristic ends of the virtuous person. But Aristotle does not say that the weight the virtuous person attaches to virtuous action exactly matches the place of virtue in happiness. One might argue that virtue is indeed a component of happiness, but virtuous people care more about it than its place in happiness would warrant.

One might, then, accept the Non-instrumental Thesis (P3) and the Stability Thesis (P4) without the Comparative Thesis (P5). Plato suggests that without P5 we undermine a rational person's commitment to virtue. But one might argue that, contrary to Plato, P4 can stand without P5. The *MM* has not yet clarified Aristotle's position on this question.

---

of 'the preferred activity' (Stobaeus, *Ecl.* II 51.10). The reference to the conditions and to the activity really refer to the same feature of virtuous activity.

[15] 'Since, then, happiness is a complete good and end, we must not fail to observe that it will be in what is complete. ... it will not be in an incomplete time, but in a complete time; and a complete time will be as long a time as a human being lives' (1185a1-6).

3. *Magna Moralia*: fortune and virtue

Later in the *MM* (II.8) Aristotle returns to the virtuous person's attitude to external goods. He affirms that happiness requires good fortune (1206b30-34), and he treats external goods as good in their own right, not only when they are used correctly by the good person. Hence he reaffirms his rejection of P1 and P2.

Since external goods are goods in their own right, virtuous people do not make them good by choosing them. Their task is to use external goods correctly. Aristotle seeks to correct a misunderstanding of 'correct use'. If we reject wealth or power on the ground that it will expose us to irresistible temptations, or that it costs us unnecessary anxiety and effort, do we thereby use these external goods correctly, and show that we are virtuous people? Aristotle answers No. In his view, we show ourselves not to be virtuous if we find that external goods tempt us to vicious behaviour; virtuous people are not troubled by such temptation. We are equally mistaken if we forgo the pursuit of these genuine goods simply because they cost us anxiety and effort.[16,17] Aristotle requires virtuous people not to limit their acceptance of external goods to a minimal level. Virtue is not to be assessed by how we use the external goods we have, but by how we both accept and use external goods.

4. *Magna Moralia*: magnanimity and fortune[18]

This demand clarifies the attitude of the virtuous person to external goods. A relevant virtue to consider in this context is magnanimity,[19] which is displayed in one's attitude to failure, dishonour, and ill fortune. Aristotle's position is most easily intelligible by comparison with the outlooks of Ajax and Socrates. These

---

[16] Some restriction on this general principle is needed. Perhaps Aristotle is right to say that if Pericles had shirked a position of power in Athens because he feared being corrupted, he would have shown himself not to be virtuous; but it does not follow that Pericles must become king of Persia, if he gets the opportunity. Even virtuous people should be allowed to recognize that some accumulations of external goods are beyond their capacities as human beings.

[17] 'One who is the sort of person who shrinks from any good so as not to have it would not seem to be fine and good. But the one for whom all good things are good, and who is not corrupted by them – by wealth and power, for instance – this sort of person is fine and good' (1207b38-1208a4).

[18] I have said more on magnanimity in 'Some Developments in Aristotle's Conception of Magnanimity', in M. Giusti (ed.), *La nocion de arete*, (Pontifica Universidad Catolica del Peru, 1999), 173-94.

[19] One might also consider Aristotle's treatment of magnificence in relation to Plato. I believe this strengthens the argument about magnanimity.

outlooks reveal two opposite conceptions of magnanimity, neither of which Aristotle endorses.[20]

For Ajax, failure and dishonour are unbearable; for Socrates they are indifferent, if they are not his own fault. Socrates claims to display magnanimity by taking the right attitude to external goods. Since he disagrees radically with Ajax about what that right attitude is, he is indifferent to those failures that make Ajax believe that life is not worth living. The Socratic attitude to magnanimity implies the Sufficiency Thesis (P2).

In the *MM* Aristotle's criticism of Ajax is restrained. He implies that Ajax valued honour from the wrong people; but he does not say that Ajax had the wrong view about what deserves honour, or that he reacted wrongly to the prospect of a life without honour.[21] Socrates' indifference to misfortune is not mentioned, and it does not fit the account of magnanimity. In eliminating the Socratic attitude from the discussion of magnanimity, Aristotle might reasonably expect to be understood as rejecting this attitude.

Since the Platonic Comparative Thesis (P5) is less extreme than the Sufficiency Thesis in its treatment of non-moral goods, it does not require as extreme an attitude as Socratic magnanimity. Plato does not suggest that just people who face all the misfortune described by Glaucon regard it as irrelevant to their happiness. Still, they retain one element of Socratic magnanimity; they do not believe that the

---

[20] Ajax and Socrates are discussed in the *Posterior Analytics*, in a purely incidental illustration of a problem about definition (97b17-25):

> For instance, if Alcibiades is magnanimous, or Achilles and Ajax, what is the one thing they all have? Refusal to endure insult; for the first went to war, the second was angry, and the third killed himself. Again <what is there in common> in other cases, e.g. Lysander or Socrates? If <this common feature> is being indifferent in both good and bad fortune, then I take these two common features and ask what there is in common between indifference to fortune and refusal to endure being dishonoured. If there is nothing in common, there will be two species of magnanimity.

[21] Magnanimity is the virtue concerned with honour and dishonour, 'not about honour from the many but the honour from virtuous people, and indeed with the latter in preference <to the former>' (1192a23-4). Aristotle is perhaps thinking of three situations; (1) the virtuous people honour x, and the many are indifferent to it; (2) the virtuous people are indifferent to x, and the many honour it; (3) the virtuous people honour x and the many honour y, which is incompatible with x. The magnanimous person will value x in the first situation, and avoid x in the second. In the third situation, he prefers x over y, even though it brings a loss of honour from the many.

The magnanimous person does not pursue honour indiscriminately, but only from the right people. This is because he cares most about the goods that they honour him for: 'for neither is he concerned about every kind of honour, but about the best kind and the sort of good that is honourable and has the status of a principle' (1192a28-9). The connection between being honoured and being an origin or first principle is explained in the initial division of goods in the *MM*, where the goods deserving honour are the source, basis, or origin, of other goods (1183b21-3).

loss of external goods matters so much that it should shake them from the virtuous course of action.

Aristotle does not mention even this element of Socratic magnanimity; he ignores both the Comparative Thesis (P5) and the Dominance Thesis (P8). In eliminating Socrates' attitude from magnanimity, Aristotle also passes over without comment the attitude appropriate to the Platonic doctrine.

5. *Magna Moralia*: eudaimonism?

Even if Aristotle rejects the dominance of virtue in happiness, he might still accept Plato's view that the just person ought to stick to justice even in ill fortune. Plato thinks the two views stand or fall together because he accepts eudaimonism. But Aristotle's treatment of self-love (*philautia*) suggests rejection of eudaimonism.

In the *Laws* Plato attacks the bad effects of extreme self-love, arguing that a virtuous person should love justice rather than himself.[22] Aristotle exploits these objections to excessive self-love, in discussing whether the virtuous person is a 'self-lover' (*philautos*).[23] First he describes the self-lover as 'the one who does everything for his own sake in things that concern expediency' (1212a29-30). By this standard, the virtuous person is not a self-lover, because in these actions[24] he acts for the sake of another (a33-4). Hence, as far as these goods are concerned, he is not a self-lover; if he is a self-lover, it must be where the fine is concerned (1212b3-4). In the choice of the fine, the virtuous person is a self-lover, but in the

---

[22] Plato considers the common view that every human being is by nature a friend to himself, and must be so (731e1-3). (In 731e3 *dein* might refer to a natural necessity (derived from *phuesi* in the previous line) or to a rational necessity (i.e. 'ought to be so').) In answer to the common view, he maintains that 'the cause of all errors arises on each occasion for each person because of extreme love of oneself' (731e3-5). Love of ourselves makes us excessively favourable and charitable to ourselves and our own point of view, since we prefer what is our own before the truth, and this makes us bad judges of just, good, and fine things (731e5-732a1). Love of ourselves makes us slow to correct our own ignorance, and prone to claim knowledge when we know nothing (732a4-b2). A truly great man, therefore, should not love himself nor what belongs to him; he should love just things, whether they are done by himself or by someone else (732a2-4). We might exploit Plato's remarks here by arguing that a purely impartial concern for justice and just action ought to replace one's concern for one's own welfare.

[23] An unfavourable sense of '*philautos*' is clearest in *Politics* 1263a41-b5: 'For each person's love (*philia*) of himself is not pointless, but a natural tendency. Certainly, a self-lover (*to philauton einai*) is justly blamed; but this is not loving oneself (*to philein heauton*), but loving oneself more than is right (*to mallon ê dei philein*), just as with money-loving (*to philochrêmaton*) – for practically everyone loves himself and loves money.' The term seems to have a more neutral sense at *Rhetoric* 1371b18-25, 1389b35-1390a1 (where Aristotle uses '*philautoi mallon ê dei*' to indicate a blameworthy condition). At *NE* 1125b14-17 Aristotle draws attention to these different uses of '*philo*'- compounds.

[24] I assume that in 1212a33 *touto prattei* refers to action *en tois kata to lusiteles*, a30.

choice of the expedient and the pleasant, the vicious person is a self-lover (1212b6-8).[25]

Aristotle now asks whether the virtuous person loves himself most. Where expediency is concerned, he loves his friend more, but where the fine is concerned, he loves himself most. This, however, shows that the virtuous person is not a self-lover, but a lover of good (*philagathos*); for if he loves himself, it is only because he is good.[26] The bad person, by contrast, really is a self-lover, because he loves himself despite having nothing fine about him; and so he is the one who would properly (*kuriôs*) be called a self-lover.[27] When Aristotle says the good person loves 'the good', he does not mean that she loves her own good; he means that she loves goodness, and that this non-self-referential love explains her love of herself.

Good people, then, are only conditional and derivative self-lovers. On this view, they primarily love goodness, whether in themselves or in others; they love themselves only in so far as they satisfy the general conditions for goodness. If Aristotle means this, he rejects the Eudaimonist Thesis (P9). Acceptance of the primacy of self-love fails, in his view, to capture the good person's overriding impartial concern for goodness without reference to any particular person's good.

This is a short passage on which to hang the sweeping claim that in the *MM* Aristotle rejects eudaimonism. I would not insist strongly on it if some other passage in the treatise made his acceptance of eudaimonism clear.[28] But I mention the passage because it is the only passage that I know of that even tends to commit Aristotle one way or the other. Since it tends to a non-eudaimonist position, it is worth mentioning, in order to show that he may not accept eudaimonism.[29]

---

[25] 'As far as these [sc. expedient] goods are concerned, [the virtuous person] is not a self-lover, but, if he is a self-lover, it must be where the fine is concerned. ... In the choice of the fine, he is a self-lover, but in the choice of the expedient and the pleasant, the vicious person is a self-lover' (1212b3-8).

[26] 'He is therefore a lover of good, not a self-lover. For if he loves himself, it is only because he is good. But the bad person is a self-lover' (1212b18-20).

[27] 'Properly' here shows Aristotle's concern to set aside the derivative or metaphorical uses of the term; we noticed this same concern in the discussion of magnificence. Aristotle differs from the *Laws* on love of oneself, since he says nothing about the connection between love of oneself and complacency about one's own ignorance or one's own defects. But he agrees with the *Laws* in describing the good person as a lover of goodness rather than a self-lover.

[28] For this reason, I would not suggest that the *Laws* passage signals Plato's intention to reject eudaimonism, since the rest of the dialogue speaks so strongly in the other direction.

[29] We might still want to discount this passage if we supposed that eudaimonism must have appeared evidently correct to Aristotle, or to his audience, or to 'the Greeks', so that anyone would be taken to accept it unless its rejection were emphatically underlined. (In the Cyrenaics the rejection of eudaimonism is emphatically underlined.) But to suppose this would be to lay too much weight on the predominant tendency of Greek moral philosophy.

In the *Rhetoric* Aristotle's account of some ordinary moral attitudes does not suggest that eudaimonism is universally accepted. I have discussed this in 'Ethics in the *Rhetoric* and in the *Ethics*', in *Essays on Aristotle's Rhetoric*, ed. A.O. Rorty (Berkeley: University of California Press, 1996), 142-74. I mention the *Rhetoric* not as evidence of Aristotle's views,

6. *Eudemian Ethics*: happiness and function

The *EE* agrees with the *MM* on the completeness of happiness, but Aristotle's reasons are less clear.[30] The *MM* argues that happiness is the best good because it is complete (1184a8-14), and the good must be complete; the *EE* simply assumes without argument that happiness is complete, in order to argue that it consists in the activity of complete virtue (1219a28).[31] Aristotle might suppose that the completeness of happiness follows from the initial assumption that happiness is best and finest, and thereby pleasantest (1214a7-8); perhaps the appeal to completeness helps to specify the sense in which happiness is best. At any rate, it is less clear in the *EE* than in the *MM* how external goods contribute to happiness.[32]

---

even his early views, but to show that his audience or readers would probably not find it strange or unintelligible if an ethical treatise failed to maintain eudaimonism. In contrasting the virtuous person with the lover of self, the *MM* relies on a contrast that most people would find familiar.

[30] The opening discussion in the *EE* differs most obviously from the *MM* in the relative prominence of questions about happiness and the relative absence of questions about goods. The *MM* concentrates on the division of goods and introduces happiness quite casually (1184a13), whereas the *EE* introduces happiness at the beginning, and says very little about its place in a classification of goods.

[31] 'Therefore this is the complete good, which was happiness. And it is clear from the assumptions laid down; for happiness was the best ...' (1219a28-30). In 1219a28 the mss actually read *pleon*, which Bekker emends to *teleon*. Perhaps one ought not to accept the emendation – despite its palaeographical simplicity – without question. But even if one rejects it, the same claim appears at a35-6.

[32] He mentions fortune briefly at the beginning (1214a24-5), but does not say how much happiness depends on it. He raises an important issue later, in considering how widely accessible happiness might be. If living finely consisted in things resulting from fortune or nature, it would be beyond the expectation of most people, because they could not acquire it by their own efforts, but if it consisted in one's character and the corresponding actions, it would be more widely shared and more divine (1215a12-19). ('Beyond the expectation' renders *anelpiston*, 1215a13. Dirlmeier: 'dann müssten viele resignieren'. Solomon's and Woods's use of 'hope' is a bit less appropriate for the precise point Aristotle is making.) This gives us a reason to expect that Aristotle will be somewhat inclined to regard happiness as consisting in character and activity, but he does not say we can completely satisfy our preference for finding happiness to be up to us; it is not up to us to make happiness the sort of thing we might like it to be. Though this remark adds an important constraint to the conditions mentioned in the *MM*, it might be satisfied by a number of views about the role of virtue and external goods in happiness.

Aristotle proceeds to dismiss various unappealing aspects of human life as candidates for happiness, and turns to the more appealing aspects that define the 'three lives'. He then begins from an agreed starting point, that happiness is the greatest and best of human goods, and, more precisely, of goods achievable by human beings (I.7). The reference to achievable goods leads to a discussion of the Platonic Form of the Good (I.8). After that discussion, the argument and the order agree much more closely with the *MM*; Aristotle introduces the threefold classification of goods, the superiority of activity over possession, and the function argument. He does not refer back to Book I, except for the claim that happiness is the best good.

The argument that results in the definition of happiness is longer and more complicated than the one in the *MM*. Like the *MM* and *Republic* I, it uses an appeal to function to explain the character of virtue.[33] In relation to *Republic* I, the *EE* differs from the *MM* on two main points: (a) In the *MM* the remark about the soul being responsible for other things besides life suggests a specific recollection of *Republic* I. In the *EE* the only function ascribed to the soul is living (1219a23-5); this is reasonable if Aristotle sees that this is the only activity that is relevant to the argument about virtue and living well. The recollection of the *Republic* is absent. (b) Unlike Plato, the *MM* does not speak explicitly of function. In the *EE*, however, the explicit mention of function recalls the *Republic*.

These two differences leave us with a strong case for seeing a close connection between both treatises and *Republic* I. In the *EE*, as in the *MM*, Aristotle assumes a close connection between living well, understood as living virtuously, and living well, understood as living happily. This assumption needs more defence than it receives in the *Republic* or in the two *Ethics*.

In the *MM* the definition of happiness as a complete good leads into observations about completeness in time, and about activity (1185a1-13). In the *EE* Aristotle defends his definition of happiness by citing common beliefs, in accordance with the method set out in Book I (1216b26-8). Among these common beliefs he mentions the temporal aspects of happiness; he connects them with completeness, as the *MM* does (1219b4-8).[34] But he also includes some discussion of objects of praise and other goods, which came earlier in the *MM* (1219b8-16). The demand for activity is illustrated by a fuller discussion of why we cannot be happy if we are always asleep (1219b16-26).

So far, then, though the *EE* offers us less detail than the *MM* offers on the specific points that concern us, it says enough to show that it agrees with the *MM*. It understands the completeness of happiness in such a way that happiness depends on external goods; hence it rejects the Sufficiency Thesis (P2). But it does not commit itself on the Dominance Thesis (P8).

7. *Eudemian Ethics*: happiness and fortune

This conclusion from the argument about happiness and virtue is confirmed by other passages in the *EE*, if we include the Common Books. The remarks on

---

[33] 'Let these assumptions, then, be made, and let it be assumed about virtue that it is the best disposition or state or capacity of each kind of things that have some use or function. This is clear from induction, for we posit this in all cases: for instance, a coat has a virtue, since a coat has a function and use ...' (1218b37-1219a3).

[34] '... and the <view> that a person is not happy for one day only, and that a child is not happy, nor any <limited> period of life (hence also Solon's advice is right, not to call anyone happy while he is alive, but when he has reached the end); for nothing incomplete is happy, since it is not a whole' (1219a4-8).

external goods clarifiy the position of the *MM* by saying that these external goods are good without qualification, even though they are not good for every type of person; the good person is the one for whom these goods are good (*NE* 1129b1-6).

In the discussion of pleasure Aristotle confirms that these external goods belong to happiness, and so he rejects the Sufficiency Thesis. Someone who is broken on the wheel and suffers the greatest misfortunes cannot be happy; to this extent happiness requires good fortune (1153b19-25).[35] The falsity of the Sufficiency Thesis follows from the completeness of happiness (1153b16-18). This is a more explicit rejection of the Socratic Sufficiency Thesis than anything we can find in the *MM*; but the *MM* accepts premises from which it follows.

The chapters on good fortune and on the fine and good person agree with the *MM* on the relevant points. Fine and good people are those for whom unqualified goods[36] are good (1248b26-37).[37] They prefer fine actions above the possession and enjoyment of external goods; but Aristotle does not say whether they take the fine to dominate all other goods.

8. *Eudemian Ethics*: magnanimity

In *EE* III. 5 Aristotle discusses gentleness, generosity, magnanimity, and magnificence, in the same order as in the *MM*.[38] He distinguishes magnanimity from virtue as a whole, by making it a large-scale virtue, requiring achievements and successes that deserve large honours, and therefore requiring the external resources needed for these successes.[39] Whereas the *MM* requires the magnanimous

---

[35] 'For no activity is complete if it is impeded, and happiness is something complete. That is why the happy person needs to have goods of the body and external goods added, and needs fortune also, so that he will not be impeded in these ways. Some maintain, on the contrary, that we are happy when we are broken on the wheel, or fall into terrible misfortunes, provided that we are good. ... And because happiness needs fortune added, some believe good fortune is the same as happiness. But it is not. For when it is excessive, it actually impedes happiness ...' (1153b16-23).

[36] Here Aristotle calls them 'goods by nature', *phusei agatha*.

[37] 'The good person, then, is the one for whom the things good by nature are good. ... Someone is fine and good by having the goods that are fine because of themselves, and by being a doer of fine actions, and for their own sake; and the fine things are the virtues and the actions from virtue' (1248a26-37).

[38] He departs farthest from the *MM* in the account of magnanimity, by introducing features of the magnanimous person that might incline us to identify magnanimity with the whole of virtue. The *MM* does not intend to suggest this; it intends to treat only the particular virtue. In the *EE*, however, Aristotle suggests that the account in the *MM* is at fault, in so far as it fails to distinguish magnanimity from the rest of virtue.

[39] 'Honour is small or great in two ways: it differs in being conferred either by many ordinary people or by people worth considering, and in what it is conferred for, since its greatness does not depend only on the number or the character of those who confer it, but also on its being honourable; and in reality ruling offices and other goods that are

person simply to be correct in his estimate of the goods he deserves (1192a32-4), the *EE* requires him to believe truly that he deserves great goods. A person with modest achievements and expectations would not obviously fail to be magnanimous according to the *MM*; but the *EE* disqualifies him (1233a16-19).

This narrower condition for magnanimity does not clarify the role of honour in a magnanimous person's conception of his good. He does not aim exclusively or indiscriminately at honour. Since he demands honour from the right people for the right achievements, he cares only about being honoured by people who are right about what deserves honour. But if he finds no such people to honour him, would he be right to agree with Ajax? Should he conclude that life without this honour is worth living? Aristotle does not say; hence he does not express a view on Socratic magnanimity. Since he does not suggest that one's attitude to ill fortune is an aspect of magnanimity, he does not treat the Socratic outlook as a part of this virtue.

Nor does he answer the question of *Republic* II. If the just person suffers dishonour as a result of being just, is he none the less better off than he would be if he were less just and had more honour? The *EE* rejects the indiscriminate pursuit of honour, but it does not say how serious a loss dishonour would be for the virtuous person.

9. *Eudemian Ethics*: self-love and eudaimonism

In comparing the *MM* with Plato on virtue and happiness we asked whether Aristotle accepted the Eudaimonist Thesis (P9). His treatment of self-love gave us grounds for answering No. We cannot compare the *EE* directly with the *MM* on this particular point, because it lacks a discussion of self-love.

This omission in the *EE* may be partly explained by a broader difference between the treatments of friendship in the two works. In the *MM* a series of chapters discusses the relation between attitudes to oneself and attitudes to one's friend. Friendship for oneself, beneficence, goodwill, and self-love (1211a16-1212b23) prepare us for the concluding argument for the goodness of friendship. Since this concluding argument considers the attitudes that are included in treating one's friend as another oneself, it is reasonable to approach this argument by considering various aspects of the proper treatment of others and of oneself. The treatment of self-love fits into this preparatory discussion.

The *EE* proceeds in this order as far as the discussion of beneficence; but then (in VII.9) it turns to friendship in different types of community. Aristotle examines the political aspects of friendship, and the relation between friendship and justice. This classification of friendships leads naturally into a discussion of the disputes that arise in different types of friendships.[40] After this, Aristotle comes back to the

---

honourable and worthy of serious pursuit are those that are truly great ...' (1232b17-23).

[40] One might mark this section as beginning at 1242b37, but Aristotle does not mark a sharp break.

topics of the *MM*, and takes up the question of self-sufficiency and the goodness of friendship.

In discussing the treatment of happiness in the *EE*, we found that Aristotle departs from the *MM*, and then returns to it, after omitting the discussion of completeness that would support his argument for the definition of happiness. Something similar, though less obvious, may be true in the treatment of friendship. As the *EE* presents it, the argument for treating one's friend as another oneself is presented without an account of how the virtuous person treats himself, and hence without a clear account of what it means to treat another person as one treats oneself. The *MM* provides an account in the discussion of self-love. The omission of this chapter creates a gap in the argument in the *EE* about friendship.[41]

Does any other part of the *EE* bear on eudaimonism? In the initial discussion of happiness Aristotle claims that everyone sets some goal with reference to which one does everything (1214b6-14).[42] This goal is identified with happiness. Hence Aristotle insists that the rational agent will be guided in all choices, including the choice between virtuous and vicious action, by the prospects of happiness.

If this is Aristotle's view, and if he sees its implications, he should not endorse the account of self-love in the *MM*; for the combination of the eudaimonism affirmed in Book I with a non-eudaimonist treatment of self-love would make his position inconsistent. A non-eudaimonist defence of the Stability Thesis (P4) fits the *MM*, but not the *EE*. Aristotle, therefore, offers no defence of the Stability Thesis. He certainly rejects the Sufficiency Thesis, since he does not believe that

---

[41] These remarks on the *EE* on friendship may be compared with A.J.P. Kenny's explanation of the omission of a treatment of self-love in 'Friendship and Self-love' (in *Aristotle on the Perfect Life* (Oxford: Oxford University Press, 1992), ch. 4, esp. 52f.). He suggests that Aristotle consciously abandons, or at least modifies, his egoist eudaimonism in his treatment of friendship in the *EE*. (I take this to be the point of his remark: '... even the *prima facie* appearance of egoism is much less in the *EE*. In both *Ethics*, however, the contorted and obscure nature of the writing seems to betray that Aristotle felt uncomfortable in the attempt to find room within his eudaimonistic system for the manifest importance of friendship' (52).) I am not initially convinced by Kenny's claims about this aspect of the *EE*. If they were correct, they would fit the treatment of self-love in the *MM* (which Kenny regards as post-Aristotelian).

[42] 'Having then in regard to this subject established that everybody able to live in accordance with his own decision sets some end of living finely – honour, reputation, wealth, or education – focusing on which he will do all his actions (since it is a mark of much folly not to have one's life regulated towards some end), one must above all define first in oneself, neither hastily nor sluggishly, in which of the things that are ours living well consists ...' (1214b6-13). I take this difficult sentence to describe what everyone does, not what everyone ought to do (and so I would reject the insertion of *dei* in b7, favoured by a marginal reading in one ms and by some editors and translators). But even if Aristotle is saying what we ought to do, the main point about eudaimonism and the comparative thesis will stand (since the virtuous person can be expected to do what everyone ought to do, and hence will aim at happiness in all his actions).

the just person is happy when he is tortured. But he does not explicitly endorse the Comparative Thesis, since he does not suggest that the just person must be happier in these circumstances than the unjust person in favourable circumstances.

10. *Nicomachean Ethics*: goods and happiness

Early in Book I Aristotle displays his interest in the questions raised by Socrates' claims about virtue and happiness. Before he turns to his own account of happiness, he criticizes some mistaken views of happiness, through his comments on the three lives. The life of virtue, like the previous two lives, is incomplete; it leaves out the goods that depend on fortune. Hence anyone who identifies the life of virtue with the happy life must maintain the untenable claim that we can be happy without the external goods that depend on fortune (1095b31-1096a2).

After this informal introduction of completeness, *NE* I.7 follows the *MM* in presenting a more formal discussion of the completeness of the ultimate good, immediately before Aristotle's own account of happiness. The discussion of completeness leads directly into the function argument.

In the function argument Aristotle diverges sharply from the other two *Ethics*. Instead of appealing to the function of F to explain the virtue of F, he uses it to explain the good of F, so that instead of saying that F's goodness consists in F's performing its function, he claims that F's good – i.e. welfare – consists in F's performing its function.[43] On this point Aristotle disagrees both with the other two *Ethics* and with *Republic* I.

Like the other two treatises, the *NE* concludes the argument for a definition of happiness with a further remark about completeness. The *MM* simply requires a complete length of time. The *EE* inserts a section on common beliefs about happiness, and mentions the temporal dimension near the beginning. The *NE* agrees with the *MM* in proceeding directly to the temporal claim (1098a18-20). But it agrees with the *EE* in including a reference to complete virtue in the definition of happiness.[44] To this demand for complete virtue, the *NE* adds a demand for a complete life, and takes this to justify a complete length of time.[45]

Aristotle considers the possibilities mentioned in the *EE* about whether happiness is achieved by our own actions or by fortune. He now states his own position more fully: (1) Virtue is not sufficient for happiness (contrary to P2)

---

[43] 'For just as the good and the well, for a flautist, a sculptor, and every craftsman, and, in general, for whatever has a function and action, seems to be in the function, the same seems to be true for a human being, if a human being has some function' (1097b25-8).

[44] Cf. 1219a35-9; contrast *MM* 1184b36-1185a1, *kata tas aretas*.

[45] 'And so the human good proves to be activity of the soul in accord with virtue, and indeed with the best and most complete virtue, if there are more virtues than one. Moreover, in a complete life. For one swallow does not make a spring, nor does one day; nor, similarly, does one day or a short time make us blessed and happy' (1098a15-20).

because happiness depends on external circumstances.[46] (2) None the less, virtuous actions, not external conditions, control happiness (*kuriai*, 1100b7-11).[47]

Aristotle now clarifies his position on the Dominance Thesis (P8). Though ill fortune can mar happiness, the happy person will never become miserable; for he is noble and magnanimous, and will therefore never do anything hateful or vicious (1100b30-1101a6).[48] A happy person may cease to be happy, if he suffers enough ill fortune, but he will not become miserable, because he will always choose the virtuous and fine action.

This virtuous person accepts the Stability Thesis (P4). But it does not follow that Aristotle agrees with the Comparative Thesis (P5). To agree with it, he must accept eudaimonism and must believe that the virtuous person's choice is rationally justifiable if and only if it is the best choice for her own happiness.

Aristotle accepts eudaimonism in *NE* I, as he does in *EE* I. He identifies the best good with the good that we wish for for its own sake and for the sake of which we wish for the other goods. If there is such a good, he claims, it is important for the conduct of our lives to find out what it is. Though at first he simply says what we ought to do if there is such a good, he clearly accepts the antecedent of the conditional. Once we agree that there is such a thing as political science, and that the highest good is the object of political science, we also agree that there is a highest good (1094a26-b7). This feature of the highest good is also a feature of happiness; that is why happiness is the highest good (1097a34-b6; cf. 1102a2-4).[49]

This commitment to eudaimonism does not imply that the virtuous person chooses virtue only for the sake of happiness; since he also chooses it for its own sake, he would still have a reason to choose it even if it did not promote happiness

---

[46] For this specific claim it does not matter whether external goods, or external goods correctly used, are components of happiness (as I take Aristotle to believe) or simply necessary conditions for the virtuous activity that wholly constitutes happiness. Some relevant issues are discussed by J.M. Cooper, 'Aristotle on the Goods of Fortune', in *Reason and Emotion* (Princeton: Princeton University Press, 1999), 292-311; and by S.L. White, *Sovereign Virtue* (Stanford: Stanford University Press, 1992). I have discussed them in 'Permanent Happiness: Aristotle and Solon', *Oxford Studies in Ancient Philosophy* 3 (1985), 89-124.

[47] 'Or is it quite wrong to take our cue from someone's fortunes? For <his doing> well or badly is not in them. Rather, a human life, as we said, needs these added, but the activities in accord with virtue control happiness, and the contrary activities control its contrary' (1100b7-11).

[48] 'And yet, even in these circumstances the fine shines through, whenever someone bears many severe misfortunes with good temper (*eukolôs*), not because he feels no distress, but because he is noble and magnanimous. And since it is activities that control life, as we said, no blessed person could ever become miserable (*athlios*), since he will never do hateful and base actions' (1100b30-35).

[49] '... <happiness> is a principle; for it is for the sake of this we all do all the other things ...' (1102a2-3). Richard Kraut (*Aristotle on the Human Good* (Princeton: Princeton University Press, 1989), 88) discusses this passage. I do not think he gives it enough weight when he argues (144-8) that Aristotle is not (in the *NE*) a eudaimonist.

(1097b2-5). But the supremacy of happiness requires the rejection of other goods if they exclude the course of action that promotes happiness. If, therefore, the virtuous person in misfortune would be better off if he were less virtuous and could secure greater external goods, he would be acting irrationally in preferring to act virtuously. Since the virtuous person does not act irrationally, he correctly believes that the virtuous action is better, from the point of view of one's own happiness, than any alternative would be.

For this reason, even though Aristotle does not state the Comparative Thesis (P5) and the Dominance Thesis (P8), he accepts them. This aspect of the *NE* marks a clear difference from the other two treatises.

11. *Nicomachean Ethics*: magnanimity

This difference between the *NE* and the other two *Ethics* re-appears in the discussion of magnanimity. Aristotle now extends the scope of magnanimity from honour to all external goods (1124a12-20).[50] The magnanimous person takes a 'moderate' attitude to all external goods, so that he is neither overjoyed by good fortune nor excessively grieved by misfortune (1124a15-16). His moderate attitude is described as calm in the face of misfortune (1100b31-2, *eukolôs*). This is the right attitude because virtuous people's character, expressed in virtuous actions as far as possible, outweighs any other loss. Though misfortune deprives them of happiness, it does not reduce them to misery (1100b33-5).

In connecting the Stability Thesis with magnanimity, Aristotle recognizes the magnanimity of Socrates in contrast to that of Ajax. Magnanimity requires the appropriate attitude to great honour; but this attitude requires the proper evaluation of honour; this proper evaluation requires the proper evaluation of external goods, since honour is one of them; and the proper evaluation of external goods results in the virtuous person's moderate and reserved view of them.

Aristotle does not, however, treat the outlook of Socrates as genuine magnanimity. Magnanimity retains its connection with ambition and the pursuit of honour. Magnanimous people think honour worth pursuing in addition to virtue; hence they care about things that Socrates would not care about. They think it legitimate to be honoured for possessing external goods, and therefore they care about acquiring them, even apart from any effect on virtuous action. This aspect of the magnanimous person marks Aristotle's preference for the Dominance Thesis over the Sufficiency Thesis.

---

[50] '... the magnanimous person is concerned especially with honours. Still, he will also have a moderate attitude to riches and power and every sort of good and bad fortune, however it turns out. He will be neither excessively pleased by good fortune nor excessively distressed by ill fortune; for he does not regard honour as the greatest good either' (1124a12-17).

12. *Nicomachean Ethics*: self-love

The treatment of magnanimity supports the conclusion derived from *NE* I, that the *NE*, in agreement with the other two *Ethics*, rejects the Sufficiency Thesis, but, in contrast to the other *Ethics*, accepts the Dominance Thesis. We can confirm these claims by comparing the treatment of self-love in the *NE* with the treatment in the *MM*.

Aristotle introduces self-love in IX.4, in the section of the *NE* that most clearly recalls the *Republic*. He argues that the vicious person is incapable of friendship either with himself or with others, since he has nothing loveable (*philêton*) about him. He concludes that since this is a miserable (*athlion*) condition, we ought to avoid vice strenuously and try to be virtuous, since this will make us friends to ourselves and with others (1166b25-9). This argument deserves some discussion, but its conclusion is especially relevant to our concerns. Aristotle regards vice as so miserable that he is justified in giving the unqualified advice to be virtuous. He emphasized earlier that a happy (and therefore virtuous) person cannot become miserable even if he ceases to be happy (1100b34-5); such a person therefore never has good reason to cease to act virtuously. He now adds that the vicious person is thereby in a miserable condition, and therefore we are better off being virtuous. Aristotle does not imply that virtue is the whole of happiness. But he commits himself to the choice of virtue over vice without qualification, and therefore without reference to the external goods that either the virtuous or the vicious person might lose or gain. In advocating this choice, he agrees with Plato's Dominance Thesis (P8).

This discussion of friendship for oneself makes it reasonable to discuss the ways in which a virtuous person is a self-lover; and so the *NE* returns to this topic that is discussed in the *MM*, but omitted in the *EE*. Aristotle still insists that the virtuous person is a self-lover in relation to the fine, not the expedient. But the *NE* does not say, as the *MM* says, that virtuous people are primarily lovers of good who love themselves only in so far as they are good.

To explain this omission in the *NE*, we might turn to a point with no parallel in the *MM*. The *MM* distinguishes the virtuous from the vicious person on two dimensions – concern for the fine versus the expedient, and love for goodness versus love for oneself. The *NE* replaces the second dimension with the contrast between reason and passion. The correct self-lover differs from the mistaken self-lover as much as life according to reason differs from life according to passion, and as much as desire for the fine differs from desire for apparent advantage (1169a3-6).[51] He lives according to reason because he regards himself as rational. Since

---

[51] 'That is why he most of all is a self-lover, but a different kind from the self-lover who is reproached. He differs from him as much as living in accord with reason differs from living in accord with passion, and desiring the fine differs from desiring for what seems advantageous' (1169a3-6). In 1169a6 I read *oregesthai tou kalou*, with Susemihl (OCT: *oregesthai ê tou kalou*).

one's rational part is most fully oneself, and since virtuous people love their rational part, they are the people who most of all love themselves (1169a2-3).

The *NE*, therefore, does not claim that virtuous people are lovers of the good rather than of themselves. The *MM* seems to deny that good people are basically self-lovers, because we might love our selves as they are without requiring them to be good, and in that case our self-love would lead us into bad action. In the *NE* Aristotle answers that it is not ourselves that we love if we do not understand ourselves correctly; if we do not recognize that we are primarily rational agents, we do not identify ourselves correctly, and so our love is not for ourselves as we really are. Self-love and virtue are connected, not because self-love needs to be restricted by love of the good, but because self-love needs to be directed by a true conception of oneself.

I have suggested that it is not an accident that the *NE* both subtracts from the *MM* the remark that the virtuous person primarily loves the good and adds the remark that virtuous people love themselves as rational. The two differences explain each other.

13. Aristotle's development

I have given some reasons for believing that Aristotle changes his mind about the Comparative Thesis and the Dominance Thesis (P5 and P8). The *NE* both discusses the relevant issues most fully and shows the most evident sympathy with the answer to Glaucon's challenge that Plato offers in the *Republic*.

Since some of the arguments I have offered are arguments from silence, one might suggest that the apparently different views expressed in the other two works are simply the result of their brevity, and that if Aristotle had stated his view fully, he would have taken the view he takes in the *NE*. But I take the silences in the earlier treatises to be systematic, and therefore significant. The *NE* mentions magnanimity in Book I and includes attitudes to fortune in magnanimity in Book IV; this connection is completely missing in the other two treatises. The complete absence of the connection is most readily explained if the other two treatises do not accept the dominance of virtue.

These aspects of the three *Ethics* suggest that I have put them in the right order. I find it difficult to suppose that the writer of the *MM* had access to the treatments of these topics in the other two *Ethics*; and the differences between the *EE* and *NE* are more easily explained if the *NE* is revising and expanding the *EE* than if the *EE* is revising and abbreviating the *NE*. Both Aristotle (supposing that the *EE* is later) and the author of the *MM* (supposing that it is post-Aristotelian) would display remarkably bad judgement in deleting those parts of the *NE* that deal with questions about the resilience of virtuous people in ill fortune. The questions are clearly relevant and important; and once Aristotle had seen the need to address them, it is difficult to understand why he would decide that they no longer needed to be addressed. This is not a conclusive reason, all by itself, for accepting the order that I have assumed. It is only one of a number of individually non-conclusive reasons that need to be collected and examined in the course of trying to grasp the relations between the three *Ethics*.

Reply to T.H. Irwin

Anthony Kenny

Professor Irwin's paper is rich and stimulating and forces one to think hard about Aristotle from unfamiliar angles. As will be seen, I agree with a very great deal of what it contains. But I must admit that I am a little uncomfortable with the structure of the paper. Essentially, Irwin offers Aristotelian answers to Platonic questions. It is not always easy to match an answer to a question, and following Irwin's discussion can feel like trying to take the measure of an Aristotle wearing an ill-fitting suit.

One problem concerns the central concept of virtue. 'Virtue' in Irwin's Platonic texts is not often *aretê*; the quotations are more likely to concern particular virtues such as justice and temperance. Aristotle might well give different answers to the questions put if 'justice' was substituted for 'virtue' in their formulation. This is partly because he made a systematic distinction between moral and intellectual virtues, and placed a special emphasis on the latter. Admittedly, in the middle books of the *Republic*, justice includes some pretty heady intellectual activity; but most of the Platonic texts on which Irwin relies concern moral virtue.

More important than the distinction between moral and intellectual virtues in Aristotle is the distinction between virtue as a state on the one hand, and the exercise or use of virtue on the other. The distinction between possession and use goes back to the *Euthydemus* passage (280b7-d7) that is Irwin's first quote – but there what is in question is the possession and use of external goods, not of virtue. By contrast, in all three of the Aristotelian ethical treatises, happiness is identified not with the having of virtue, but with the exercise of virtue. This is in my view the most significant advance in Aristotle's theory. Irwin is of course well acquainted with the distinction; but my principal difference from him is that I believe he underplays its importance.

In *NE* I.8 Aristotle, having said that the human good is 'activity of the soul in accordance with virtue', goes on to relate this definition to those offered by others. With regard to those who define it as virtue, or a virtue, he says, 'It makes no little difference whether we place the supreme good in possession or in use, in state (*hexis*) or in activity' (1098b31-4). It is the view of all three treatises that the mere possession of virtue, as opposed to its exercise, does not amount to the supreme good for human beings.[1] The terminology used to contrast the possession and the

---

[1] *NE* 1098b32-1099a2: 'the state may exist without producing any good result, as in a man who is asleep or in some other way quite inactive, but the activity cannot.'

exercise of virtue differs, however, in the *NE* from the other two treatises. Virtuous behaviour, as contrasted with the mere possession of virtue, in the *NE* is by preference described as a person's 'activity in accordance with virtue'; in the *EE* and (to a lesser extent) the *MM* it is described as a 'use of virtue'. The contrast is striking, but I do not believe that it denotes a difference of substance between the treatises.[2]

The importance of the distinction means that we have a complicated task in giving Aristotelian answers to Irwin's Platonic questions. When the word 'virtue' appears in the question we may have to give two different answers, one related to the possession of virtue, the other to the exercise of virtue. Aristotle's answers to the Platonic questions will often need bifurcation.

Bearing this distinction in mind, I will now try to give my own answers to Irwin's Platonic questions, but I will reverse Irwin's order of tackling the treatises, and I will start with the *NE*, and then move to the *EE* and to the *MM*. The chronological sequence that will probably come naturally to most people here is neither Irwin's order nor mine, but rather *EE*, *NE*, *MM*. I am not putting my own ordering forward as a chronological one, for I believe the relationships between the ethical writings in the corpus are too complicated to be explained by a simple temporal sequence. I am simply adopting another approach to the detection of differences of doctrine between the treatises. It is, of course, only if we regard the differences between the treatises as being due to chronology that we can regard the differences as being evidence of a *change of mind*. In considering the individual texts I will concentrate on their treatments of happiness, not magnanimity and self-love.

The *Nicomachean Ethics*

I will first set out the *Nicomachean* position in respect of the theses enunciated by Irwin.[3]

NE 1176a33-5: '[happiness] is not a state; for if it were it might belong to someone who was asleep throughout his life, living the life of a plant, or again, to someone who was suffering the greatest misfortunes.'

AE 1153b19-21: 'Those who say that the victim on the rack or the man who falls into great misfortunes is happy if he is good are, whether they mean to or not, talking nonsense.'

EE 1219b9-10, 16-20: 'We crown the actual winners, not those who have the power to win but do not win ... This clears up the difficulty sometimes raised – why for half their lives the good are no better than the bad, for all are alike when asleep; the cause is that sleep is an inactivity, not an activity of the soul.'

MM 1185a10: 'That [happiness] is an activity can be seen also from the following consideration. For supposing someone to be asleep all his life, we should hardly consent to call such a man happy.'

[2] Statistics of usage for the *NE* and the *EE* are given in my *The Aristotelian Ethics* (Oxford: Clarendon Press, 1978), 68.

[3] Like Irwin, I find no answer to the question whether the *NE* accepts P1 (the conditionality of goodness).

P2. Is virtue sufficient for happiness? Virtue itself is not: the virtuous man may be asleep or overtaken by disaster. The exercise of the appropriate virtue, however, is not only sufficient for happiness: it is what happiness consists in.[4]

P3. Is virtue choiceworthy for its own sake? Yes: both virtue itself (1097b2-4) and also virtuous actions (1176a6-9).

P4. Should virtue be stuck to at all costs? It is hard to give a precise answer, because of the vagueness of 'stuck to'. But we can point to the following relevant passages, which support a positive answer. There are some actions one must never do (1107a14-18). Virtuous actions are the most stable thing in human life, and the happy person will always by preference do and contemplate what belongs to virtue (1100b12-20).

P5. Is virtue the choice most productive of happiness? Since happiness consists in the exercise of virtue, no one can be happy without virtue, which is a necessary condition for its exercise. But the mere possession of virtue is not sufficient for happiness, if the exercise is obstructed (e.g. by illness, or by the lack of necessary means, or grave misfortune). A virtuous person who, because of one of these impediments, is not in a position to choose virtuous actions ceases to be happy. However, such a person will never become wretched because he will never do anything wicked (1100b30-1101b8).

P6. Is the supreme good composite? In an earlier version of his paper Irwin gave the answer yes, but he now seems to have withdrawn this claim. I believe he is right to do so. The supreme human good that is happiness, for the *NE*, consists in philosophical contemplation and that alone.[5] It is true that at 1101a14-17 Aristotle says:

> Why then should we not say that he is happy who is active in accordance with perfect virtue, and is sufficiently endowed with external goods, not for some chance period, but through a perfect life?

Some have taken this as indicating that the endowment of external goods is an element constitutive of happiness.[6] But this passage is not a definition of happiness – it is a thesis about the happy person. At any given time a happy person will be doing many other things (e.g. digesting and breathing) besides the activity, or

---

[4] This is so whether one regards Aristotle as holding an inclusive view of happiness (it consists in the exercise of all the virtues) or a dominant view (it consists in the exercise of the virtue of *sophia*).

[5] I have argued for this in many places, notably in *The Aristotelian Ethics*, 190-214; *Aristotle on the Perfect Life* (Oxford: Clarendon Press, 1992), 86-93; and *Essays on the Aristotelian Tradition* (Oxford: Oxford University Press, 2001), 17-31.

[6] E.g. John Cooper, in 'Aristotle on the Goods of Fortune' (*Philosophical Review* 94 (1985), 173-96), an article I have discussed in *Aristotle on the Perfect Life*, 40-42.

activities, that constitute his happiness. The wise man will need the necessities of life, but it is not in the use of them, but in the exercise of his mind that his happiness consists (1177a28-33, b19-24).

P7. Is the supreme good comprehensive? It is complete and self-sufficient, but that does not mean that it includes all goods worth choosing for their own sake.

P8. Is virtue the dominant component in happiness? Virtue itself is not; it is insufficient for happiness. But the exercise of the appropriate virtue is not only the dominant but the sole component of happiness.

P9. Are all reasons for action premised on the pursuit of happiness? Yes, on the face of it: 'it is for the sake of [happiness] that we all do everything else' (1102a2). However, there is room for discussion about the appropriate interpretation of 'for the sake of' in this and similar passages.

So, once we pay attention to the distinction between virtue and its exercise, we can tease out, from the *NE*, answers to the questions set us by Irwin; but in several cases, as we have seen, the answer is neither 'yes' nor 'no' but '*distinguo*'. If we turn to the *EE*, however, matters become more complicated, but also, in certain ways, clearer.

The *Eudemian Ethics*

One clarification introduced in the *EE* is an explicit distinction between the constituents of happiness and the necessary conditions of happiness (1214b11-14, 26-7):

> We must first define for ourselves without haste or presumption in which of our possessions the good life consists, and what are the indispensable conditions of its attainment ... Some people take as elements of happiness things that are merely its indispensable conditions.

Among those proleptically condemned by the *EE* we must include, I think, the author of the *MM* as interpreted by Irwin, who regards external goods as part of happiness; we must also include a number of modern authors. Their error, according to the *EE*, is parallel to that of someone who thought that meat-eating and walking after dinner were parts of, and not just necessary conditions of, bodily health.

Keeping in mind this distinction, as well as the one between virtue and its exercise (which is emphasized in 1218a30-38), let us put Irwin's questions to the *EE*.

P1. Are goods other than virtue only conditional goods, whose goodness depends on their proper use? The *EE* answers by a distinction: they are good by nature, but good for individual people only conditionally (1248b26-31):

> The goods people compete for and think the greatest – honour, wealth, a wonderful body, fortune and power – are naturally good, but may be hurtful to some because of their dispositions: neither a foolish nor an unjust nor an intemperate person would get any good from making use of them.

P2. Is virtue sufficient for happiness? As in the *NE*, virtue by itself is insufficient to be the supreme good, the reason now given being that an activity is better than a state, and therefore happiness, which is the best thing in the soul, must be not so much the best state of the soul, as the best activity of that best state (1218a31-35).

P3. Is virtue choiceworthy for its own sake? Here again Aristotle explicitly distinguishes between virtue and virtuous action, though he gives a positive answer in each case. Among goods, he says, those that are chosen for their own sake are ends. Some ends, like health and strength, are merely good; but some ends are not merely good but noble. A good is noble if it is an object of praise. Into this class fall both the virtues (justice and temperance, for instance) and the actions to which they give rise (1248b18-24). But there is an important difference, in the *EE*, between the choiceworthiness of virtue and the choiceworthiness of virtuous action. Every good person chooses virtuous actions for their own sake (i.e. because they are virtuous, and not because of their consequences). But among good people some choose virtue because of the non-moral goods that result from virtue: Aristotle calls these people Laconians. Other good people choose not just virtuous actions for their own sake, but virtue itself for its own sake. These people, Aristotle says, are not just good, but noble, *kaloikagathoi*.[7]

P4. Should virtue be stuck to at all costs? As in the *NE*, Aristotle insists that there are some acts that are in themselves wicked (1121a22).

P5. Is virtue the choice most productive of happiness? To answer this question, I turn, like Irwin, to the Disputed Books, which I regard as belonging with the *EE*. There we learn (1153b19-21) that the good man on the rack is not happy; but this does not mean that by giving up virtue he could be more happy, because he would then not be in a position to exercise virtue, and it is in this alone that happiness consists.

P6. Is the supreme good composite? There is an important difference here between the *EE* and the *NE*. In the *EE*, I believe, (and in the Disputed Books) the supreme

---

[7] The subtlety of Aristotle's argument at this point has been well expounded by Sarah Waterlow Broadie in her *Ethics with Aristotle* (Oxford: Oxford University Press, 1991), 376ff., which I followed in *Aristotle on the Perfect Life*, 9ff.

good is composite: it consists in the exercise of all the virtues, and not just in the philosophic contemplation of the intellect.[8]

P7. Is the supreme good comprehensive? Not if being comprehensive means including, in addition to the exercise of virtue, also the natural goods – the *haplôs agatha* or *prima facie* goods – which are in the gift of fortune. These are, up to a point, necessary conditions for happiness, but not constituents of it – though of course the virtuous *use* of them may be part of happiness, for instance the use of wealth in the expression of liberality.

P8. Is virtue the dominant component in happiness? As in the *NE*, the answer to this falls out immediately from the thesis that happiness consists solely in the exercise of virtue.

P9. Are all reasons for action premised on the pursuit of happiness? There is, I think, a difference between the eudaimonism of the *NE* and the *EE*. The *NE* seems to state eudaimonism as a fact about human nature; the *EE* seems to propose it as a desirable human attitude, (or perhaps, rather, a desirable gentlemanly attitude). 'We must enjoin everyone that has the power to live according to his own choice to set up for himself some aim of noble living – whether honour, or reputation, or wealth, or culture – to keep his eye on in all of his actions.' In several ways the *EE* formulation seems to me preferable. Factual eudaimonism seems a false thesis about human nature and 'keeping an eye' on the supreme good seems a more reasonable program than always 'acting for the sake of' happiness. Exhortatory eudaimonism, unlike factual eudaimonism, is compatible with the recognition, in the third of the common books, of the existence of incontinent people (i.e. most of us) who act for the sake of pleasure now and then without thinking it will contribute to our overall happiness (1146b23-45).

The *Magna Moralia*

I have left myself little time to discuss the *MM*. I do not regret this since it has been very fully dealt with by Irwin in his paper. I will merely note a few disagreements.

P1. Are goods other than virtue only conditional goods? The *MM*'s answer is similar to that of the *EE*: office, wealth, strength and beauty are goods, but they are not choiceworthy without qualification, because they can be used ill (1183b28-31, 1184a3). Irwin sees this as a disagreement with Plato, since in the *Euthydemus* we are told that wealth, health and beauty are in themselves worthless. But the reason that the *MM* gives for saying that they are genuine goods – namely that their worth

---

[8] I have argued this in *The Aristotelian Ethics*, 191-200, 206-214, and in *Aristotle on the Perfect Life*, 93-102.

is to be judged by the good person's use of them – is one which would surely commend itself to the mature Plato.

P2. Is virtue sufficient for happiness? Irwin argues that the *MM* denies this, since it says that if we are happy we lack nothing else and that the best we are seeking is not a simple thing (1184a11-14, 33-4).[9] But the suggestion that happiness includes also non-moral goods seems to go counter to the statement repeated several times in chapter four of the first book that happiness consists in living in accordance with the virtues (1184b27, 30, 36, 39).

P3. Is virtue choiceworthy for its own sake? Irwin claims that the *MM* gives a positive answer to this; but the passage he cites (1184b1-6) merely says that virtue, as one of the goods of the soul, belongs to the best class of goods. The *MM* comes nearer to a positive answer when it says that justice and the other virtues are everywhere and everyhow choiceworthy (1184a2).

P4. Should virtue be stuck to at all costs? I believe the *MM* would say yes, but like Irwin I find it difficult to give chapter and verse.

P5. Is virtue the choice most conducive to happiness? Irwin thinks the *MM* leaves this question open; but this is because he thinks that happiness includes goods other than the exercise of virtue, which I contest.

P6 and P7. Is happiness composite and comprehensive? Irwin credits the *MM* with a positive answer to both questions. I believe that like the *EE*, the *MM* accepts that happiness is composite, in the sense that it involves the exercise of more than one virtue (1184b37) but not that it is comprehensive in the sense of including all non-moral goods. The good man will not be corrupted by wealth and power, but there is no reason to believe that their possession will constitute part of his happiness (1208a3). Not even all activities of the soul are part of happiness (1185a35).

P8. Is virtue the dominant element in happiness? Irwin believes that the *MM* takes no account of this principle, but for my part I can see no difference between the *MM* and the *EE* on this point.

P9. Are all reasons for action premised on the pursuit of happiness? Irwin believes that the *MM*'s treatment of self-love shows that it rejects eudaimonism, but he is prepared to give this up if some other passage supports it. I have been unable to find such a passage.

---

[9] Irwin bases his claim also on the long argument about 'counting together', 1184a15-39.

Aristotle's Development

Like Irwin, I conclude with a brief note on Aristotle's philosophical biography. I find the treatment of happiness in the *EE* superior to that in the *NE*. The *NE* is an easier read, but the *EE* (even if we leave the Disputed Books out of consideration) is philosophically more sophisticated. (1) A clear distinction is made between constituents and necessary conditions of happiness. (2) An inclusive conception of happiness is more credible than a dominant one. (3) Exhortatory eudaimonism is preferable to factual eudaimonism. (4) The subtle distinction between the good person and the *kaloskagathos* adds a degree of philosophical reflection absent from the *NE*. However, the differences between these two treatises may be explained by differences of audience or editor, rather than chronology, and in any case I am unconvinced that our *NE* existed as a single whole in Aristotle's lifetime. With regard to the *Magna Moralia*, I do not find it possible to take it seriously as an authentic work of Aristotle. The crawling pace of its myopic pedantry seems a whole world away from the cavalier intellectual charge of Aristotle in full tilt. I continue to think that it is most likely to be a student's notes of a course closely resembling the *EE*.

Chapter 5

Plato and Aristotle on 'Finality' and '(Self-)Sufficiency'

John M. Cooper

I

In the first part of chapter 7 of the first Book of the *Nicomachean Ethics* Aristotle proposes two criteria for the specification of that good which he has been investigating since the first two introductory chapters of the work (i.e. *to zêtoumenon agathon*, 1097a15). This is the 'end of action(s)' (*telos tôn praktôn*, 1094a18-19) or 'the good and the best' (*tagathon kai to ariston*, a22) or 'the highest of all the goods achievable by action' (*to pantôn akrotaton tôn praktôn agathôn*, 1095a16-17). Aristotle's proposed criteria are that this good should be one that is 'unqualifiedly final' (alternatively, 'unqualifiedly an end', *haplôs teleion*, 1097a33), and that it should be 'self-sufficient' (*autarkes*, b8). He takes care to explain what he means by these criterial terms and to connect the criteria together (I will come back in sect. III to these explanations); and he concludes that this good is in fact *eudaimonia* (1097a34, b15-16) – I leave this Greek word untranslated (for reasons I will explain later, beginning of sect. IV). In the remainder of the chapter Aristotle first gives an argument that *eudaimonia* itself is to be equated with exercise or activity of the soul that derives from and expresses the soul's excellence or virtue (*psuchês energeia kat' aretên*) – or perhaps it is activity deriving instead from the soul's 'best and most final virtue' (*kata tên aristên kai teleiotatên*) (1098a16-18). Then (a20ff.) he comments upon the limited informativeness of this equation, while nonetheless emphasizing its importance, since for him it provides the basic principle (*archê*, b3, 7) for the philosophical understanding of how human life should be organized and led.

It has long been recognized that in proposing his two criteria for the specification of the highest good – finality and self-sufficiency, as I will call them – Aristotle is indebted to, and somehow follows, Socrates' discussion with Protarchus in Plato's *Philebus* 20b-23b. There Socrates argues, and Protarchus is brought to agree, that neither pleasure (*hêdonê*) nor mind or reason (*nous, phronêsis*) can be that by having which in it a life is made happy,[1] i.e. that neither

---

[1] See 11d4-6: Socrates announces at the outset that the debate concerns which 'possession or disposition of the soul' (*hexin psuchês kai diathesin*) can provide for all human beings a

of these can be '*the* good' (*tagathon*, cf. 14b4, 22b4). Instead, Socrates argues and Protarchus agrees (eventually), only some or other so-called 'mixed life' (mixed: *sunamphoteros* 22a1, *koinos* a2, c7, d1, *meiktos* d7), one that has both pleasure and reason in it, would be a, or the, life worth choosing. It follows, Socrates says, that the good would be whatever that mixed life has in it that makes it choiceworthy and good (*hairetos hama kai agathos*, d7). Neither pleasure nor reason is *the* good; *the* good is some third thing yet to be discovered. Only this third thing, then, being *the* good, can be what makes a life choiceworthy, good and happy.

Socrates begins his argument for these conclusions (20d) by obtaining Protarchus' preliminary agreement on three apparently distinct, and perhaps even mutually independent, conditions on, or criteria for, what can count as *the* good: it is because they fail these conditions that he will go on to argue that neither pleasure nor reason is the good. He says first, that the good must be *teleon* (final or end-like),[2] then that it must be 'sufficient' (*hikanon*), and thirdly that 'anything that knows the good hunts and pursues it, wishing to choose it and possess it for its own, and does not bother about anything else except what is accomplished always together with things that are good'.[3] Socrates does not explain how he understands the first two criteria, those of finality or end-likeness and sufficiency. Nonetheless, despite the variation from Plato's *hikanon* to his own *autarkes*, to which I will return (130-32 below), it is plain that these requirements must correspond closely somehow to Aristotle's pair: Aristotle must have this passage in mind in *NE* I.7, and must somehow be developing Socrates' point when he uses his criteria of finality and self-sufficiency to identify the highest good as *eudaimonia* and to specify it as activity deriving from and expressing the soul's virtue. However, as I

---

happy life, *tên dunamenên anthrôpois pasi ton bion eudaimona parechein.* See also Protarchus' reformulation at 19c5-6: *pros to dielesthai ti tôn anthrôpinôn ktêmatôn ariston.*

[2] I translate Plato's *teleon* here as 'final' or 'end-like', rather than, for example, 'complete' partly in anticipation of Aristotle's understanding, which he carefully explains at *NE* I.7, 1097a25-34, of this same word (in a variant spelling) to express one of his own criteria for the highest good – a criterion obviously borrowed from Socrates in this passage. (See my discussion in sect. III paragraph 2 ff. below.) But I also think, independently of Aristotle's apparent understanding of what the term means in Plato, that the translation 'complete' would not convey correctly what Socrates has in mind (although, as I point out below, Socrates says nothing at all to explain what he understands by being *teleon* or why he thinks that is a suitable criterion for the identification of the good). Socrates endorses these three criteria as guides in his own search for the good, after rejecting the claims of pleasure and reason, and the account he finally accepts (see below, sect. II last paragraph) does not make the good some 'complete' combination of lots of independently good things, with nothing missing – as the translation 'complete' would necessarily imply. On the contrary, it is a value-property a life possesses because of the way its ingredient leading goods are combined together. To be sure, Socrates does insist that the good be 'lacking in nothing' but that is the burden, not of this criterion, but of 'sufficiency' – and the latter turns out also not to require that the good *be* some complete combination of good things.

[3] The Greek for the third condition is this: *pan to gignôskon auto thêreuei kai ephietai boulomenon helein kai peri hauto ktêsasthai, kai tôn allôn ouden phrontizei plên tôn apoteloumenôn hama agathois.*

will explain, the conclusion Aristotle reaches through the use of his two criteria is in fact very different from Socrates': it goes in a direction Socrates thought actually precluded by acceptance of his closely related triplet of criteria. In order to understand and assess Aristotle's conclusion, and his use of his criteria to reach it, it will be necessary to spend time first considering this passage of the *Philebus* quite closely.

II

I mentioned that Socrates presents his three criteria (20d) one after the other, as separate and independent conditions. And later, in declaring his verdict that neither pleasure nor reason is the good, he clearly mentions each of the three. He clearly thinks he has shown that each of the candidates has failed each of the tests. In order to test the claims of pleasure and reason to be the good he has discussed the life chockfull of pleasure but totally lacking all functions of reason, and the life chockfull of reason but devoid of pleasure. In declaring his verdict, he says (22b3-6): 'So isn't it perfectly clear about these [lives], that neither of the two had in it the good? For it would have been sufficient, and final, and choiceworthy for all plants and animals, whichever ones were able to live in that way always throughout their life'.[4] In fact, however, he has argued in two steps, not three: first, that each life needs (*prosdeisthai* 20e6, *prosdein* 21a11) something else beyond the pleasure and the reason that each respectively is fully supplied with, and then, in consequence, that neither life is choiceworthy. This is quite explicit in his examination of the life of pleasure (as I will explain just below), and it is plainly implied also for the life of reason.[5] Now, needing or not needing something further seems plainly linked to the sufficiency criterion; and the choiceworthiness or not of a life is plainly linked to the third criterion ('anything that knows the good wishes to choose it'). So Socrates argues from the insufficiency of these lives to their

---

[4] *Môn oun ouk êdê toutôn ge peri dêlon hôs oudeteros autoin eiche tagathon; ên gar an hikanos kai teleos kai pasi phutois kai zôiois hairetos, hoisper dunaton ên houtôs aei dia biou zên.*

[5] The examination of the life of reason, which follows immediately upon that of the life of pleasure, is abbreviated (21d6-e4). Socrates simply asks Protarchus whether anyone would 'accept' that life (*dexai' an*), and Protarchus answers 'no' immediately in this second case, without further explanation. Socrates begins his examination of the life of pleasure (21a8) with the same question ('Would you accept ...?'). But in that case Protarchus responds, 'Why not?' So Socrates does not need to go through the details in the case of reason, as he has had to do for pleasure. However, he has indicated at 20e5-21a2, in announcing the tests to be administered to the two lives, that the question will be whether either 'is in need at all of anything else' (besides its pleasures or reasonings respectively); and when Protarchus finally does (implicitly) agree that he would not, after all, 'accept' the life of pleasure he does so on the basis that that life is not choiceworthy, because something else is needed that it does not provide or contain (21d3-5). So both steps are implied also for the second examination too, that of the life of reason. Protarchus' rejection of that life is implied to be on the basis that, because it needs something further, it is not choiceworthy.

unchoiceworthiness – thus linking his criteria of sufficiency and choiceworthiness to one another. But there is nothing in Socrates' argument that specifically draws upon or relates to the good's being final or end-like. If nonetheless, as I have said, in giving his verdict Socrates thinks he has shown that neither pleasure nor reason satisfies the finality criterion any more than his other two, this is presumably because he silently presupposes that if some good is insufficient it is also not final. Any good that was insufficient, Socrates may think, would thereby show that there was some further end lying beyond or above it that was still unachieved when one possessed just it. (I return to this point below, 130.)

Let us then consider Socrates' argument – his argument against the life of pleasure, since that is the only one he sets out in full. He imagines a person living his whole life through while experiencing *the greatest pleasures* at every moment, but devoid of all rational capacities. Would Protarchus, an announced proponent of pleasure's claim to be the good, not think he needed anything further? Naturally enough, Protarchus at first replies that he would not (21a13): after all, having no deficiency of pleasure, what else could he need in order to be leading the best and the happy life, if indeed pleasure is the good – his announced position in the debate? Socrates points out, though, that if *ex hypothesi* he were devoid of all rational capacities he would not be able, first, to realize that he was enjoying those pleasures at any moment when he was in fact enjoying them (i.e. enjoyably aware of them); also, second, he could not remember that he enjoyed the extreme pleasures of the past, since no memory would remain of any pleasure enjoyed in any present moment;[6] and, third, he could not figure out (and so anticipate) that he was going to enjoy great pleasures in the future (even if he was in fact going to). Present awareness *that*, memory, and calculation as to the future are all functions of reason; so, lacking reason *ex hypothesi*, he would have no capacity for awareness *that*, memory, or calculation, not even in relation to these very great pleasures (the greatest, 21a9) that he would nonetheless be enjoying, i.e. aware *of*.

---

[6] Plato writes quite carefully here. The memory that Socrates says Protarchus would lack if he were deprived of reasoning 'and everything related to it' (21b1) is memory that: 'that he had ever enjoyed himself'. This memory is 'propositional' just as the present awareness and anticipation of the future here referred to are. The Greek is: *anankê dêpou mêd' hoti pote echaires memnêsthai.* However, Socrates immediately adds, as if in explanation: *tês t' en tôi parachrêma hêdonês prospiptousês mêd' hêntinoun mnêmên hupomenein,* 'and [it is necessary that] no memory at all would remain of the pleasure befalling you at the moment'. If by this addition Socrates means to say that the reason why you would have no memory that you had enjoyed yourself when you did is that no trace of that pleasure survives in memory for you to recall at all, then Protarchus might well have objected. Presumably at least some irrational animals have memories, though they don't have memories-that; so merely by being deprived of all reasoning power Protarchus would not necessarily have lost all his memories of his experiences. However that may be, I take it that Protarchus has understood Socrates correctly about the principal point intended, viz. that he would lack all memory-that. He accepts that this, alongside failure to be aware-that and to anticipate-that, would be a very great loss; he values highly that kind of memory (in addition, perhaps, to its presupposition, bare event-memory). This seems to me a reasonable admission on Protarchus' part.

Now, we need not, and certainly we should not, suppose that Socrates or Plato is cheating here, and that when Protarchus abandons his position in the face of these facts he does so simply because he thinks that having such awareness (awareness that), memory, and anticipatory powers would give him additional pleasures, very great ones. In that case, his devotion to pleasure as the good would itself require that he have these powers if in fact he is to live throughout his life enjoying the greatest pleasures (as Socrates hypothesizes he would in fact be doing). If that is what he had in mind, then of course he ought never to have allowed Socrates to construe him as giving up the idea that pleasure is the good because of the admitted need for awareness that, memory, and calculation for the future. And Socrates should never have said that Protarchus' acceptance of these needs entailed the denial of his earlier position. No: in posing his hypothesis Socrates is explicit that even without these powers a person might enjoy the *greatest* pleasures throughout his life, without remission (21a8-9). Therefore, if Protarchus understands the position, he cannot be accepting the need for reasoning because without it he cannot obtain the greatest pleasures, as it were in the first place. And even if Protarchus does value reasoning (as, presumably, he does) only insofar as it makes available to him the use of these powers *in relation to* present, past, and future enjoyments of pleasure, his response shows that he recognizes some extra and inherent value in reasoning itself (but only when so related), in addition to the value that, of course, he has accorded to the enjoyment of pleasure (including any pleasure he might get in using reason in these ways). At any rate, even if Protarchus is too stupid to follow the argument, and agrees that he would need reasoning in addition to pleasure if his life is to be happy only because he thinks that even having (or enjoying) all the greatest pleasures requires reasoning directed to present, past or future states of pleasure, no reader should suppose that that is what Socrates (or Plato) is arguing. Socrates is arguing that anyone who thinks about it (see the *tis* at 21d9, and similar language at e4, 22a5-6, b1-2), not just Protarchus in his presumed stupidity, will have to agree that reasoning does matter, that however much they might value pleasure, they also value reasoning (awareness that, memory, calculating anticipation) quite independently of any relation these may have to getting pleasure: reasoning powers are needed, in addition to pleasure, if any human being is to lead a happy life.[7]

To me, Socrates seems undoubtedly right in this claim. Protarchus was right to concede that more than pleasure is needed for any acceptable human life. Anyone who considers the matter must see this, even someone who loves pleasure with an

---

[7] As I mentioned, Protarchus presumably only concedes this need because he recognizes some added value in being aware that one is enjoying pleasure when one in fact is enjoying it, or recalling it or reliably expecting it for the future – a value beyond that of any pleasure one takes in such acts of reasoning. Socrates goes on, as we will see, to speak as if some value has been conceded to reasoning without these limitations of subject matter. I think that is fair enough: once anyone sees the need, even on Protarchus' presumed ground, for the concession, it is clear enough that they have no good basis for insisting on the limitation. Whatever value there is inherent in any given acts of reasoning, qua acts of reasoning, must surely be replicable in some other acts with different contents or of different types.

overwhelming passion. In fact, Socrates says and Protarchus obviously agrees, the life chockfull of pleasure but devoid of all reasoning is not a human life at all, but that perhaps of a sea-lung or oyster (21c6-8). When, having said this, Socrates asks (d3, invoking now his third criterion) whether such a life would be choiceworthy for us (*hairetos hêmin*), Protarchus is stymied, he has nothing to reply. He sees clearly, or thinks he does, that it would not be. And this is to the detriment of his candidate for the good, since according to the third criterion anything that knows the good chooses it: if pleasure really were the good, then, we would have to choose it, and so also the life that contains it in abundance. Such a life would be among the things that are 'accomplished always together with things that are good', and things so accomplished, according to the third criterion, are the sorts of things, and the only ones besides pleasures themselves, that we would have to concern ourselves for, if pleasure were the good. But it is not only *for us* that this life, chockfull of pleasure, would not be choiceworthy, according to Socrates' argument. It would not be choiceworthy for any animal (not even the sea-lung or oyster who if lucky lived that way) or indeed for any *plant*, he says (22b5-6) – adding plants to what Protarchus himself claimed about all animals (22b1-2)! This too seems to me an entirely reasonable claim, when properly understood. Socrates' claim is that an oyster or plant whose natural capacities limited it so that the only good thing it can be aware of is pleasure would have nothing in its life that would make that life worth *choosing*. To be sure, one could prefer on its behalf, and hope, that it got a life of continuous extreme pleasure, and one could certainly rank such a life ahead of the alternatives available to it (ones with lots of pain, say). One could even, I would grant, count the life chockfull of pleasure as a *better*, indeed a *good* life, for such a creature. But that would not make it one worth choosing: better still, perhaps, not to be born at all, or to die immediately after birth and not have to live a life – better than to be condemned by this 'unhappy necessity' of your nature (cf. *tinos anankês ouk eudaimonos*, 22b6-7) to a life chockfull of pleasure but devoid of all functions of reason as the best you can live. Of course, the plant or oyster does not have any choice in the matter; indeed, the very absence from its nature of all powers of reason carries with it the absence of the power of choice. So it will live on, or not, helplessly – whether with a life of unending greatest pleasure, or one with some pain, or one with nothing but pain all the way through. But if it did have the power to survey lives beforehand and to make a choice, before losing the power to choose anything at all by coming to life, it could not choose *this* one, however good for the one living it it might nonetheless recognize it to be. To *choose* a life, it seems, implies that there is something in it so good that you would choose life itself, because of its presence in it, in preference to not coming to life at all – and pleasure is not a good of that kind. So anyhow Socrates seems to be thinking.[8] And very reasonably so, I should say.

---

[8] I should emphasize that the connection I have made here, and subsequently, between the choiceworthiness of a life and that life's being worth living at all is mine; Socrates himself does not explicitly draw it. Nonetheless, it seems to me the best way of understanding and making good sense of his repeated claim that a life chockfull of pleasure but devoid of reasoning would not be choiceworthy – not even for an oyster or a blade of grass.

Now, as I mentioned, Protarchus also thinks that the life chockfull of reasoning is not choiceworthy (21e7-8) – no one could choose a life that did not have *some* pleasure in it. Pleasure, too, is needed in a choiceworthy life, he thinks, as well as the reasoning that he has already conceded is needed. Thus the life chockfull of reasoning too, in his opinion, is lacking in something, and so (on both grounds) reason also – Socrates' initial candidate – cannot count as the good. However, the mixed life – that is, one chockfull of both the greatest pleasures and all sorts of reasonings about everything (d9-10)[9] – seems to him choiceworthy, and the only one of the three that is. Socrates agrees (22b3-8).[10] If that is so, then, the good must be contained in some life that has both pleasure and reasoning in it: as the third criterion has made explicit, those who know the good choose it and so far as other things go (including lives) concern themselves solely with those that are accomplished with goods. What then can the good be – this thing that is in the mixed life and that by its presence makes that life a good and happy one? That is the main question with which Socrates' and Protarchus' discussion is occupied through the remainder of the dialogue.

Now, we can speak of the constituents of a life as all the activities and experiences, whether conscious or not, which make it up. So far, then, Socrates' argument has excluded the two principal constituents of the choiceworthy mixed life, at least if taken singly, from being the good: neither the reasonings nor the pleasures that this life contains can be counted as the good in it, by the presence of which it itself is a happy one. So it is no surprise eventually to learn that, on Socrates' view, not even the combination of these needed constituents – the reasonings and the pleasures *taken together* – are the good. Instead, he argues, the good in the mixed life derives from the *way* the two ingredients are combined. I will not go into his arguments, but his final view, set out at 64c-65a, is this: The good – that is, that in the mixed life which is responsible for its being a good and

---

[9] At 22a3 Socrates specifies the mixed life, upon his introduction of it, simply as mixed 'from pleasure plus reason and reasoning' (*nou kai phronêseôs*), but I take it from the preceding context that, when Protarchus agrees that the mixed life is choiceworthy we are to understand him as meaning one that merges the other two – and those were not merely lives of pleasure and reason respectively, but of each at its highest and most complete level. As the dialogue proceeds, however, Socrates treats the mixed life more loosely, as simply one that has both pleasures and reasonings in it – it being left open for further consideration both which pleasures and which reasonings these will be, and how they are to be combined and mixed.

[10] A bit later Socrates confusingly appears to revoke his acceptance of Protarchus' judgement that the life of reason too is not choiceworthy, and so he seems to maintain that reason can be the good, after all (22c5). However, he restricts his claim that reason might after all be the good to divine reason – human reason, the subject of the earlier discussion, he grants, is in a different condition. As reason exists *within* the physical world, reason and reasoning are not the good, then, Socrates continues to think. The conclusion of the preceding argument stands: a life that had the highest degree and extent of reasoning in it would still not be choiceworthy for us, or any other animal or plant that was naturally equipped to lead it, if it totally lacked pleasure.

happy one – is the beauty (*kallos*), harmony or proportionedment (*summetria*), and truth (*alêtheia*), of the mixture of pleasure and reasoning in the version of a mixed life that Socrates and Protarchus have constructed in the preceding discussion – these three properties being taken together as a single characteristic found in the mixture. Thus for Socrates in the *Philebus* the good is none of the good constituents of the happy life, not even some or all of the good constituents taken together. The good is rather a certain complex single property of the happy life's constitution – namely, the way in which the included ingredients are beautifully and truthfully proportioned and harmonize with one another.

III

Now let us return to Aristotle in *NE* I.7. I said that by using his criteria of finality and self-sufficiency Aristotle reaches quite a different conclusion from that of Socrates in the *Philebus* about the highest good – the source of the happiness of the best life.[11] Though we would need to consider many intricate detailed questions (some of which I address below) before we could claim properly to understand Aristotle's view about the highest good in the work as a whole, and his intentions for its articulation, it cannot be doubted that beginning in I.7 he identifies it with some constituent(s) or ingredient(s) of the best life. He does not at all think, as Socrates did, that the application of these criteria inexorably leads to the denial of that title to any constituent, and its reservation for some normative or evaluative feature of the choiceworthy life itself – for example, a feature of the way its constituents, or the good ones among them, are combined together. As I mentioned in my initial summary of the chapter (sect. I), Aristotle tells us there that *eudaimonia*, i.e. the highest good, is a certain exercise or activity of the soul that derives from and expresses the soul's excellence or virtue (never mind for the moment whether he means an activity deriving from the sum of the virtues, or from some particular one or ones). Any such activity is of course just one constituent or ingredient (maybe a vastly complicated and flexible one, varying to fit varied circumstances). It is neither the totality of the good ingredients (at any rate, pleasure is a further ingredient left out of account) nor yet any feature of a life as a whole, for example of the way its ingredient activities and experiences are combined together to constitute it. In fact, Aristotle makes it clear that the activity he is referring to is an activity in one way or another of reason, using now neither of Socrates' terms for it (*nous* and *phronêsis*) but rather *to logon echon*, 'what (in

---

[11] I am greatly indebted to Gabriel Richardson for discussion on this point, and have learned a great deal from her own treatment in her Ph.D. dissertation (Princeton 2001) of the relation between Aristotle's discussion of finality and self-sufficiency in the first part of *NE* I.7 and Socrates' use of much the same criteria in the *Philebus*. (See her book, *Happy Lives and the Highest Good: Aristotle's Nicomachean Ethics*, a revision of the dissertation, Princeton University Press, forthcoming 2003.) My discussion in this section is indebted to her account.

or of the soul) has reasoning' (1098a3-5):[12] it is an activity of the soul 'in accordance with [i.e. deriving from] reason or not without reason' (*psuchês energeia kata logon ê mê aneu logou*, a7-8; cf. *psuchês energeian kai praxeis meta logou*, a13-14). So Aristotle's conclusion simply flies in the face of Socrates' argument. According to Socrates, neither pleasure *nor* reason can be the good; a life chockfull of reasonings still lacks something that is needed; such a life would not be choiceworthy. Aristotle plainly thinks that in fact, somehow or other, reason (maybe reason of some special restricted sort, or used in some particular way) is the good, the highest good, making any life that contains it choiceworthy. Our task will be, then, to see, if we can, how Aristotle intends to reach that conclusion from the very criteria that Socrates in the *Philebus* had used to deny it.

We can begin a closer examination of Aristotle's argument by reverting to something I said in my opening summary. Unlike Socrates, Aristotle is careful to explicate his two criteria before applying them. To be unqualifiedly 'final' or *teleion* (which he and Socrates both agree any successful candidate for the good must be), Aristotle says (1097a33-4), is to be 'choiceworthy for itself always and never because of anything else'.[13] Thus a good that is unqualifiedly final is such that it really is in the strongest possible way an *end* of action: it is always choiceworthy for itself, as ends must be, *and* in being choiceworthy it is never in any way referred to anything else – whether as a productive means to something further, or some sort of constituent in a larger whole, or in any other way owing any part of what is choiceworthy about it to any relationship it might bear to anything else. Aristotle then claims that this condition is fulfilled most notably (*malista*) – so anyhow we think – by *eudaimonia*.

I need to make two comments on this argument before proceeding to Aristotle's handling of the second criterion, that of self-sufficiency. First, Aristotle has not yet given on his own account any characterization of *eudaimonia*, however vague.[14] He has mentioned (ch. 4-5) that the vast majority of people agree in using this term to refer to 'the highest of all goods achievable by action' (1095a18-20), and he has mentioned pleasure, honour, virtue, wealth, and (by implication) the highest level of theoretical or philosophical knowledge, as candidates that different people or groups of people have themselves shown in one way or another that they favoured as being that highest of all goods. Presumably, then, when he says 'we think' (*dokei*) that *eudaimonia* is 'unqualifiedly final' he means merely that each of us thinks this, whatever candidate he or she may favour (if any). Despite the wide variation among specifications people make for *eudaimonia*, then, it is something

---

[12] Notice, however, that in the *Philebus* Socrates occasionally adds to his specifications of reason, besides *nous* and *phronêsis*, *logismos* and *logizesthai* (see 21a14, c5-6).

[13] *kai haplôs dê teleion to kath' hauto haireton aei kai mêdepote di' allo*, 1097a33-4.

[14] In rejecting some of the popular conceptions of *eudaimonia* and the good in chapter 5 Aristotle does draw upon certain, as he thinks agreed, pre-conceptions about *eudaimonia*, for example that it cannot be easily taken away from one who has it, or that it cannot be something that would suit even farm animals. But he is not engaged there yet in any direct characterization on his own of *eudaimonia*.

that stands agreed on that *eudaimonia* is an 'unqualifiedly final' good. Thus even if we think that lots of other things are choiceworthy in themselves, we also choose them for the sake of *eudaimonia*, whereas no one ever chooses *eudaimonia* for the sake of any of them, or indeed for anything else whatsoever (1097b1-6).[15] My second comment concerns the form of Aristotle's argument. His argument goes like this: the best or the highest good is clearly something final (1097a28); *eudaimonia* most notably is thought to be something final, indeed unqualifiedly so (a35); therefore *eudaimonia* is the best or highest good. That is manifestly not a deductively valid argument: it only identifies *eudaimonia* as having a feature or fulfilling a condition that the highest good is admitted to require, without showing that nothing else does the same – something which, in that case, could dispute the claim of *eudaimonia* to be the highest good. In fact, this is an argument of the kind Aristotle refers to in the *Prior Analytics* and *Rhetoric* as being 'from a sign' (*ek sêmeiou*) and he indicates in those contexts, quite rightly, that some such arguments are good ones even if they are not deductively valid, as this one is not.[16] Plainly, however, this is one of the good ones of that sort: *eudaimonia*'s being unqualifiedly final surely is a good indication, a good reason for thinking, that it is the highest good. Not a proof, but a solid indication. What else could anyone think of that might possibly give this same 'sign', by being final in an unqualified way?

   In turning to his second criterion, of self-sufficiency, Aristotle proposes not to argue directly that *eudaimonia* is the highest good because it is a self-sufficient good, but rather to bolster his previously given reasons for thinking that

---

[15] Aristotle instances here 'honour, pleasure, intelligence and every virtue' (*timên kai hêdonên kai noun kai pasan aretên*, 1097b2) as things we choose 'for themselves' (we would choose them 'even if nothing resulted from them') but also choose for the sake of *eudaimonia*. I take him to mean that we would choose these things even if no other good of their same order resulted (in particular, even when each did not result in any of the others, or when e.g. no money, no, as one might say, 'reward' followed): as we will see later, *eudaimonia* as something for the sake of which they are also chosen is not in the relevant sense a 'result' of them. (See section IV below.) Hence in saying we would choose e.g. pleasure even if nothing resulted from it, he is not implying that pleasure would still be choiceworthy apart from *eudaimonia*, i.e. (for example) in a life that was in no way or degree devoted to, or inclusive of, the highest good (whatever that turns out to be). This qualification is needed because, as I argue in sects. IV-VI (see especially VI, second paragraph) Aristotle thinks that no good 'subordinate' to *eudaimonia*, such as pleasure, is choiceworthy at all except when it is chosen for the sake of *eudaimonia*. (I thank Robert Heinaman for making me see the need to take note of this qualification here.)

[16] See *Prior Analytics* II.27, *Rhetoric* 1357a33-b25, 1401a9-14, 1402b12-20, 1403a2-5; and the many places where Aristotle uses the term *sêmeion* in particular contexts listed in the index to *Aristotelis Ars Rhetorica*, R. Kassel (ed.) (Berlin: De Gruyter, 1976), 244. See now James Allen, *Inference from Signs* (Oxford: Oxford University Press, 2001), Study I, and 8, 14-15, 29-38. See also M.F. Burnyeat, 'Enthymeme: Aristotle on the Logic of Persuasion', in D.J. Furley and A. Nehamas (eds.), *Aristotle's Rhetoric: Philosophical Essays* (Princeton: Princeton University Press, 1994), 3-55; and 'The Origins of Non-deductive Inference', in J. Barnes, J. Brunschwig, M.F. Burnyeat, and M. Schofield (eds.), *Science and Speculation* (Cambridge: Cambridge University Press, 1982), 193-238.

eudaimonia is unqualifiedly final. He begins, 'The same thing also clearly follows from self-sufficiency, since the final good is thought also to be self-sufficient' (1097b6-8).[17] Here the 'same thing' that follows has to be the immediate conclusion for which he has just been arguing, namely that *eudaimonia* is an unqualifiedly final good.[18] Thus we get again an argument from a sign: the unqualifiedly final good is self-sufficient; but *eudaimonia* is self-sufficient; therefore *eudaimonia* is the unqualifiedly final good. I think that in arguing so Aristotle is intending to correct or clarify Socrates' argument in the *Philebus*, by explicitly establishing what Socrates merely assumed, that if something is (self-) sufficient it is also final. As I pointed out (120-21 above), Socrates does infer (but only implicitly) from the fact that pleasure is not sufficient, that it is also not final. Aristotle is explicit in claiming that any final good is also (self-)sufficient (the presupposition of Socrates' inference):[19] he introduces that claim when he argues here from the premise that the (unqualifiedly) final good is self-sufficient. The effect of Aristotle's argument is to relate the two criteria to one another in the following way. The highest good is (agreed to be) unqualifiedly final; and what is unqualifiedly final is (agreed to be) self-sufficient. Since it follows by valid deduction from those two claims that the highest good is self-sufficient, it is no error to speak, as I have been doing and as other commentators do, of finality and self-sufficiency as two distinct criteria of the highest good for Aristotle, as finality and sufficiency are of the good for Plato. Still, it is important to see that Aristotle explicitly subordinates self-sufficiency to finality in making it a sign of the latter. For Aristotle, the criteria though distinct are not independent of one another. This is one revealing indication of the close attention Aristotle gave to Socrates' argument in the *Philebus* while working out his own views in the *NE*.

There is another such indication. Before making his claim that *eudaimonia* is self-sufficient Aristotle, as I remarked already, explains what he understands by

---

[17] *phainetai de kai ek tês autarkeias to auto sumbainein: to gar teleion agathon autarkes einai dokei.*

[18] J.A. Stewart (*Notes on the Nicomachean Ethics* (Oxford: Oxford University Press, 1892)) followed by F. Dirlmeier (*Aristoteles Nikomachische Ethik* (Berlin: Akademie Verlag, 1966)) in their nn. *ad loc* both mistakenly take 'the same' to mean the further conclusion aimed at in the previous argument, namely that *eudaimonia* is the highest good. That cannot be right, however, because in that case the argument that Aristotle goes on to give (1097b8-16) would have to run differently from the way in fact it does. Aristotle uses as one premise in this argument (as is indicated in the passage just quoted, 1097b6-8) that 'the final good is self-sufficient', but for the conclusion that *eudaimonia* is the highest good to follow, even by a deductively invalid sign-argument, once one adds as a second premise (b15-16) that *eudaimonia* is self-sufficient, this first premise would have to be instead that the *highest good* is self-sufficient (not that the final good is). T.H. Irwin sees the logic here correctly: in his translation (*Aristotle: Nicomachean Ethics* (Indianapolis: Hackett, 1985, 2nd edn. 1999) he adds the correct supplement '[that happiness is complete]' to explicate 'the same conclusion'.

[19] Socrates' assumption that anything that is not sufficient is also not final is logically equivalent to the claim that nothing can be both not sufficient and at the same time final. So it follows for Socrates that anything that is final has to be sufficient.

self-sufficiency: 'that which is self-sufficient we put down as that which, isolated on its own, makes life choiceworthy and lacking in nothing'.[20] It is noteworthy that in this account of self-sufficiency Aristotle combines the second with the third of Socrates' three criteria: for Socrates, not needing anything in addition was the mark of sufficiency (being *hikanon*), while making the life that contains it choiceworthy was the burden of Socrates' separate third criterion. Thus when Aristotle introduces his new term, *autarkeia*, it is not in fact a mere substitute for Socrates' term (*hikanon*) as a way of referring to Socrates' second criterion (i.e. not needing anything in addition); rather, Aristotle uses this term to denote a *new* criterion that combines the idea of not needing anything in addition with the idea of making a life choiceworthy. Thus, besides subordinating (self-)sufficiency as a criterion to the criterion of finality, Aristotle also eliminates Socrates' third separate and further criterion, of being choiceworthy-making, by incorporating it into a revised conception of sufficiency, i.e. *self*-sufficiency.

It seems very probable that Aristotle took the trouble to find a new word (*autarkeia*, self-sufficiency, as I am translating it) to replace Socrates' sufficiency with, precisely because he was acutely aware of the correction or clarification in Socrates' scheme that he was adopting. By announcing sufficiency and choiceworthy-making as if they are two independent criteria Socrates suggests that if anything is the good it must satisfy first the one condition and then, in addition, the other. This leaves open the thought that something *might* be such as to make a life choiceworthy by its presence, but nonetheless, because it was not a *sufficient* good, it could not be *the* good. (Or vice versa.) For example, pleasure might indeed not be sufficient, as Socrates argues: even if you have the fullest share possible of the greatest pleasures, you would still reasonably want something further; not all your wishes would be satisfied; you would prefer a life with pleasure if it were supplemented so as to satisfy those remaining wishes. But nonetheless, the life in question might be *choiceworthy*, despite containing the unmet need. In fact, however, in applying these criteria Socrates does not treat them as independent of one another. He begins his argument against the claim of pleasure to be the good by getting Protarchus to see that even if he lived throughout his life with the fullest supply of pleasure, there would still be something he needed – articulate belief, memory, calculated anticipation, in short the power of reasoning. And Socrates goes immediately from that to the conclusion, which Protarchus himself accepts, that such a life would not be choiceworthy (not even choiceworthy for the luckiest possible oysters and sea-lungs, which would in fact lead it). But even if this conclusion about a life devoid of all reasoning is true, as I have suggested it is, and even if the premise is also true (that the life of pleasure would *lack* something needed), the inference is apparently not valid. For all we have been told to the contrary, there really might be an unmet need in a nonetheless choiceworthy life: you would be glad to be alive and to have a life to lead even with the lack, because of the value to you of other things the life brings. Why not? The effect of

---

[20] *to d' autarkes tithemen ho monoumenon haireton poiei ton bion kai mêdenos endea*, 1097b14-15.

Aristotle's definition of *autarkeia* is to close this gap in Socrates' argument against pleasure, by making it clear that a choiceworthy life could still lack something needed – even though what the life of pleasure lacks (reasoning) is indeed something needed for choiceworthiness. On Aristotle's definition we are asked to read together the two conjoined conditions as constituting a single criterion: 'makes a life choiceworthy and lacking in nothing'. The result is that now Socrates' separate criterion of lacking in nothing is replaced by a narrower one: lacking in nothing *needed for choiceworthiness.*[21] (Thus some life might meet this condition even if it did lack something one would merely prefer to have in it, something one would miss if it were absent – so long as its absence did not make the life not worth living, not choiceworthy.)[22]

---

[21] In construing in this way the force of Aristotle's criterion of self-sufficiency I am guided by two considerations. First, there is no doubt that Aristotle means this criterion to differ from that of (mere) sufficiency as explained by Socrates in the *Philebus*. There would be no point in combining Socrates' language of 'lacking in nothing' with his language of 'choiceworthiness' in explaining this replacement-criterion if the effect were simply to replicate Socrates' analysis: the self-sufficient good makes a life lacking in nothing (at all) and (so) choiceworthy. Second, we know that Aristotle is going to draw on these criteria to defend his conclusion that *eudaimonia* is in fact a single activity (excellent reasoning of some sort); but Socrates had used his criteria, apparently validly enough, to exclude any such ingredient of a life as constituting the good. Aristotle does not dispute Socrates' inference from his criteria understood Socrates' way. And since one of the effects of adopting self-sufficiency understood in the way I suggest, in place of sufficiency, is that (see the next paragraph) it permits Aristotle to argue (as in fact he does) that a *eudaimôn* life might lack some goods that were still needed (i.e. while not satisfying Socrates' criterion of sufficiency), he *needs* to understand self-sufficiency in this way if he is to maintain consistency.

[22] One should bear in mind, in considering Aristotle's difference from Plato over sufficiency vs. self-sufficiency as a criterion, that Plato proposed criteria for the specification of the good (*tagathon*) whereas Aristotle speaks variously of 'the good and the best' (*tagathon kai to ariston*), 'the end of actions' (*to telos tôn praktôn*) and 'the highest of all goods achievable by action' (*to akrotaton tôn praktôn agathôn*). If one thinks of '*the* good', as presumably Plato did think in the *Philebus*, as referring to something that is the universal source of the goodness of anything and everything else that is good, it could seem quite plain, as Socrates maintains in proposing sufficiency as a criterion, that if anything good (i.e. anything one would need *as* a good) were lacking in a life that nonetheless possessed some candidate, then that candidate could not possibly be *the* good. If you already had in your life what makes anything that is good good, it might easily seem, how could you still have unmet needs for something good? If you did need to add something, surely you would have to say at the very least that, not the original candidate alone, but it plus this new thing was the sought-for good? Aristotle, of course, rejects any such conception of a universal single source of the goodness of anything good (see his arguments in *NE* I.6); so, for him, the target in seeking 'the good' becomes a single organizing goal of life, which however cannot be presumed to be the metaphysical or even the moral source of the goodness of any and every other good thing a person might enjoy. So for him it seems obvious that even by achieving that goal in one's life one might still possibly have needs for additional goods. Hence Socrates' (mere) sufficiency cannot be a valid criterion for the (Aristotelian) good. (On this see further below in my text.)

This limitation is important in itself, and it is needed if Aristotle is to complete successfully his own preliminary account of *eudaimonia* in *NE* I. For he allows later on in his discussion (ch. 8) that in fact *eudaimonia* does 'need in addition external goods' (*tôn ektos agathôn prosdeomenê*, 1099a31-2), using the very verb that Socrates used in applying his criterion of sufficiency (20e6, 21a11): things like friends, wealth, political power, good looks or at least no really gross ugliness, good children or anyhow no scandalously awful ones. Aristotle does not mean here that you do not have *eudaimonia* without such goods, as if they were included as among its constituents or parts – he completed his definition of *eudaimonia* already in chapter 7, without mentioning any of these goods as included in it.[23] He means rather that even with *eudaimonia* you need them too if your *eudaimonia* is to be perfectly satisfactory – he says that *eudaimonia* needs them, implying, as I say, that even when you have *eudaimonia* these are further things you need.[24] Yet he has argued, in chapter 7, that *eudaimonia* does satisfy his criteria of finality and self-sufficiency for being the highest good, and is in fact that good. So, if self-sufficiency had been understood simply as Socrates' sufficiency, Aristotle could not say, as he does, that it satisfies that criterion: it would lack something, as Aristotle grants in chapter 8 that it does. On the other hand, with Aristotle's own understanding of this criterion, *eudaimonia* can satisfy the requirements for the highest good, because although indeed there are good things lacking in a life provided only that it has *eudaimonia* in it (lots of external goods, certainly many sorts of innocent pleasure, might be lacking), these missing goods, Aristotle can argue, are not ones that are needed *for the choiceworthiness* even of the resulting deprived life. The life of *eudaimonia* would be more satisfactory if it has them as well; they remain things to be wished and hoped for; they remain goods and every good is worth wanting and trying to get and concerning oneself over. But in a certain way they are not important: they are not make-or-break conditions for a life worth choosing, or worth living. Only *eudaimonia* is important in that way, for only it makes the life that has it worth choosing and worth living – and it does that all by itself, without needing the help of any other good to yield that result. It is *self*-sufficient, though not *sufficient* – if sufficiency is understood in Socrates' way.

Aristotle's limitation of 'lacking in nothing' to what is lacking in nothing needed for choiceworthiness of life is important for a second reason as well. In the *Philebus* Socrates argues, as we saw, not only that a life chockfull of pleasure but

---

[23] Hence one must understand '*eudaimonia* needs these goods in addition' at 1099a31-2 and b6-7 not as indicating that it needs them in addition to virtuous activity in order to be achieved at all, but rather as a supplement to itself. This is, in the context, the most natural reading in any event. In the lines preceding neither occurrence of 'needs in addition' is there a reference to virtue as something *eudaimonia* needs in the first instance, which might support the other interpretation.

[24] For now, I do not go into the precise way that Aristotle thinks *eudaimonia* needs these external goods – whether as conditions needed before *eudaimonia* (some activity) can be fully present, i.e. engaged in fully, or as further goods needed even when *eudaimonia* is engaged in fully.

lacking all use of reason would be unchoiceworthy but also, *pari passu*, that the life chockfull of reason but lacking all pleasure would be so likewise. Although, as I pointed out above (sect. II), his argument about the life of reason is truncated, it certainly does appear that Socrates intends to argue for this parallel conclusion about reason on precisely the same ground as he argued for the conclusion about pleasure. That means that Socrates goes seamlessly from the premise that the life chockfull of reason lacks all pleasure (something needed if a life is to be satisfactory) to the conclusion that it is not worth choosing. As we saw, that inference is not obviously correct. Here is where Aristotle evidently objected. So long as lacking something means merely lacking something desirable, to be wished and hoped for, needed if the life is to be fully satisfactory, there would be an important further question to consider: is the missing good of such a sort or weight that its absence does render the life not worth choosing? Perhaps a missing good (for example, pleasure missing from the life of reason) is like wealth or other external goods, as Aristotle reasonably conceives them, in that it certainly is a good thing, worth desiring and worth being concerned for, worth regretting if it is absent, yet still not really all that important. It might not be a make-or-break condition for a life worth choosing, or worth living.

It is at this point in his careful study of Socrates' argument in the *Philebus*, I suggest, that Aristotle saw the flaw that permitted Socrates to conclude – erroneously, we can now see – that not even reason can be *the* good. Even if, as we can agree, pleasure is not a good by having which in it a life is made choiceworthy (no matter whatever else is lacking, for example all reasoning), it need not follow, *pari passu*, that reasoning is not such a good. Yes, a life with lots of reasoning in it might lack things one would like to have, things one would miss if one didn't have them, but nonetheless it might still be *choiceworthy*, worth living. Once, with Aristotle, we abandon (mere) sufficiency as a criterion and combine sufficiency with choiceworthy-making into the more acceptable Aristotelian criterion of *self*-sufficiency (sufficiency *for* choiceworthiness), we open up the possibility of arguing (contrary to Socrates) that excellent activity of reason (or, perhaps, some particular such activity) is the good. Such activity can be argued to be a good that is not only unqualifiedly final, but one that makes life worth living whether or not it is accompanied by any other goods – goods other than itself plus any consequences for the life that followed immediately and solely from its presence in it. If so, it would be *the* good, the good whose presence in a life makes it a happy one. Plato's error in the *Philebus*, as Aristotle sees it, then, was to suppose that simple sufficiency (sufficiency for a satisfactory or a fully satisfactory life) is a valid criterion for the identity and specification of the good. In fact, the relevant valid criterion is *self*-sufficiency – sufficiency for a life that is choiceworthy, one worth living (even if it might possibly lack some further good things).

In sum, then: Aristotle makes three major adjustments in taking up Plato's criteria for the good in the *Philebus* and reworking them for his own search for the identity and specification of the highest good. First, he does away firmly with any suggestion that his own criteria of finality and self-sufficiency are independently satisfiable: though they are distinct, self-sufficiency is subordinated to finality, as a sign of the latter. Second, he rectifies the unclarities in Socrates' application of his separate criteria of sufficiency and choiceworthy-making (why must something whose presence leaves a life insufficient also fail to make it choiceworthy?), and avoids the unsatisfactoriness of Socratic sufficiency as a criterion at all by proposing his new criterion of self-sufficiency to replace both of these Platonic ones. Third, he carefully explains what he means not only by self-sufficiency but also by finality.

IV

With these innovations in the criteria for the highest good achieved, the way is open for Aristotle to think that perhaps, after all, the good might be some ingredient or constituent of the happy life – precisely what Plato had used his own criteria to rule out. In following up this thought we need to consider next Aristotle's arguments, using his revised criteria, first to identify the highest good with *eudaimonia* and then to specify it further as some activity of reason: as Aristotle argues in the last half of *NE* I.7 *eudaimonia* is an activity of the soul 'in accordance with [i.e. deriving from] reason or not without reason' (see beginning of sect. III above). As we have seen, *eudaimonia*, as the highest good, must both be unqualifiedly final and self-sufficient, according to Aristotle's careful explanations of these two criteria. The first thing to notice is that in this context (as most often in Aristotle) *eudaimonia* means not the happy life itself, but something in it that is responsible for the happy life's being happy (*eudaimôn*).[25] That is why I have left this term untranslated. First of all, if we gave 'happiness' as our translation of *eudaimonia* into English here that would probably be quite misleading: to say that happiness is what in a life makes it a happy one would inevitably invite the erroneous interpretation that what Aristotle is referring to is the quality, whatever one might then say about it, in having which a life is happy (*eudaimôn*): unperturbedness, we might think, or the smooth flow of one's life, as Epicureans or Pyrrhonean sceptics or Stoics might later have said – and then telling us that that quality is in fact an activity of reason. That, however, would make the initial claim that *eudaimonia* is what makes a life happy quite tautologous: Aristotle would then be saying that to be happy, a life needs to have that quality having which constitutes its being happy. (Though of course one might then dispute whether Aristotle has specified correctly which quality that is in fact.) Second, however,

---

[25] See Cooper, 'Contemplation and Happiness: A Reconsideration' in *Reason and Emotion* (Princeton: Princeton University Press, 1999), 212-36, at 219-220. In I.7 Aristotle is proposing some activity of reason as the correct answer to the question what *eudaimonia* is, where that competes with the answers canvassed in chapters 3 and 4 – pleasure, honour or virtue, wealth, and so on. Manifestly Aristotle is not understanding that question as asking for a specification of the happy life itself – except insofar as opting for one of these candidates, or something else, would indicate, derivatively, that the life having it would be a happy one. See also S. Broadie, *Ethics with Aristotle* (New York: Oxford University Press, 1991), 26-7 and nn. 14 and 15.

and much more decisively, Aristotle is clearly following Plato in the *Philebus*, so that he intends from the beginning to be proposing an answer to the question what *the* good is, i.e. what that particular good, among other goods, is that by having it a life is made happy, and he is calling that good (as Plato does not) *eudaimonia*. Proposing such an answer presupposes acceptance of a substantive thesis, namely that there is something specifiable in a good and happy life (whether an ingredient or not) that gives it the quality of happiness (whatever that quality may be), and is the only thing that does convey that quality. Given the inadequacy of 'happiness' and any other English term that comes to mind to convey his meaning, then, I will continue simply to use Aristotle's Greek word.[26]

Before proceeding to consider Aristotle's answer to the question what *eudaimonia* so understood in fact is, we need to bring into our discussion the brief passage, much discussed and disputed recently, which Aristotle appends to his argument, discussed above (sect. III), to show that *eudaimonia*, being the self-sufficient good, is the final good as well. This passage (1097b16-20), introduced by 'And further ...' (*eti de ...*), is sometimes interpreted as a third criterion for the good, alongside finality and self-sufficiency.[27] But that is clearly a mistake. Immediately after this passage Aristotle concludes the whole preceding discussion of the criteria by saying: 'So *eudaimonia* appears to be [or is clearly] something final and self-sufficient, being the end of things achievable by action'.[28] Here he mentions only the two criteria of finality and self-sufficiency. So, it would seem, this appendage (1097b16-20) does not introduce a third criterion. In fact, this passage seems intended to tell us something about how Aristotle understands a certain requirement implied in the self-sufficiency criterion as that has been explained just before, namely that the good, i.e. *eudaimonia*, should itself be *most* choiceworthy (since, as self-sufficient, it is what makes the life that has it a *choiceworthy* one, lacking in nothing that would be needed to make it worth choosing). His purpose, then, is to explain in just what way we are to understand the good's, i.e. *eudaimonia*'s, being most choiceworthy, inasmuch as it is the source of the choiceworthiness of any life that possesses it, and is thereby the self-

---

[26] Perhaps I should emphasize that this worry about 'happiness' as a translation is unrelated to worries I expressed in *Reason and Human Good in Aristotle* (Cambridge: Harvard University Press, 1975; Indianapolis: Hackett, 1986), 89, n.1. Even if, as I suggested there (not of course intending to say how any one offering a complete translation of the work should render the Greek term), 'human flourishing' more accurately conveys the word's meaning (or Aristotle's understanding of it), that translation would be equally open to the concerns I have expressed here. If *eudaimonia* is (possibly) to designate some constituent activity or activities of a good and happy human life, neither 'happiness' nor 'flourishing' can well render the term in such a use.

[27] See Irwin's translation (1985 ed.), where it is set off with a special heading, coordinate with those for finality and self-sufficiency: '(5) The good is most choiceworthy; so is happiness'.

[28] *teleion dê ti phainetai kai autarkes hê eudaimonia, tôn praktôn ousa telos*, 1097b20-21.

sufficient good.[29] The passage reads as follows (in what I intend as an interpretatively neutral translation):

> And further, it [*eudaimonia*] is most choiceworthy of all things without being counted together – if counted together, it is clear that it is more choiceworthy taken along with the very least of goods, since that which is put together with it makes [lit., becomes] a larger quantity of goods, and of goods the greater is always more choiceworthy.[30]

In interpreting Aristotle's explanation here it is important to bear clearly in mind that for him the superlative choiceworthiness of *eudaimonia* is a function of the role it plays *as an end*, indeed as an end in relation to any and everything else in a properly conducted human life that is choiceworthy at all.[31] The passage to which these remarks are appended, and which they are intended to clarify, is an argument to show that *eudaimonia*, being a self-sufficient good, is also unqualifiedly final or 'endlike', i.e. an end 'choiceworthy for itself always and never because of anything else' (1097a33-4). Aristotle reminds us of this when, as I just mentioned, he

---

[29] That this is the right way to understand this passage is confirmed by a passage of *NE* X.2 discussed below in sect. V: 1172b26-35. Questions about the choiceworthiness of the good, and of other goods, are raised there with clear reference to Plato's discussion in *Philebus* 20-23, where, as we have seen, issues about the sufficiency of the good are at the forefront.

[30] *eti de pantôn hairetôtatên mê sunarithmoumenên – sunarithmoumenên de dêlon hôs hairetôteran meta tou elachistou tôn agathôn: huperochê gar ginetai to prostithemenon, agathôn de to meizon hairetôteron aei*, 1097b16-20. I have translated with the intention to leave undecided which of two ways to take the participle *sunarithmoumenên* in its first occurrence: does *mê sunarithmoumenên* ('without being counted together') mean 'because or in the sense that it is not the sort of thing to be counted together with other goods' or 'under the condition that it is not counted together with other goods'? Depending on how you take it in its first occurrence, the second one will either express something counterfactual ('if it were the sort of thing to be added together with other goods, it would be more choiceworthy along with the least of goods, since that is how it always goes with goods that get counted together with one another') or something merely circumstantial ('but when it is counted together [as of course it can be] it is more choiceworthy along with the least of goods'). Aristotle's purpose here is to tell us in which sense or way the good is most choiceworthy, and he distinguishes from that way a different way that something might be most choiceworthy, namely in relation to other goods along with which it is being counted. It is not necessary for his purposes here to say whether the good is such (somehow) that it *cannot* be coherently counted together, or whether instead it can be so counted (in which case it is not most choiceworthy in the other sense or way). So long as he makes it clear in what way he understands that *eudaimonia* or the good is most choiceworthy, we do not need to know whether there is a different sense of 'most choiceworthy' that coherently applies to it but that it does not satisfy, or none. So it would be a mistake to translate this passage in any way that made Aristotle opt for either of these understandings. His Greek is simply uncommitted either way on this question. (See further below, n. 47 and my discussion in the text there.)

[31] Gabriel Richardson in discussion and in preliminary writing toward her dissertation (above, n. 11) has particularly, and particularly effectively, emphasized this point.

concludes the whole discussion of the criteria immediately afterward (1097b20-21) by putting forward the fact that *eudaimonia* is 'the end of things achievable by action' in explication of its satisfying both of the two criteria, self-sufficiency as well as finality. Such an end is the constant and single source of the detailed organization of the way any person making it their end lives their life. Such an end, then, as such, lies beyond all other goods, even all other ends, that are ingredient in their life: for them, it is the focus for the choice and pursuit of all other goods, and all stand together as subordinate to it (however they may otherwise be differently related to one another). In this addendum Aristotle is saying that this good is most choiceworthy 'without being counted together', and he contrasts this way with another way of being more or most choiceworthy, one that involves being counted together with other goods. Clearly enough, then, he is drawing attention to this categorial distinction between the way that this good is a good for the person and their life, and the way that all the subordinate goods are good. It is by relation to it that the latter are choiceworthy when, in the way, and to the extent that they are. As such, i.e. in that relation, they can be compared with one another as better or less good, more and less choiceworthy. Likewise, they can be added together, in that considering some one of them and its value in relation to the single ultimate end permits rankings both with individual other goods and with combinations of them: one such good is improved (and more choiceworthy) if another such is added together with it. And there might be some one subordinate good that is most choiceworthy, in the sense that it, taken singly, is more choiceworthy than any other subordinate good also taken singly.

Aristotle's point, then, is that *eudaimonia*, *the* good, is 'most choiceworthy' in a different way from this, i.e. from the way that some single subordinate good might be most choiceworthy in relation to other subordinate goods. *It* is most choiceworthy in the way that an end is most choiceworthy in relation to anything whose value is subordinated to it, anything that is in some way or other pursued for its sake. It is that for the sake of which, ultimately, any of them is ever chosen, or to be chosen, at all. It is the extreme, the final object of choice whenever any of them is chosen. *This* is the sense or way that it is most choiceworthy in relation to them, and better than any or all of them – indeed, the absolutely best thing. It is not most choiceworthy or best in the way that some one among such subordinates might be ranked as most choiceworthy among them all.[32]

---

[32] Some light is cast on these issues by a passage of the *Magna Moralia* that also discusses *eudaimonia* and 'counting together' (I.2, 1184a14-25). The example there of health in relation to healthy things (healthy foods, practices, etc., are presumably intended) in fact illustrates clearly and precisely the sort of orientation of some goods to an end that is the source of their value that, on my interpretation, Aristotle's account in *NE* I.7 of the 'most choiceworthiness' of *eudaimonia* relies upon. So, in fact, the reason why, as the *MM* says, the way that *eudaimonia* is *ariston* and most choiceworthy is not one that involves 'counting together' is simply that no end is to be spoken of as most choiceworthy in relation to the things that are subordinate to it by being ranked as the best among them. As the *MM*'s author correctly says, to speak that way will result in the incoherence of its being better than itself – it as overarching end will be better than it as subordinate to that end. So far, then,

Further issues can be and have been raised in connection with this brief passage, but we can take this much as clearly established, I think – even though many who have written on the passage have not interpreted it in this way – and it suffices for my present purposes.[33] Aristotle envisages here some way that some single end might be the most choiceworthy of or for *all* things (all goods, all other ends), which could permit that end to be the (sole and self-sufficient) source of the choiceworthiness of any life in which it was achieved and present. From what Aristotle has said so far, the end that fulfills this role could even, in itself, be just one of the good ingredients or constituents of that life. Its special character as a good, even though there are other goods as well, subordinated to it, might be such that it and it alone rendered the life possessing it 'choiceworthy and lacking in nothing'. So what he says here fits together well, as it certainly ought to, with the conclusion he is going to argue for in the next section of the chapter, that the human good or *eudaimonia* is, quite simply, activity of soul deriving from the excellent or virtuous condition of its reason-possessing part.[34] For that *is* a single activity (perhaps a complex or even variegated one) ingredient in the life, alongside others some of which, of course, are also, as ingredients, further goods. Nothing, in short, in his explication of how *eudaimonia* is most choiceworthy suggests or

---

this *MM* passage is illuminating. However, the author remarks that 'we put *eudaimonia* together from many goods' (1184a19) and he seems to make that part-whole relationship what produces the incoherence when, as best, *eudaimonia* is 'counted together' – confusingly, he does not focus clearly on the fact that then an end is being improperly counted together as far as goodness or choiceworthiness is concerned with its subordinates. But any part-whole incongruence is clearly not what Aristotle has in mind in the *NE* I.7 in saying that *eudaimonia* is most choiceworthy without being counted together. Furthermore, appeal to the idea that *eudaimonia* is a whole of parts would seem to go counter to the very illustration via health of how *eudaimonia* stands related to its subordinates that the *MM* passage provides: health does not have healthy food, etc. as its *parts*. This difficulty would be removed if we could take the healthy things subordinate to health in the illustration as e.g. the health of the foot, the health of the eyes, the health of the stomach, etc. – not foods, practices, etc. – so that health itself, the end, would simply be a whole put together from these 'healthy things'. (And then we could proceed to understand the *MM* as consistently and throughout deriving the incoherence of 'counting *eudaimonia* together' with other goods from its character as a whole put together from them.) But that is an odd and non-standard way of speaking of healthy things (*hugieina*) in relation to health (for the standard one, which I have adopted above, see e.g. Aristotle *Metaphysics* Γ.2, 1003a3-37). Hence I think we have to regard the remark in *MM* 1184a19-20 that 'we put *eudaimonia* together from many goods' as an excrescence, representing a misunderstanding of the view the author is presenting, and out of kilter even with the example he presents to illustrate the way the 'most choiceworthiness' of *eudaimonia* is supposed to be understood. The view he is intending to present is in fact the one I have attributed to Aristotle in *NE* I.7.

[33] See further X.2, 1172b26-35, and my discussion below, sect. V.

[34] Here and in the next section my attention focuses on questions about whether and if so in what way Aristotle's implicit claim that *eudaimonia* as he specifies it in this conclusion satisfies his two criteria for the highest good. I leave aside, as not relevant to my concerns in this paper, consideration of the argument itself by which he works out his specification (the so-called 'function argument').

should be thought to suggest, that a 'most choiceworthy' end as Aristotle understands that title would have to be some combination of all the intrinsic goods of life, or even any subset of them, aimed at as a sum total.[35]

Now in fact, as I indicated in my initial summary, in reaching his conclusion in the next section of the chapter Aristotle actually adds 'or, if there is a plurality of virtues, then it is activity deriving from the soul's best and most final (*teleiotatên*) virtue' (1098a16-18).[36] And of course, as he makes explicit already in the last chapter of Book I, he thinks there are indeed a plurality of virtues. On the one hand there are moral or ethical virtues (many of those) and on the other hand intellectual ones (more than one of those too). Moreover, while he never explicitly ranks the virtues in terms of 'finality', upon beginning his discussion of the life of contemplation in Book X (promised already at 1096a4-5 in chapter 5 of Book I), he does argue (1177a13-18) that the activity of *nous* or intellect deriving from its proper virtue is 'final' (*teleia*) *eudaimonia* – and that this activity is 'contemplative' (*theorêtikê*), that is, consists in theoretical thinking. So, in Book X, a specific virtuous activity – namely, excellent theoretical contemplation – is identified as 'final' *eudaimonia*. Presumably, then, the virtue that gets exercised in this activity will itself be the most final of the virtues, the finality of the virtue being the basis for its activity's constituting final *eudaimonia*. This suggests pretty explicitly that the human good announced by Aristotle in *NE* I.7 is in fact already being conceived as some single activity, a contemplative one, deriving from the one virtue (the 'most final' of them) that constitutes the perfection of our ability to know, in a foundational way, i.e. to contemplate, the fundamental principles on which the universe is grounded. I will say more about this conception in the next section; for now, it is enough to notice that it, too, could fit together well with his explanation of how *eudaimonia* is 'most choiceworthy'. If excellent theoretical contemplation were the unqualifiedly final and self-sufficient good, that would mean that it is the single highest end for the organization of a good and happy human life, whose character and value were such that simply by achieving it one's life would be made worth choosing and lacking in nothing needed for it to be choiceworthy; other goods, of which of course there could be many, would find their place in the life under some controlling subordination to this good activity as

---

[35] This was the view of J.L. Ackrill, most fully argued for in 'Aristotle on *Eudaimonia*', *Proceedings of the British Academy* 60 (1974), 3-23. See also his *Aristotle's Ethics* (London: Faber, 1973), 243-4. Irwin, *Aristotle: Nicomachean Ethics*, ed. 1 (1985), 304, holds the same view (though in the ed. 2 commentary [1999], 181-2, he proposes this only as one of two possible interpretations of the passage).

[36] He immediately adds, 'in a complete life' (*eti d' en biôi teleiôi*). Here it seems clear that Aristotle is using his term *teleion* with its most common ordinary acceptation, not his specially explained one of 'final or end-like': he means a life that has had some normal human range of time, development, and experience, over which to play itself out. I take it that this addition is intended to be part of the 'definition' of *eudaimonia* or the human good that Aristotle adopts here in *NE* I.7, but for my purposes in this paper I do not need to take it specially into account.

final and highest end. Various detailed questions would need to be addressed, but this certainly sounds like a viable conception.

In the past I have resisted accepting this interpretation and have proposed more than one way of reading Aristotle's texts so that they do not involve this idea, because I did not see how to make good sense of his ethical theory (his theory of moral virtue and of the value of the moral life) on the basis of it.[37] I now think, though, that there might be hope of accepting it, without wreaking havoc on Aristotle's moral theory; and, besides, the philosophical view that emerges is of considerable interest. So without going (again) into the question whether this interpretation really is the correct or best available given all the evidence, let us see what we can do about Aristotle's moral theory if we are prepared at least to relax our resistance to it.

V

Let us return to Aristotle's thoughts about finality and self-sufficiency, and the criticisms of Socrates' argument in the *Philebus* that are implicit in them. On the view that excellent contemplative activity is (all by itself) the good, Aristotle will be maintaining that this activity is the 'end of things achievable by action', the end that is always somehow ultimately in view whenever those living a good human life do anything at all that they choose to do: it organizes and gives structure to the whole of their active, practical life. Further, its presence in their life is sufficient of itself to make it worth choosing, and so worth living. If that activity is present in their life, absolutely nothing is lacking (nothing additional is *needed*) for the choiceworthiness of the life they lead. Thus, as Aristotle sees things, Socrates' mistake in the *Philebus* was to think that *no* ingredient activity or experience in life can be an adequate grounding for its choiceworthiness, that one must look instead to some principles of organization applied from outside, as it were, in combining into a life whatever principal ingredients there would be. No, says Aristotle: excellent contemplative activity itself, though an ingredient, can serve in all the ways that the good must function, given acceptable criteria: both as an unqualifiedly final end that organizes and structures all other activities, and as a self-sufficient good. We need next to consider how this might be so.

As I pointed out (sect. III), the self-sufficiency of the good leaves open that something else might still be needed from some other point of view than the choiceworthiness of the life led with ultimate reference to it. Accordingly, in discussing the contemplative life in chapter 7 of Book X Aristotle admits that even excellent contemplation still leaves one in need[38] of some other things (the necessities of life, as he calls them), just in fact as morally excellent activity may

---

[37] See *Reason and Human Good in Aristotle* (above, n. 26), 91-115; 'Contemplation and Happiness' (above, n. 25).

[38] Aristotle's word for 'need' here is *deisthai*. Socrates' term in applying his criterion of sufficiency in the *Philebus* is the same, but with the prefix *pros-* ('in addition') (20e6, 21a11).

do (except that the latter needs yet more, beyond the necessities).[39] Moreover, even the wise person (the *sophos*), the one who possesses the virtue for contemplation, will find that his surpassingly excellent activity is better (*beltion*) if he has fellow-contemplators to share his thought-work with. In both these cases (the necessities alluded to, whatever exactly those are, and the fellow-contemplators whose co-work will make one's own a better thing) Aristotle is clearly recognizing the additional value of something such that by having it in your life your life will be improved – just, as we have seen (sect. III, fourth paragraph from the end), as with external goods like friends and good looks and good children in *NE* I.8. That is what it means to say that you need it (in addition).

In what way(s) are these additional things needed by the person devoted to the exercise of his virtues for contemplation? As for the 'necessities of life', needed both by the contemplator and the morally virtuous person, I assume that something that was needed simply in order to make possible virtuous activity, or indeed activity of any sort at all (something needed just for remaining alive and active, such as a minimum regular supply of food and water or air, or a climate at least minimally hospitable for human life, or those things plus being loved by some other people), should not be counted as something beyond those activities that was needed in addition to them, as providing some improvement in one's life. In fact, in the absence of those conditions there would be no activity, or no virtuous activity, at all. So I take it that by 'necessities of life' here Aristotle is thinking not so to speak of such barest necessities, but of other things that we may think life needs, even if it can be conducted without them – just as contemplation can be engaged in on one's own, but goes better if pursued in association with co-workers. Hence, I do not think it would distort Aristotle's thought here to suppose that, like Protarchus in the *Philebus*, he thinks any life that had none of the ordinary sorts of pleasures we all get and take an interest in while eating and drinking and so on was one that lacked something valuable: these, one could say, are themselves 'necessities of life' and so among the necessities Aristotle alludes to (Plato calls these pleasures 'necessary pleasures' in the *Republic*).[40] Aristotle's insistence is only that even without them a life that had excellent contemplation in it as an ingredient would still be choiceworthy: *any* life's choiceworthiness would be directly guaranteed by the presence in it of this activity (provided only that any conditions actually necessary for engaging in it in the first place, and continuing to engage in it, are present).

Before proceeding to examine this claim we need to take into account one last passage, so far left aside, where Aristotle is responding to Socrates' argument in

---

[39] X.7, 1177a28-b1: *tôn men gar pros to zên anankaiôn kai sophos kai dikaios kai hoi loipoi deontai, tois de toioutois hikanôs kechorêgêmenôn ho men dikaios deitai pros hous dikaiopragêsei kai meth' hôn, ... ho de sophos kai kath' hauton ôn dunatai theôrein ... beltion d' isôs sunergous echôn, all' homôs autarkestatos.*

[40] See 554a, 559dff. Plato speaks first of 'necessary' and 'unnecessary' kinds of desire or appetite, but he speaks also, by extension from those, of the corresponding pleasures as necessary or unnecessary (cf. 558d5, 561a3-4, 7, 581e3-4).

the *Philebus*. This comes in *NE* X.2, where Aristotle is reporting and commenting upon Eudoxus' defence of a hedonist theory of value.[41] Among other arguments for value-hedonism, Eudoxus had argued, according to Aristotle, that pleasure must be the good, because pleasure when added to other sorts of things that are good makes those other goods more choiceworthy (i.e. better), while 'the good [or goodness] is increased [only] by itself' (1172b23-5).[42] Aristotle immediately objects (b26-7) that this argument can really only make the claim (*apophainein*) that pleasure is *among* the good things, no more a good than any other good. We can grant Eudoxus (this was his example) that an act of justice becomes more choiceworthy if the agent enjoys doing it, and we can grant that anything that increases anything's goodness has to be itself good. But from those premises it only follows that pleasure is a good (one type of good), one type perhaps among others. As Aristotle says (b27-8), the general principle Eudoxus is relying on here, in this argument, is that 'every good is more choiceworthy together with another good than on its own (*monoumenon*)', so that his example of just acts becoming more choiceworthy if enjoyed only shows that pleasure is one good, one type of good (the just act itself being of another type, good independently of any relation it bears to pleasure).[43]

Aristotle adds (b28-31), plainly reporting the contents of *Philebus* 20-23, that Plato used this same argument (the one Aristotle himself has just set out in

---

[41] I am indebted to Gavin Lawrence's discussion of this passage in 'Nonaggregatability, Inclusiveness, and the Theory of Focal Value', *Phronesis* 43 (1997), 32-76, at 58-64.

[42] *prostithemenên te hotôioun tôn agathôn hairetôteron poiein, hoion tôi dikaiopragein kai sôphronein, auxesthai de to agathon hautôi*, 1172b23-5. Eudoxus' examples here of goods of another sort than pleasure are just actions and temperate ones. To be consistent with the hedonism he is here advancing we must suppose Eudoxus to have envisaged that just acts when no pleasure is taken in doing them are good because of future pleasure to which they will lead (he cannot think just acts good in themselves, or for any other reason than some connection they have with pleasure). So if we accept the general principle that 'the good is increased [only] by itself' this will apply to such acts in the following way: these acts are good because of pleasure they involve (in the future); so when their goodness is increased (as everyone must admit) by pleasure in the acts themselves being added, that confirms that indeed pleasure, being the good, is increased by itself (= more of itself, further instances of itself). Thus anyone who grants that virtuous acts are improved if enjoyed in the doing is driven by Eudoxus' argument to identify the goodness of the acts insofar as not immediately enjoyed with some consequent pleasures.

[43] Here it is important to see that Eudoxus is claiming that a just act itself is more choiceworthy when enjoyed, because of the addition to it of the pleasure. He is not saying merely that a just action plus the pleasure taken in doing it – that sum or package – is more choiceworthy than the act taken on its own. So the principle in quotation marks in my text makes the following claim: any good thing is itself made more choiceworthy when taken together with another good. (In Eudoxus' instance, a just act is made more choiceworthy by the addition of another good to it, the pleasure taken in it.) This principle is one that Aristotle, as we will see shortly, himself disputes (1172b32-5). If the good in question is the good, then it is not true that that good becomes more choiceworthy if some other good is added to it. So Aristotle accepts this principle in application only to goods other than the highest one.

response to Eudoxus, using Eudoxus' premises to derive the conclusion that pleasure is one good among others) to *refute* the claim that pleasure is *the* good. Plato, Aristotle says, argued that the life of pleasure is more choiceworthy with reasoning than without it, so that if that mixture or combination is preferable (*kreitton*), pleasure cannot be the good. For, 'the good does not become more choiceworthy by having anything added to it'.[44] In fact Plato's argument in the *Philebus* does rely (in effect) on Eudoxus' general principle, and it could be interpreted as counting pleasure (along with reasoning, too, of course) among those goods that become more choiceworthy when together with another good. I say only that Plato's argument could be so interpreted, because in fact he does not say anything at all in the *Philebus* passage about the choiceworthiness of goods such as pleasure, much less of the good itself: he only speaks of the choiceworthiness of the three lives he compares, those chockfull of pleasure and of reason, plus the mixed life (21d3, 22a5, b1, 5, 7). However, it does seem not unreasonable to reconstrue Plato's argument as Aristotle does here, making it focus on the way that the good itself is and is not choiceworthy: as I have said (sect. IV) in discussing Aristotle's account of self-sufficiency in *NE* I.7, whatever makes lives choiceworthy by its presence is reasonably taken itself to be in some prior way choiceworthy, in fact the *most* choiceworthy thing.[45] Still, this is Aristotle's own gloss on Plato's argument, intended to show how Plato could be construed as responding to Eudoxus' claims on behalf of pleasure: if with Eudoxus 'every good is more choiceworthy with another good than on its own', but the good itself is not made more choiceworthy by the addition to it of anything, then Plato's argument in the *Philebus* tells us, in effect, that pleasure cannot be the good because *it* is made more choiceworthy if reasoning is added to it.

At the end of the passage, Aristotle then adds, now in his own voice, the following remark (1172b32-35):

> And it is clear that [not only pleasure, but] nothing else could be the good that becomes more choiceworthy when together with any [other] thing that is

---

[44] *toioutôi dê logôi kai Platôn anairei hoti ouk estin hêdonê tagathon: hairetôteron gar einai ton hêdun bion meta phronêseôs ê chôris, ei de to mikton kreitton, ouk einai tên hêdonên tagathon: oudenos gar prostethentos autôi tagathon hairetôteron ginesthai*, 1172b28-31. In paraphrasing the first part of this passage as claiming that with this argument Plato 'refutes the claim that pleasure is the good', I am taking the content of the *hoti* or that-clause in the Greek ('pleasure is not the good') as expressing the conclusion of Plato's refutatory argument; that-clauses after verbs such as *anairein* ('refutes') do not necessarily express instead the proposition refuted.

[45] One might point to *helein* (aorist of *hairein*, the root verb in *haireton*, choiceworthy) at 20d9 (taken together with *phrontizei* in 10) as having this implication (I quote this text above n. 3, and see my discussion in sect. II): Socrates might be thought to be saying here that nothing else is chosen (e.g. a life) except insofar as it is accomplished with the good, the latter being chosen in some prior way.

intrinsically (*kath' hauto*) good. What then is of this kind, that we can have a share in? That is what we are seeking.[46]

Now, of course, at this point in his discussion (X.2) Aristotle has not yet declared his discovery of what he is seeking, namely the good that does *not* become more choiceworthy when together with any other intrinsic good. He will do so, however, only a few chapters farther on, in X.7: the highest good or *eudaimonia*, he there declares, is the activity of excellent contemplative thought. So, in his view, excellent contemplative thought is a good that does not become more choiceworthy when taken together with any other good – not when taken together with ordinary pleasures, not when taken together with any other of the goods of life, not when taken together with good co-workers adding their contemplative thought to one's own and making it better.[47] This goes contrary to the Eudoxan assumption that 'every good is more choiceworthy with another good than on its own' if that is taken without restriction, and made to apply not merely to subordinate goods (with that restriction Aristotle would endorse it) but also to the highest good itself. It also goes counter (as we have seen in sect. IV) to Plato's argument in the *Philebus*, that no particular good, no good kind of thing or kind of activity (neither pleasure nor reasoning) can be *the* good. Thus Aristotle accepts the principle that he says Plato used in order to refute Eudoxus – that 'the good does not become more choiceworthy by having anything added to it' – but he disagrees with Plato's own conclusion drawn from it, that *the* good cannot be any *particular* good.

When we add what we have learned about Aristotle's view from this passage of X.2, then, we see that Aristotle holds the following. He holds that any life having excellent contemplative thought in it, as its ultimate and constantly organizing end, is good and choiceworthy – worth living – whatever else it has or lacks. It is worth living *because* contemplation occupies this position in it (and because of nothing else, not even in part). He holds that some such lives are better – even, if you like, more choiceworthy – than others, because they have additional goods that are not present in the others. He holds, however, that when contemplative thinking is ingredient as the organizing end in a life with such additional goods, that thinking is not *itself* more choiceworthy than when it is similarly ingredient in lives without them. Contemplative thinking, we could say, is for Aristotle absolutely or

---

[46] *dêlon d' hôs oud' allo ouden tagathon an eiê, ho meta tinos tôn kath' hauto agathôn hairetôteron ginetai. ti oun esti toiouton, hou kai hêmeis koinônoumen; toiouton gar epizêteitai* (1172b32-35).

[47] This shows that Aristotle's view that *eudaimonia* is most choiceworthy 'without being counted together', as that notion is explained in I.7, 1097b16-20, does not include the thought that if or when it is counted together with other goods then it becomes more choiceworthy than it is without them. Thus the counterfactual reading of the participle *sunarithmoumenên* (see n. 30 above) gives a correct interpretation of Aristotle's actual view on the 'most choiceworthiness' of *eudaimonia*, even though, as I argued above (sect. IV), it is not necessary – indeed, it is a mistake – to insist on understanding Aristotle's comments on the 'most choiceworthiness' of *eudaimonia* in I.7 as excluding the thought that it is more choiceworthy when counted together.

unqualifiedly choiceworthy (*haplôs haireton*) – *nothing* can increase *its* choiceworthiness, even if the addition of further goods alongside it can increase the choiceworthiness of a life in which it is found.

VI

We can now return to the difficulty I alluded to at the end of section IV. If excellent contemplative thinking is (all by itself) the unqualifiedly final and self-sufficient good, what are we to make of the value of morally good actions and of moral virtue itself? Precisely how do they relate to this highest good in being subordinate to it – chosen and arranged or organized with a view to it – while it all by itself is the ultimate end of a good human life? We are left to a considerable degree to our own devices in attempting to answer this question on Aristotle's behalf, since it is a noteworthy (and, at least for us, a highly regrettable) fact that he nowhere takes this question up, or even seems to feel that it poses any special problem. In the first chapter of Book VI of the *NE* Aristotle raises the question of the *horos* or principle of delimitation for choosing the 'mean' in ethical action and passion, but even if by the end of that Book (see 1145a6-9) he has indicated that this principle is somehow to be equated with theoretical wisdom or its activity, he nowhere in Book VI (or elsewhere) attempts to tell us anything directly and in detail about how this function of delimitation is supposed to be carried out. We can only attempt to construct an answer for ourselves, drawing on the somewhat scattered materials that Aristotle does provide us, together with other ideas that were available to him in his own intellectual milieu.

For present purposes the briefest sketch of how this might be done will suffice.[48] The first point to notice is that as I interpret him, Aristotle recognizes a vast array of things that are, in a certain way, good independently of any orientation to the highest good. Bodily pleasure is good just because it satisfies natural desires of ours, food is good just because our bodily substance and the continuation of our physical lives as well as other aspects of our lives depend upon it. Likewise, I would take it, companionship is good because again of complicated and perhaps in some ways obscure natural desires of ours. Similarly for all kinds of games and sports; fulfilling work; music and art and literature; perhaps even having power and control over others. All these things, and many others as well, answer to natural capacities and needs of human beings, as such. (Corresponding things are good for corresponding reasons for other animals, too.) These remain good for us whether or not we recognize moral or any other type of virtue as the highest good, or even as a good at all; they are good without reference to any other good, even the highest. They are good for every human being simply because of fundamental, universal,

---

[48] Gabriel Richardson has a great deal to say on this question in her dissertation (see n. 11 above). My own thinking has been very much improved by reading her work and discussing it with her, and my sketch draws on some of her ideas. I do not mean to suggest, however, that she would accept everything I say here.

unalterable facts about every human being's physical and psychological constitution. Where, for Aristotle, the orientation to the highest good comes in is with our *choosing* instances of such goods. When, and in what manner and way, shall we select and make use of such goods? Even if they are good independently of being oriented to the highest good, they are not *choiceworthy*, on Aristotle's conception, except when, and in ways that, such orientation provides. The orientation of these goods, in worthy choices, to the highest good seems to proceed, for Aristotle, in two stages, which we need to take up separately.

To begin with, to a very great extent moral virtue as Aristotle conceives it simply consists in moulding our capacity for choosing in such a way that we do select such independent goods only on certain occasions or in certain circumstances, and only in certain particular ways and manners (and not others).[49] This reflects the fact or has the consequence that from the perspective of the chooser the value of those independent goods is subordinated to the values encapsulated in such correct choice, as such. The timing and the manner of the selection and use of such goods, deriving from the act of choice, are regarded as reflecting special values, ones that stand a level above in worth the worth of the independent goods themselves that are selected. The latter are choiceworthy only if chosen when and as they ought to be, and the inherent excellence of those acts of choice and its expression in the regulated use and enjoyment of the independent goods is seen by the choosing agent, and is to be seen, as ranking more highly in worth than any of the objects chosen. Thus the way the independent goods are selected and used is of higher value than the value itself of the items selected and used. In that precise sense, moral action and moral virtue, which expresses itself in moral action, is a distinctly overarching end for the moral chooser. It constitutes a higher level of value than the value of the independent goods. Moral action and moral virtue are thus something inherently better than the independent goods, inasmuch as they constitute the end that (in the first instance, anyhow) controls the choice and use of the latter. The choice of those goods can never be made in a correct manner if this difference of level is not fully reflected in the very making of the choice. The independent goods are in that sense subordinated to moral virtue and morally virtuous action, as to an end that organizes and controls their pursuit. So, for Aristotle, moral action and moral virtue are important and higher-level ends to which any proper concern for these independent goods, as I am calling them, must be subordinated.[50] They are and remain good for us, as I have indicated,

---

[49] On this conception – common to all the Greek moral philosophers – the 'moral' virtues are not limited to, and have no original connection to, serving the needs or interests of others besides the agent. They can encompass all kinds of personal and private concerns. Not only justice, but temperance and personal courage too, count as virtues.

[50] I leave aside here all questions about what sort of considerations about action go into a moral choice, as Aristotle understands it. Even if it consisted entirely in some process of assessing, in their own terms, the independent values of the independent goods, and then figuring out some way of obtaining some maximum, or some satisfactory quantity, of the lower sort or level of value attaching to these goods, the level-distinction I have insisted on would remain. The value of choosing well, and getting the choice right, would still function

simply because of the ways that they respond to needs (physical, psychological, social) that human beings simply by their nature all have. What moral virtue does is to direct our selection and use of them in such a way as to make us constantly aware of the higher value of our rationality itself – including our rationality in making orderly, suitable, overall coherent use of them.

However, according to Aristotle (if we accept the interpretation according to which excellent contemplation is, all by itself, our highest good), moral virtue itself is oriented toward excellent contemplative activity as to an end. So he also holds that the independent goods, being subordinated to the values of moral choice, are at the same time subordinated, through the subordination of the latter to the highest good or *eudaimonia*, to excellent contemplative activity as well – and indeed, ultimately. But in what way are moral virtue and moral value oriented toward and subordinated to excellent contemplative activity as their end? One point to make right away is this. On this interpretation, Aristotle's view implies that just as in using the independent goods it is crucial, if that use is to be choiceworthy, for them to be chosen and used in the awareness that there is something better (so to speak, categorically better) than they are (namely correct choice, or more generally, moral virtue); so, that choice, insofar as it is *moral* choice, must itself be aware that there is something better even than it – namely, excellent contemplative activity. Moreover (and this is my second point), moral virtue and moral choice are, of course, excellences of the reasoning part of the soul. So one might expect to be able to work out some understanding of how excellent moral reasoning functions (for example with respect to its focus on the truth) that could make it mirror in some suitable way the excellent processes of excellent contemplative thinking. In other words, one might expect the two aspects of reason that Aristotle distinguishes, the practical and the theoretical, to be internally related in such a way that the excellences of practical reasoning could be seen as lesser instantiations of the very same values fully instantiated in and only in theoretical thought. This would be a second way that the excellences of the practical use of the mind could be subordinated to the excellence of its theoretical use, precisely as to an end.

Thus in valuing the rational perfection present in practical thinking when that is subject to the procedures and constraints of the moral virtues, one would be valuing this (1) in recognition of its subordination as a value to the higher value of pure theoretical knowledge of the world order as a whole in its relation to the (rational) first principles on which it depends (a much larger and more complex system than the system of human life); and simultaneously (2) recognizing the purer and more thoroughly reason-governed way of grasping the truth that is found in excellent theoretical thinking as a model for the less fully reasoned-out grasp of truth that moral understanding of human life can, at its best, achieve.[51] One would,

---

as an end to which the values of the independent goods would be subordinate in the way I have indicated.

[51] In this connection one should take note of Aristotle's emphasis on the limitations of moral knowledge – its exceptionability, its reliance on perception for establishing some basic truths, etc. See *NE* 1094b22-1095a13, 1126a31-b10.

as a result, be fairly described as pursuing even in one's moral actions the ultimate end of excellent theoretical thinking – as on this interpretation Aristotle would imply any morally virtuous person would do who also grasped the true highest end, contemplation, as the ultimate goal of human life. That would always be in view, as a finally controlling value, both in choosing morally virtuous actions themselves, and in one's selection, through moral virtue and its standards of evaluation, of independent goods to pursue and enjoy.

Much more, of course, would need to be looked into and thought about before an interpretation along these lines could be made finally presentable. However, I think this sketch does show how we might understand Aristotle's idea that *eudaimonia* or the highest good is excellent contemplative thinking (all by itself) in such a way that it would not undermine the values of moral choice and moral action taken on their own as fundamental goods, and ends, for human life. I do not think an interpretation along these lines would undermine these values in either of two distinct ways. It would not commit Aristotle to holding that the superior value of contemplation might in some circumstances so outrank moral values so that one would, on his theory, be entitled simply to override the claims of morality and do something horrible in order to make room in one's life for some extra contemplation. And it would not commit him to any bizarre and unacceptable account of what is actually morally required, or permitted, of us: as if it would all of a sudden become an act of justice to do what in other circumstances would be a horrible violation, in consequence of the position at the top of the hierarchy of values assigned to contemplation – because by doing it one could make possible some extra contemplative thinking. On the view I have sketched moral virtue and contemplative virtue, and the goods that I have been calling independent, are related to one another so to speak each *en bloc*, as values of different orders or at different levels. Thus moral value is subordinated to contemplative activity as a kind of value, or in terms of the values that they are. Nonetheless, it is moral virtue, and only it, that tells us what is rationally required of us, or permitted, to do – what our choices among subordinate goods, and so our actions, should be. These choices are made in light of the totality of our human nature and our needs and interests as human beings – even if, as Aristotle recommends, we take our theoretical and contemplative powers as our most distinctive and highest capacities. We remain full human beings, no matter what.

So there is no call (and, I think, in fact no room) to raise questions about what, given that contemplation is the final and highest good, we should do if a *prima facie* requirement of moral virtue (say some *prima facie* duty of justice) should, as things have worked out willy nilly, force us to neglect an opportunity to do some heavy contemplating that without that requirement we would certainly give ourselves over to. On the view I have sketched such a question would not arise, or would be easily and immediately answered. On this view, a life is made choiceworthy simply by the presence in it of contemplation as the good that is recognized as the highest.[52] As I have explained, that good is taken to be unqualifiedly choiceworthy: when carried out over a greater extension of time it does not become more choiceworthy than it would be over a lesser extent. So there would be no extra value achieved by the extra time contemplating that one could set against the values (both that of the independent goods and that of moral action itself) involved if one did the (normally) virtuous thing. In fact, on this view, the thing to do, clearly, is to meet all the legitimate requirements of morality first, including any that might take you away from contemplative thinking that without them you would have engaged in, and then give yourself over to such work when and as circumstances – including in the first instance various moral relationships and commitments – permit. So I do think that on the view I have been proposing, Aristotle's understanding of moral virtue, however unusual and indeed extraordinarily interesting it may be from other points of view, does not strain our credulity.[53]

---

[52] I have not had occasion to point this out, but of course a life devoted simply to moral virtue as if that were the highest good, which did not recognize any special – and certainly not the superior – value of contemplative understanding, would also be for Aristotle a life worth living, and choiceworthy. I take Aristotle's view about the choiceworthiness of lives to be that any life in which rational functioning and its virtues are included as ends is worth living, and choiceworthy. I have not had room to go into these and other consequences of *NE* X.8, where Aristotle makes a 'life of moral virtue' (i.e. one devoted to moral virtue and moral values as the highest good, without recognition of the in fact higher value of contemplative excellence) a *eudaimôn* one, though in a secondary way.

[53] In preparing this final version I have been assisted by valuable written criticisms and queries on the penultimate draft by Robert Heinaman, T.H. Irwin, and my commentator at the Colloquium, Anthony Kenny. I thank them and all the participants in London, November 2001, when I first presented the paper, for a challenging and helpful discussion.

Reply to John M. Cooper

Anthony Kenny

I agree with Cooper that the discussion between Socrates and Protarchus in the *Philebus* is a key to understanding important passages of Aristotle's *Ethics*. Indeed, I shall argue that it provides a framework that embraces much more than the concepts of finality, self-sufficiency, and choiceworthiness which (as Cooper shows) Aristotle extracts as criteria for *eudaimonia*.

First, a note about the Greek words '*teleion*' and '*autarkês*' which correspond to the 'finality' and 'self-sufficiency' of Cooper's title. In my book *Aristotle on the Perfect Life*[1] I translated '*teleion*' as 'perfect' in order to be neutral between two different translations suggested by different paraphrases of the word given by Aristotle in different places. The translation 'final' (or, as some have it, 'supreme') appears to fit some passages better, while the translation 'complete' seems preferable in other contexts.[2] It is one of the attractive features of Cooper's paper that it shows us a way of avoiding the choice between the two translations, since in the appropriate context they will always (for Aristotle) be equivalent in reference, if not exactly in sense.

To be unqualifiedly *teleion* in the sense of 'final' is to be ultimately choiceworthy (cf. *NE* 1097a33-4), never chosen as a means to an end or (Cooper adds) as a constituent of a larger whole. But if something is final it is also self-sufficient (*autarkês*, *NE* 1097b8), that is to say it is something that, 'isolated on its own, makes life choiceworthy and lacking in nothing' (*NE* 1097b14-15), that is to say (according to Cooper), lacking in nothing that is needed for choiceworthiness. These two glosses of Cooper's seem to me very helpful and well inspired.

That they must coincide can be shown thus. Suppose that the ultimately choiceworthy life did not contain all that was needed for choiceworthiness. Then it could not be ultimately choiceworthy, because it could be chosen as a constituent of a larger whole that contained in addition the missing elements. On the other hand, suppose that a life that contained all that was needed for choiceworthiness was not the ultimately choiceworthy good: in that case it could not contain all that is needed for choiceworthiness: since there must be something left out in order to make something else the ultimately choiceworthy life. So if we try, in the consideration of lives, to separate perfection in the sense of finality from perfection in the sense of completion, we get a *reductio ad absurdum*. The

---

[1] (Oxford: Clarendon Press, 1992).
[2] Final: *NE* 1097a28-34, 1098a18 (1), *EE* 1249a16; complete: *NE* 1097b7, 1098a18 (2), 1100a4, 1177b24-5, *EE* 1219a35-9.

relationship between the two criteria is very well brought out by Cooper's discussion.[3]

The coincidence of the two meanings of *'teleion'*, however, occurs only when we are discussing lives: it cannot be taken for granted when the adjective is attached to some other noun. Since Aristotle's prime interest is in defining *eudaimonia*, the perfect life, this point may seem unimportant. But in his definition of *eudaimonia* he makes use of the notion of perfect virtue (*NE* 1100a4, 1102a6; *EE* 1219a39, 1249a16). In the case of virtue, choiceworthiness and completeness do not coincide: virtue can be something *teleion* but it is not something ultimately choiceworthy in the way that *eudaimonia* is (1097b1-5).

For some decades there has been much discussion of the *Nicomachean* definition of *eudaimonia* as the activity of soul in accordance with virtue, and if there are several virtues in accordance with the best and most perfect virtue (1098a16-18). I am glad to see that Cooper and I are now agreed that 'most perfect virtue' in this and parallel *NE* passages does not mean 'most complete virtue' or 'all the virtues', as many scholars have argued. He is now willing to consider that for Aristotle the human good is some single activity, a contemplative one.

I agree with Cooper that *eudaimonia* is one ingredient of the life of the happy person – many other things go on in his life beside the contemplation in which *eudaimonia* consists. But it is a controlling or dominant ingredient, which gives shape to the whole of his life, and for this reason Aristotle is from time to time content to equate *eudaimonia* with living well and with the happy life as a whole.[4] I find attractive Cooper's account, in his final section, of how contemplation may be related to the activities of the moral virtues in the life of the *Nicomachean* happy person.

It will be seen that I am in very considerable agreement with Cooper's paper. Such dissatisfaction as I have with it concerns not what he says, but what he leaves unsaid. His paper seems to omit Aristotle's final answer to the *Philebus* question, which is that *phronêsis* and pleasure are, as properly understood, not in competition with each other as candidates for happiness.[5] The exercise of the highest form of *phronêsis* is the very same thing as the truest form of pleasure; each is identical with the other and with happiness. To reach this conclusion he needs three characteristically Aristotelian theses: (1) that happiness is virtuous activity; (2) that the intellectual virtues are superior to the moral ones; (3) that pleasure is identical with the activity enjoyed.

---

[3] I do not wholly understand Cooper's discussion of the 'counting together' passage but I am glad to see that he does not now regard it as establishing that *Nicomachean eudaimonia* is an inclusive rather than a dominant activity. I also agree with him that the parallel passage in the *MM* is confused in itself, and is a misunderstanding of the *NE* argument.

[4] As Cooper notes in 'Contemplation and Happiness: A Reconsideration', *Reason and Emotion* (Princeton: Princeton University Press, 1999), 212-36, at 219. I am less unhappy than Cooper is with 'happiness' as a translation of *eudaimonia*, but I think this may be a disagreement about the meaning of the English word rather than the Greek one.

[5] According to Cooper (124) pleasure is a further ingredient of the best life, but it is left out of account when we describe the highest good.

The argument, I shall maintain, is most forcefully set out in the *Eudemian Ethics* (including the Disputed Books), but I see no difference of substance on this issue between that treatise and the *Nicomachean Ethics*. In the *NE* the ground is already laid in the eighth chapter of the first Book, the chapter where the *endoxa* are reconciled to the definition of happiness as *energeia kat' aretên*. The following passage is significant (1099a8-16):

> Their life is also in itself pleasant. For pleasure belongs to the soul, and everyone who is called a lover of X finds X pleasant: a horse is pleasant to a horselover, and a drama to a drama-lover, but in the same way just deeds to the lover of justice and in general virtuous deeds to the lover of virtue. Now most people's pleasures clash with each other because they are not naturally pleasurable; but for those that love what is noble it is the naturally pleasurable things that are pleasant: namely, actions expressive of virtue, which are pleasurable for such people as well as in themselves. Their life has no need of pleasure as an additional ornament: it has its pleasure in itself.

It is the mark of the genuinely virtuous person to take pleasure in his virtuous deeds, rather than doing them painfully or grudgingly. Now happiness consists of the best, most virtuous, activities (or the best one of these best activities). So happiness is the pleasantest of all things – in accordance with a famous inscription at Delos (1099a17-31).

The *Philebus* dichotomy is already undercut, but a number of things are left unclear. We are not yet told what is the relation between Plato's *phronêsis* and the virtues whose exercise is pleasant. Though pleasure is no mere ornament, we are not yet told its precise relationship to pleasant activity. And while we may agree that a genuinely virtuous person finds virtuous activity pleasant, we are not here given reason to believe that this pleasure is greater than pleasure taken in other activities – unless it be that concentration on virtue is less likely to lead to a clash between competing pleasures.

However, when *eudaimonia* comes to be finally identified with philosophical contemplation in Book X, one of the reasons we are given is that contemplation is the pleasantest of virtuous activities. The very pursuit of philosophy provides unmixed and stable pleasures, and the contemplation that results from success in the pursuit is even more exquisitely delightful (1177a22-7). 'Pleasure' is not to be thought of as a good or bad thing in itself: the pleasure proper to good activities is good and the pleasure proper to bad activities is bad (1175b27). This doctrine leaves it open for the pleasure of the best activity to be the best of all human goods.

This last doctrine is stated explicitly only in one of the Disputed Books (1153b7-11):

> If certain pleasures are bad, that does not prevent the best thing from being some pleasure – just as knowledge might be, though certain kinds of knowledge are bad. Perhaps it is even necessary, if each state has unimpeded activities, that whether the activity (if unimpeded) of all our states, or that of some one of them is

happiness, this should be the thing most choiceworthy; and this activity is a pleasure.

The problem with *NE* X is that the long discussion of pleasure that introduces it leaves most readers uncertain whether pleasure is identical with, or supervenient to, the activity enjoyed.[6] But the corresponding (*Eudemian*) discussion in the third of the Disputed Books is unambiguous that pleasure is to be identified with (unimpeded) activity. The unimpeded activity of (one or more) virtues, which is identical with the greatest good, is also identical with the greatest virtue.

Aristotle's definitive resolution of the *Philebus* problem is most clearly set out in the *Eudemian Ethics*. Unlike the *NE*, the *EE* regards *eudaimonia* as the exercise of all the virtues, not just of a single dominant virtue: it includes the exercise of the moral virtues, and of both the intellectual virtues, wisdom and understanding, that correspond together to Plato's *phronêsis*.[7] In his final book, having earlier established that happiness is the exercise of perfect virtue, Aristotle explains that perfect virtue is *kalokagathia* (1249a16).[8] He continues thus (1249a17-20):

> Pleasure has already been discussed: what kind of thing it is, and in what sense it is a good; and how things which are pleasant *simpliciter* are noble *simpliciter*, and things which are good *simpliciter* are also pleasant. But there cannot be pleasure except in action: and so the truly happy man will also have the most pleasant life.

The backward references are to the context we have just discussed and to the *Eudemian* book on friendship. Things that are pleasant *simpliciter* are noble *simpliciter* because what most rightly deserves to be called pleasant is that which the wise man calls pleasant; and to him it is good and noble things that are pleasant (1235b36-36a7). Things that are good *simpliciter* are also pleasant, because it is natural goods that are good *simpliciter* and these are naturally pleasant: this natural pleasure is nature's road to virtue (1237a5-9).

Thus, for the ideally virtuous person the concepts '*agathon*', '*hêdu*' and '*kalon*' coincide in their application. If what is pleasant for a man differs from what is good for him, then he is not yet perfectly good but incontinent; if what is good for him does not coincide with what is noble for him, then he is not yet *kaloskagathos* but only *agathos*. For the nobly virtuous person the natural goods of health and wealth and power are not only beneficial but noble, since they subserve his noble virtuous activity. So, for him, goodness, nobility, and pleasantness coincide. The bringing about of this coincidence is the task of ethics (1237a3). But whereas

---

[6] In *The Aristotelian Ethics* (Oxford: Clarendon Press, 1978), 233-38, I have argued that there is, in the end, no real difference of substance between the treatments of pleasure in the two treatises; but the notorious 'bloom on the cheek of youth' passage (1174b23-32) has led many people to believe that the *NE* refuses to identify pleasure and activity.

[7] See my *Aristotle on the Perfect Life*, 19-22.

[8] The perfection of the virtue of a *Eudemian kaloskagathos* is both final and complete: final, because, as I explained in my response to Prof. Irwin, the *kaloskagathos*, unlike the Laconian, chooses not only virtuous action, but virtue itself, for its own sake; complete, because his happiness consists in the exercise of all the virtues (not just contemplation).

something can be *kalon* or *agathon* whether it is a *hexis* or an *energeia* (1248b35-7, b23-4), it is only an *energeia* or *praxis* that can be pleasant. So it is in the noble activities of the good man that the highest pleasure is to be found, and that pleasure, goodness, and nobility meet.

We met earlier, in considering *NE* I, the inscription from Delos:

> *Kalliston to dikaiotaton, lôiston d'hugiainein*
> *Pantôn hêdiston d'hou tis erai to tuchein.*

In the *Eudemian Ethics* Aristotle takes this text and puts it at the beginning of the book as a challenge. He will set out to prove that *eudaimonia* alone is the best, the noblest, and the pleasantest of things. In the final book the challenge is met. The noble activities of the good man are the activities of perfect virtue in which *eudaimonia* consists. But it is in these noble activities that pleasure, goodness and nobility meet. So Aristotle has carried out the promise of his first paragraph to show that *eudaimonia* combines the three superlatives – noblest, best, and pleasantest – of the Deliac inscription.

Chapter 6

Justice in Plato and Aristotle: Withdrawal *versus* Engagement

Richard Kraut

1. Socrates' disengagement from ordinary politics

I will be discussing a significant difference in the political orientations of Plato and Aristotle, but I want to begin by saying that in one important respect Aristotle is a faithful adherent to a line of thought initiated in Plato's dialogues.[1] The figure of Socrates who speaks to us in the *Gorgias* and the *Republic* takes the proper task of politics – a task that has seldom been recognized or achieved – to be the moulding of the souls of citizens. 'Statecraft as Soulcraft' is the way the journalist George F. Will expresses (and endorses) the Socratic-Platonic-Aristotelian idea.[2] It is an idea that the liberal political tradition views with great suspicion, but today I will refrain from taking sides in this dispute. I merely want to set the stage for what is to come by emphasizing one of the ways in which Aristotle's political thought is continuous with that of Plato. I will briefly return to this point, later, for not every student of Aristotle's *Politics* would wholeheartedly agree with it. But in any case, one of the central ideas I want to get across today is that despite Aristotle's adherence to the tradition initiated by Socrates and Plato, there is one respect in which his political orientation is strikingly different from theirs. To put my point quite simply: I believe that Plato advises his readers to withdraw from politics in all but the most unusual circumstances: by contrast, Aristotle, as I read him, holds that justice requires a significant degree of engagement in political activity. If I am correct, we have here a striking contrast in their portraits of what a just person is like, and what justice requires us to do. There is nothing surprising or original in my idea that we find this sort of difference among the ancient philosophers. It is a familiar fact that in the Hellenistic world the Epicureans and Stoics differed in precisely this respect, the Epicureans advocating withdrawal from politics and the Stoics favouring engagement. But it is not so widely noted that a similar difference exists between the political orientations of Plato and Aristotle.

---

[1] This essay replicates, with only minor changes, a lecture given as part of the Keeling Colloquium in November 2001. Many of the ideas it contains are developed more fully in Chapter 4 of *Aristotle: Political Philosophy* (Oxford: Oxford University Press, 2002).

[2] George F. Will, *Statecraft as Soulcraft* (New York: Simon and Schuster, 1983).

I begin with a reminder of something that Socrates says to his jury in Plato's *Apology* (31c-32a, Grube trans.):

> It may seem strange that while I go around and give this advice privately and interfere in private affairs, I do not venture to go to the assembly and there advise the city. You have heard me give the reason for this in many places. I have a divine sign which Meletus has ridiculed in his deposition. ... This is what has prevented me from taking part in public affairs, and I think it was quite right to prevent me. Be sure, gentlemen of the jury, that if I had long ago attempted to take part in politics, I should have died long ago, and benefited neither you nor myself. Do not be angry with me for speaking the truth; no man will survive who genuinely opposes you or any other crowd and prevents the occurrence of many unjust and illegal happenings in the city. A man who really fights for justice must lead a private, not a public life, if he is to survive for even a short time (see too 32e).

When Socrates says that he has been commanded not to *prattein ta politika* (31d5: take part in politics) he does not mean, of course, that he shuns all of his political responsibilities. As he emphasizes in the *Apology*, he fought in several battles, and he served as a member of the *boulê* (Council), when it was his turn to do so (32b). What he means when he says that he did not practice politics was that he did not make it his business to attend meetings of the assembly; he had no ambition to rise to a level of leadership in its debates; he was not active in any political clubs or factions; he sought and held no high office; he did not volunteer to serve on juries. All of his efforts to improve the city were carried out by means of conversations in small groups. And in those conversations, he did not address himself to the details of civic affairs or partisan politics, but to the broadest issues of human life.

It is true that in the *Gorgias* he claims to be one of the few Athenians to have undertaken the true art of politics (521d). But that boast merely serves to emphasize the point I am making: Plato's readers are expected to recognize this as a radical re-conception of what politics really is. It is not something practised by ordinary leaders, who talk about walls, ships, alliances, enemies, war, and peace. Socrates withdraws from all of that, because such talk bypasses the deeper issues of human life, and is a mere attempt to gratify the many. Success in democratic politics is inevitably corrupting. The only way to keep oneself free from such corruption is to practise a different kind of politics, a politics of one-on-one conversation, for this is the only way one can make an improvement in someone else's life.

2. *Republic* and *Laws*

All of this is familiar ground. What I want to emphasize is that this disengagement from normal political life had a profound effect on the political philosophy of Plato's *Republic*. There are two passages in this work in which Plato gives his readers unequivocal guidance about how they are to conduct themselves in relationship to the ordinary (and therefore highly defective) cities in which they live. The first occurs in Book VI, at a point where Socrates is explaining why those who have a talent for philosophy and political leadership are so easily corrupted. He says that only extraordinary circumstances have prevented a few of these exemplary people from entering political life and destroying their souls. Some live in exile; others are citizens of small cities; Theages has been saved by his physical weakness, he himself by his divine sign (496b-d). Each has for some special reason taken refuge from the storm of political life, and each 'does his own' by keeping himself aloof from the lawlessness and madness around him (496d-e). The use of Socrates' definition of justice – *ta hautou prattôn* (496d6: doing one's own) – at this point in the text is quite striking. Plato is signaling that even though a talented philosopher will be assigned onerous political tasks in an ideal city, he is not only free to withdraw from politics in ordinary cities, but in fact justice consists precisely in such withdrawal.

That point is endorsed once again later in the *Republic*, at the end of Book IX, where Plato comes to the end of his description of the perfect city and the ideal condition of the human soul. He says that his portrait of the best city will retain its value even if it never comes into existence, because we can use it as an image of the harmony we should try to establish in our souls. He then adds one further thought: political activity must be shunned whenever it is corrupting, and therefore the politics of the ideal city are the only politics we ought to practise (592b). We are here given an unmistakable warning not to misinterpret the politics of the *Republic*: though much of it is about civic matters, the deeper subject is the soul, because it is only in extraordinary conditions that we should participate in political life. In all but the rarest of circumstances, the description of the ideal city is to serve no practical purpose other than to be the model we look to, as we withdraw from politics in order to save our souls.

It might be suggested that Plato's *Laws* reflects a greater interest in the politics of ordinary cities, and that the implicit message of that work is that we should be engaged in the political life of whatever city we happen to be living in, however defective its constitution is. But to interpret the *Laws* in this way would be to read far more into it than is warranted. No doubt, by describing a model city in which non-philosophers play an active role in political life, Plato is implying that if his readers have an opportunity to establish a colony that resembles the one he depicts, then their efforts will certainly be worthwhile. But colonies cannot be established whenever and wherever one pleases: their creation is an extraordinary event, and most people never have an opportunity to do so. Suppose, realistically, that the only politics a 4th century reader of the *Laws* can practise require active citizenship in some quite ordinary democracy or oligarchy, filled with all of the corrupt practices that are so distant from the ones described in the *Laws*. So far as I am aware, nothing in this dialogue suggests that its reader should play an active role in the political life of that kind of city. So, the counsel of withdrawal issued by Socrates in the *Republic* still stands: it is only in the most unusual circumstances that one should take an active part in the political life of one's city.

3. Aristotle: a program of political engagement

Turn now to the first chapter of Book IV of Aristotle's *Politics*. Here we are told that the student of politics must not confine himself to the study of an ideal regime. Nor would it be sufficient to supplement the study of an ideal regime with an investigation of the city that is the best that can be achieved by ordinary people. Politics must be a far more comprehensive discipline than that. It encompasses these four components:

    (A) the best constitution (1288b22);
    (B) which constitution is 'suitable for which' cities (b24);
    (C) the 'assumed constitution' (b28);
    (D) the constitution that is 'most suitable for all cities' (b34-5).

These are not perspicuous descriptions, but Aristotle gives us a better idea of what he has in mind as he proceeds. When we examine IV.1 carefully, and also consider the way its language re-appears in the remainder of Book IV, we can grasp his meaning easily enough. It emerges that the objects studied by the four branches of politics are these:

    (A) the constitution examined in Books VII-VIII: a colony established under the best possible circumstances;
    (B) regimes that cannot be called democracies or oligarchies because they are mixtures of both;
    (C) the various forms of democracy and oligarchy;
    (D) the constitution studied in Book IV, Chapter 11: the rule of the middle class.

Now, although I wish to emphasize the ways in which Aristotle departs from Plato, it must be admitted that, in proposing this way of organizing political theory, Aristotle is, in a sense, following his lead. For the *Laws* already contains the idea that one should not study only the very best constitution, but in addition one that is more easily put into practice by ordinary human beings. But we should not allow that point of similarity to obscure an equally important way in which Aristotle goes far beyond, and departs from, Plato. Aristotle is telling his students that they must study not simply the best and second-best types of political system, but *every* political system, including the ordinary democracies, oligarchies, and mixtures that are found throughout the Greek world. Aristotle is willing, as Plato is not, to advise his readers about how to take any political situation, no matter how bad, and make significant improvements in it. He even goes so far as to include advice about how a tyranny can be made less harsh. My thesis is that by insisting that students of political science make a comprehensive study of every type of constitution – and even of forms of rule that cannot be characterized as constitutional – Aristotle implicitly abandons the Socratic-Platonic thesis that participation in ordinary political life is inevitably corrupting.

Here is one further piece of evidence for my thesis: Ancient lists of Aristotle's works attribute to him a collection of 158 constitutions, and he alludes to them near the close of the *NE* (X.9, 1181b17). No doubt, he did not write all or many of them; but no scholar has ever questioned whether he was the guiding force in their collection and examination. This confirms the point I have been making, that Aristotle shows a strong interest in the workings of ordinary and highly defective cities. Furthermore, I do not believe, as Jaeger did, that this deep interest in bad constitutions as well as good represents only one stage of Aristotle's thinking.[3] For some reason, Jaeger made the mistake of thinking that Aristotle could not have simultaneously believed that political theory must examine both ideal and defective constitutions. But that this is the task of the legislator and political leader is precisely what we are told in *Politics* IV.1. And Aristotle commits himself to the same idea at the end of the *Nicomachean Ethics*, where he urges his students to make a study of existing constitutions, and then to turn to the topics that are explored in the *Politics*, including the question of which sort of political system is best. Jaeger convinced himself that Aristotle's career as a metaphysician involved a move away from high Platonism, to a modified form of Platonism, ending finally in an anti-Platonic embracing of empirical reality. And he then transferred this scheme to political theory, even though the evidence makes it obvious that it simply will not work.

Even so, it might be pointed out that I have not yet proved one of my claims. I hold not only that Aristotle is interested in defective constitutions and requires his students to study them, but that his reason for doing so is that he wishes to improve the lives of citizens who live in such cities. In other words, my thesis is that 'statecraft is soulcraft' can serve as the guiding idea behind the entire study of politics – not simply that part of it that investigates the ideal regime. Politics must study democracies and oligarchies in order to determine the ways in which the habits of those who are citizens in these regimes may be improved. The study of politics always has as its goal the good of all citizens, even when it examines the highly defective cities that are so prevalent in Greece.

Here is an alternative to my way of thinking: It might be said that when Aristotle carries out his study of defective regimes in the central books of the *Politics*, he is interested exclusively in the problem of how to make these regimes more stable – that is, more long-lasting, and less vulnerable to alteration or revolution. And why is he interested in this problem? Because he wants to make them safer places for a few people who possess the ethical virtues and who simply want to be left alone in order to pursue their interests in science and philosophy. According to this picture, Aristotle sees political activity in defective regimes as a mere means to an end: the creation of a safe environment for the philosophical-ethical life. He admits that political activity can be worthwhile for itself, but only when conditions are ideal or nearly so. If we adopt this way of reading the *Politics*, then there is far more similarity between Plato and Aristotle than I have proposed.

---

[3] Werner Jaeger, *Aristotle: Fundamentals of the History of his Development* (London: Oxford University Press, 1948), 2nd edn., Chapter 10.

I do not believe that the alternative reading of the *Politics* that I have just sketched can stand up to examination. To begin with, we should notice an often-overlooked remark that Aristotle makes in the final chapter of the *Nicomachean Ethics*, where he is considering the problem of how to complete his project by putting his ethical theory into practice. Arguments often fall on deaf ears, he admits. The many live by their feelings, and are motivated more by fear than shame. Habits are hard to change. What are we to do, then? Part of Aristotle's response to this question is that we must lower our sights: 'Perhaps we should be satisfied if, when all the things are present through which we seem to become decent, we get some share [*metalaboimen*] of virtue' (1179b18-20). I take that to mean that it is worthwhile to alter the habits of ordinary people, even when one does not successfully inculcate the virtues, because virtue is not an all-or-nothing matter. The excellences of character described in the ethical treatises can be approximated in varying degrees. That suggests that politics always has as its goal the inculcation of virtue – 'statecraft as soulcraft' – but that in corrupt regimes nothing better can be expected of most citizens than 'some share of virtue'.

When we turn to the *Politics* to see whether we can find Aristotle carrying forward this project, we find plenty of evidence that this is precisely what he is doing. In Book III Chapter 4, he makes a distinction between being a good man and being a good citizen: the former requires practical wisdom and does not vary from one place to another, whereas the latter merely requires right opinion, and involves skills that vary according to the kind of constitution that prevails in one's city. The virtue of a good citizen is apparently less demanding and impressive than the virtue of a good human being. It is, in other words, the best kind of virtue that one can reasonably expect the leading citizens of a democracy or an oligarchy to acquire.

Furthermore, when we turn to Aristotle's description of a city dominated by a large middle class, we find him saying that it is the best constitution 'for most cities and most human beings, judging neither by a virtue that is beyond the reach of ordinary people, nor by a kind of education that requires natural gifts and resources that depend on luck ...' (IV.11, 1295a25-9, trans. Reeve). Here it is unmistakable that Aristotle is lowering his sights: if one can create conditions favourable to the growth of a large middle class, then many citizens will have something that is similar to, though less impressive than, perfect virtue. And Aristotle's general formula for the reform of democracies and oligarchies is to make them resemble a city in which the middle class is dominant: the rich and the poor must be balanced against each other, so that the dominance of one class over the other is made less extreme.

I believe it is far-fetched to read all of Aristotle's theorizing about how to achieve some balance between rich and poor to be a mere strategy for making the world a safer environment for the few who are truly virtuous and enlightened. We should instead take Aristotle at his word, and regard his project in the *Politics* to be an attempt to find ways in which all citizens acquire 'some share of virtue'. If this interpretation is accepted, then there really is a striking difference after all between the political orientation of Plato and Aristotle. One of them counsels withdrawal from politics in all but the most favourable circumstances; the other sees politics as a worthwhile endeavour in nearly every kind of political environment.

4. Plato: doing one's own as political withdrawal

I now want to suggest that this contrast in political orientation corresponds to differences in the way Plato and Aristotle conceive of the virtue of justice. When they ask themselves what justice is, they emerge with different answers in part because they have radically different estimations of what it is possible to achieve, and what we are required to strive for, in the political arena. More specifically, my claim is that Plato's definition of justice in the *Republic* makes room for his conviction that a just person must withdraw from ordinary politics, whereas Aristotle's dual definitions of justice in Book V of the *Nicomachean Ethics* cater to his conviction that justice requires engagement in even highly defective political arrangements.

We have already seen some evidence in favour of this reading in a passage I cited earlier. Socrates says in Book VI of the *Republic* that talented people like Theages and Socrates have been prevented by one happy accident or another from entering the storm of political life, and so each 'does his own' by keeping himself aloof from the lawlessness and madness around him (496b-e). Here the formula that defines justice is applied to the disengagement from civic life. One of the jobs that Plato's formula does, one of the reasons he finds it appealing, is that he can use it to praise those who live a quiet life sheltered from the corrupting effects of politics.

We specialists in ancient philosophy have become so familiar with Plato's main ideas about justice that we are apt to forget, or perhaps never to realize in the first place, how remarkable it is that justice should be defined as the relationship a person has to himself. Plato takes the edge off his proposal to some degree by first looking at justice in a social setting. But he insists that his portrait of justice at work in an ideal social setting provides us with an image that we are to apply to the individual soul. The justice or injustice of a whole community is the product of the justice or injustice of some of its individuals, and therefore it is the latter that most fully reveals what justice is. This thought leads him to the conclusion that an act of justice need not involve two or more people; on the contrary, one can perform an act of justice in social isolation, provided that one's act flows from a proper understanding of one's good and a balance among the parts of one's soul. For example, when someone who has a harmonious soul gracefully passes up an opportunity to eat an extra piece of cake, because that would harm his body and make it less useful to his reason, that act of restraint counts for Plato as an act of justice. His contemporaries would find it a stretch, or worse, to call a solitary act of self-restraint *dikaion*. They would have no trouble seeing it as *sôphrôn* (temperate, moderate), but would resist the idea that it is *dikaion*. Plato, however, does not balk at using *dikaion* in unfamiliar ways, if doing so serves his philosophical purposes.

For similar reasons, he would insist that a philosopher who is contemplating the Forms is engaging in a just activity. The rule of reason is most fully expressed through the love of learning and the subordination of the rest of the soul to the project of leading a philosophical life. That thesis allows Plato to secure the conclusion that anyone who seeks to live a life of justice, but who has no opportunity to participate in the politics of an ideal regime, is best advised to lead a philosophical life. Philosophical activity is not a means to justice, and is certainly not merely a way of staying out of trouble. It constitutes just activity of the highest order, for it is in philosophy that reason finds its grandest vocation. The apolitical philosopher living in an ordinary (and therefore corrupt) society 'does his own' in two ways: on the outside, he minds his own business, and does no wrong to others; more profoundly, on the inside, each part of him does its own, because he is devoted with his whole soul to philosophy and the Forms.

Plato does not deny that the justice in the soul of one person *can* be of enormous benefit to others. In the right social conditions, the just person will rule the city and all other citizens will benefit from his wisdom. But his power to do good to others will lay dormant in circumstances that are far removed from what is ideal. That is why Plato's attempt to portray justice at work in a community is necessarily a picture of an ideal society. It is only here that we can see that justice is a good for the whole community, and not merely for the person who possesses it. Placing justice in the context of an ideal society is not merely a heuristic device – a way of teaching us a deeper lesson about what it is in the individual soul. It is part of Plato's attempt to persuade us that the virtue he calls *dikaiosunê* really deserves the name.

5. Aristotle's rejection of Platonic justice

Aristotle makes no mention of Plato's proposed definition of justice, when he offers his own definitions in Book V of the *NE*. He characterizes a just person as having two principal features: lawfulness and equality. The facts that he decides not to propose a single definition, and that neither of the two he offers says anything about doing one's own, reflect his profound differences with Plato. Surprisingly, he does not so much as mention Plato in this portion of the *Ethics*. But it is clear nonetheless that he regards Plato's conception of justice as bizarre, and hardly worthy of discussion. At a late point in Book V, he says: 'It is possible for there to be a sort of justice, by similarity and metaphor, not of a person to himself, but of certain parts of a person – not every kind of justice, but the kind that belongs to masters or households. For in these discussions the part of the soul that has reason is distinguished from the non-rational part' (1138b5-9, after Irwin). The allusion to the *Republic* is unmistakable. Aristotle is saying that he is willing to countenance talk of the rational part of the soul being just to the non-rational part, so long as we understand such talk as derivative, resting as it does on an analogy: reason is to the non-rational soul as a master is to a slave or a father to a son.

A defender of Plato would surely object as follows: Aristotle is dismissing the whole conception of justice in the *Republic* with not so much as an argument. He claims that the way of talking proposed by Socrates in the *Republic* is merely analogical. But nothing entitles Aristotle to dismiss Plato's entire project in this way.

Before we assess that criticism of Aristotle, we should take note of an equally breathtaking piece of dismissiveness nearby: at *NE* V.11, 1138a28-b5, Aristotle takes up one of the major questions raised in Plato's *Gorgias*: is it worse to suffer injustice or to do it? He gives the issue no more than a few lines, and simply says that theory can go only so far in answering it. That suggests that he regards the *Gorgias* as a work devoted to a question of little moment.

Aristotle's low regard for Plato's attempt to define justice is discernible in one of the opening moves of Book V: He claims that justice in the broad sense – justice as lawfulness – is an extraordinary quality: it is not just one virtue alongside others, but is in some way 'complete' or 'perfect' virtue. That might sound like a point of agreement with Plato, because the *Republic* also treats justice as a master-virtue. But no sooner does Aristotle make this point than he adds another, which is surely directed against Plato: justice is not complete or perfect in an unqualified way, but in relation to others. The inter-personal aspect of justice is built into Aristotle's conception of it from the start. The point he makes later in this book, that one can talk only by extension or metaphor of the justice between parts of the soul, is based on the premise that to be just is to be just in relation to other human beings.

It might be thought that Aristotle's rejection of Plato's thesis that justice is primarily an intra-personal relationship rests at bottom on a linguistic conservatism. Aristotle's goal, according to this interpretation, is to capture the way such terms as *dikaoios* and *dikaiosunê* are used by his contemporaries. He notes, correctly, that an act of refraining from over-eating could not normally be described as a manifestation of *dikaiosunê* – unless there is a background story according to which the real motives for such an act are to promote the common good.

But we should not think of Aristotle as a slave to the ordinary use of terms. His professed methodology requires him to pay close attention to the views of the wise as well as those of the many. And in his account of the virtues he often proposes that there are excellent qualities for which the Greek language has no names. If he had warmed to the idea that justice is basically an intra-personal relation, a desire to stick to common usage would not have kept him from agreeing with Plato.

I suggest that Aristotle dismisses Plato's idea that intra-personal justice is the paradigmatic form of justice for a combination of metaphysical, political, and empirical reasons. To begin with, he believes that Plato is deeply confused in his metaphysics. Although he agrees with Plato that there are other kinds of objects besides the ones we observe by means of the senses, he has no temptation to think of these objects as paradigms of orderliness, beauty, and justice. Justice is necessarily a quality of the human realm: it applies to human beings, the cities and constitutions that they construct, and the actions they perform. There simply are no objects besides these that can be called just or unjust. Accordingly, when we study what lies beyond the ken of the senses, we cannot claim to be performing just acts, for we are not entering into a relationship with anything that can be called just. If a philosopher wants to do what is just, then he must turn his attention to the changeable world of human beings, and seek improvements in those less than perfect objects. And he will find that his study of a world beyond the senses makes him no better able to pursue justice in this world than anyone else. It is practical wisdom one needs, in order to do justice in the world of the polis, not theoretical understanding.

Plato holds that those who (perhaps for motives that are at first quite honourable) pursue political careers in oligarchic or democratic constitutions while accepting their inherent limitations and accommodating themselves to them will almost inevitably become corrupted by them. The power of the crowd to influence their thinking and the lure of wealth and elite status will be difficult or impossible for them to resist, even when they start out with philosophical dispositions and talents. Or, if they refuse to make compromises, and overtly oppose these corrupt regimes, they are likely to be put to death. That is why Plato advocates withdrawal (in all but extraordinary circumstances): no great harm is done to ordinary cities when philosophers withdraw from them in order to do their own, because those cities are incapable of significant improvement, so long as they maintain their current constitutions.[4]

By contrast Aristotle's *Politics* rests on the assumption that Plato's pessimism is unfounded. Aristotle believes that although oligarchies and democracies are filled with injustices, it is nonetheless of great practical importance to make moral distinctions among these regimes, because some are far worse than others. And he also believes that there are ways for a good person to make improvements in these constitutions, or to prevent them from becoming even worse, without corrupting his soul. If Aristotle is right, then he has a serious charge to make against Plato and his followers: those who refuse to participate in the politics of imperfect but moderately decent cities not only fail to be paragons of justice – they can even be accused of *in*justice. They are in a position to make significant improvements in civic life, but rather than doing so, they stand by, as these cities grow increasingly corrupt. Although they refrain from doing injustice, that is not enough to qualify them as just people, because they care nothing for the ordinary legal systems in which the common good can be promoted, and some degree of lawfulness and equality achieved.

It should be emphasized that Aristotle's definition of justice in *NE* V makes it clear that the just person must be politically active. He is not merely someone who benefits some one person or some small handful of people besides himself; rather,

---

[4] In this paragraph, I am drawing on Plato's depiction, at *Republic* 492b-d, of the powerful influence exerted by the public life of democracies even on philosophical natures. For the distorting effects of wealth and status, see 494c-e. At 496b-d, he claims that the price to be paid by a good person fighting for justice in a democracy is death – implying that those who accommodate themselves to its limitations, in order to make reforms, will have compromised their virtue. In the *Statesman*, Plato continues to be deeply pessimistic about the possibility of improving democratic and oligarchic constitutions, for those who accept their basic frameworks: the best they can do is to enforce a legal rigidity (300e-301a) that would make life unbearable (299e). For his harsh words about such regimes in the *Laws*, see 712e, 715a-b, 832c. I am grateful to Robert Heinaman for seeking clarification of these points.

he must actively participate in politics. We should not be misled by his characterization of one form of justice as lawfulness (*nomimos*) into thinking that the person who is just in this sense merely obeys the laws and follows the customs of his community. No genuine virtue can be as passive and easy as that; a real ethical virtue requires practical wisdom. I take Aristotle's meaning to be that the application of laws to particular situations is often a difficult matter; so too is the matter of creating new laws, when they are needed. Someone who is just in the broad sense (that is, someone who is lawful) has the emotional and intellectual skills that allow him to carry out those difficult tasks. This feature of justice – that it requires political activity – becomes all the more evident when we turn to the other component of Aristotle's dual definition of justice: the just person is equal. Justice in this sense is a virtue that enables one to make astute judgements about how to distribute goods and to make good decisions about how to correct matters when they have gone wrong. Aristotle's analysis of this skill presupposes that justice as equality operates in a political context: the kind of distribution he is talking about is one that takes place in the assembly, and the kind of correction he is talking about takes place in the courts. In other words, anyone who possesses the virtue of justice is active in the assembly and the courts: someone very different from the man who is praised in the final words of the *Phaedo* as being the most just man of his time.

Notice the similarity between Aristotle's characterization of justice as a political virtue and his idea that courage is displayed preeminently on the battlefield. The courageous person, as Aristotle conceives him, is prepared to die in the defence of his community. Aristotle does not say anything to imply that the community that is defended by the courageous person must be ideal or nearly so. Rather, he seems to be assuming that one owes it to one's city to defend it in battle, even when that city is a democracy or an oligarchy, and is therefore the site of significant injustices. Similarly, in his discussion of justice in Book V, he seems to be assuming that a just person's lawfulness and equality will be put into action even in defective regimes. The ethical works do not presuppose an ideal or nearly ideal social setting as the background to their definitions of the virtues. That, I think, is not an oversight on Aristotle's part. Rather, it represents a deliberate move away from Plato's idea that we will never understand what justice is unless we see it in operation in an ideal setting. Aristotle's portrait of an ideal city, in Books VII and VIII of the *Politics*, is not even present in the same treatise as his analysis of the virtue of justice.

It might now be asked whether Aristotle's conception of justice allows for the possibility that he could count himself as a just man. He attends no meetings of the assembly, and is a member of no jury, because he lacks the status of a citizen. Does he have to concede, then, that he fails to possess justice both in the sense of lawfulness and that of equality? And if he lacks this one virtue, then must he not admit that he lacks all of them? What then makes it possible for him to write with so much confidence about what the virtues are?

The mistake embodied in this line of questioning lies in its too narrow conception of what is involved in being a lawful and equal person. Aristotle, after all, is someone who devotes a considerable amount of time to the study of law and equality, and to the training of students who play a leading role in the life of many Greek cities. One need not confine one's political activity to one city, in order to count as a just person. One need not be a citizen to affect the lives of cities. On the contrary, if one organizes the study of the legal systems of many scores of cities, and trains students to make what reforms they can in these cities by aiming at a greater degree of equality, then one can be counted as a lawful and equal person. Aristotle can point to himself as the paradigm of someone who shows how it is possible to lead both a life of contemplation and a politically active life.

6. Commercial and conventional justice

In the time that remains, I want to call attention to three further differences between Plato's and Aristotle's theories of justice. The first has to do with Aristotle's division of justice as equality into the spheres of distribution, correction, and reciprocity. By dividing justice in the narrow sense into these three spheres, Aristotle is saying, in effect, that to be a just person (in this narrow sense) requires that one perform well in all three respects: one must be an equal person when one allocates honours (and especially political offices), when one makes judgements as a juror, and when one exchanges goods with others. I suggest that we read Aristotle's account of justice in commercial exchange as his way of correcting Plato's idea that we can find a kind of justice in the activities of ordinary craftsmen, farmers, and the like. Plato's thesis is that in an ideal polis the justice of a craftsman would consist precisely in his practising his craft and leaving the jobs for which he is ill suited to others. But nothing in Aristotle's analysis of justice leaves room for the strange idea that when a cobbler makes a pair of shoes, he is acting justly. Aristotle agrees with Plato that there is a kind of justice that craftsmen, farmers, and traders can practise; but it does not consist in crafting, farming, and trading, but rather in fair (that is, equal) practices in one's commercial interactions with others.

A second piece of anti-Platonism can be found in the distinction Aristotle makes in *NE* V.7 between natural justice on the one hand and legal or conventional (*nomikos*) justice on the other. I would like to focus on the latter half of this distinction, because it is here that I detect a further departure from Plato. Legal justice is 'that which at first makes no difference whether it is done one way or another, but does make a difference, after it has been established' (1134b20-21). Aristotle's examples of legal justice are these: it costs one mina to ransom someone; a sacrifice consists in one goat rather than two sheep. Later in the chapter, he says that legal justice depends on agreement and expediency (1134b35), and compares it to the variability of measures: 'the measures for wine and corn are not everywhere equal, but in wholesale markets are larger, in retail markets smaller' (1135a1-3).

Legal justice evidently has three characteristics: First, it exists only by virtue of being recognized and practised by some human community. Second, any rule of legal justice has a number of close cousins that could have served the community as well. There is no reason why a measure of wine has to be precisely this size or that, or why the ransom of a prisoner must be exactly this sum rather than another. Anything within a certain range would have done as well. In this sense, there is something arbitrary in all legal justice. (Nonetheless, some or all of the members of the community may fail to recognize that their way of doing things is not uniquely correct. Blind habit may incline them to suppose that only one goat will please the gods.)[5] Third, because legal justice rests on an arbitrary choice within a certain range, we will often find variations in what is legally just in different communities. It would in fact be surprising if all communities had the same practices, when their norms depend on some arbitrary starting point.

Legal or conventional justice is by definition a creation of human beings, and does not exist apart from their activities and thoughts. What is conventionally just is at first a matter of indifference, and then it comes to seem just only because it is widely accepted in a community. Plato can have no use for such a notion. According to his way of thinking, whatever is just is so apart from what we do or say. We cannot make a practice just merely by participating in it; rather, we must participate in it because it already is just.

Furthermore, the examples Aristotle gives of legal justice suggest that Plato's portrait of ordinary political life as a cesspool of corruption is highly exaggerated. Aristotle has no difficulty giving examples of existing practices that are just: they are as mundane and simple as the price of ransom or the price of an animal to be sacrificed. The justice of these practices consists simply in the fact that they promote the common good in existing cities. There is no need to show that they would be adopted in some ideal city, in order to certify that they really are just. (In fact, they might not be adopted in an ideal city, because as Aristotle points out, some close cousin of these practices would serve their purpose equally well.)

Aristotle's general point is that if we take the world as it is, we should have no trouble finding examples of just laws. No doubt, there is considerable injustice as well, but Aristotle believes that it is a serious mistake – one made by Plato – to draw a uniformly dismal picture of ordinary civic life and to claim that whoever gets involved in it will inevitably lose his soul. Even if it is conceded that on balance existing cities are unjust, we can find some justice in them, in all but the most extreme cases.[6]

---

[5] The examples of legal justice that Aristotle gives in *NE* V.7 may mislead us into supposing that these conventions always regulate matters of little concern, and that their arbitrariness is easily recognized. But that may not be the case. For example, at *Pol.* 1335b19-25, he implies that prohibiting the exposure of normal infants is a matter of legal but not natural justice. See Kraut, *Aristotle Politics Books VII and VIII* (Oxford: Clarendon Press, 1997), 154-5.

[6] For a fuller treatment, see *Aristotle: Political Philosophy*, chapter 4, and especially the discussion of his dictum that 'everything lawful is in a way just' (*NE* 1129b12).

7. The false unity of Platonic justice

The very idea that justice is not one thing – that it must receive two definitions (lawfulness on the one hand, equality on the other) is of course already a departure from Plato. But one of Aristotle's two definitions seems to be an attempt to acknowledge that there is a sense in which justice is, as Plato claims, the major virtue. For he says (*NE* 1129b26) that justice as lawfulness is *teleia* – complete, perfect. It is not one ethical virtue among many (as is justice as equality) but the whole of it.

He then adds: it is not complete or perfect in an unqualified way, but rather in relation to others (b26-7). What he means can best be conveyed by way of example: The actions of a temperate person can be divided into those that are concerned solely with his own affairs and those that bear on his relations with others. For example, there are times when the exercise of his ability to refrain from overeating benefits no one besides himself; when there is an abundance of food, he need not confine himself to a modest portion for anyone's sake but his own. But when there is just enough food to go round, temperance benefits others as well; by taking modest portions, the temperate person leaves others their due. Similarly, there may be times when a courageous person benefits no one but himself. For example, in isolated hand-to-hand combat, his control over fear may enable him to save his life, even though no one else besides himself is at risk. But on many other occasions, courage enables one to save the lives of one's comrades.

When an act of temperance or courage is done for the good of the political community, then it is not only an act of temperance or courage, but an act of justice as well (1129b17-19). For that is precisely what justice in the broad sense is: the exercise of the other ethical virtues in accordance with law for the good of the political community. Notice how different it is from those other virtues. It is not exercised on its own, but is always tied up with the employment of one of the other moral skills. A courageous act is not at the same time a temperate act or a generous act. But an act that exercises justice in the broad sense always expresses one of the other ethical virtues at the same time: it is courageous, or temperate, or just in the narrow sense, and so on. That is what Aristotle means to convey when he says that justice in the broad sense is the whole of virtue. Justice involves every other virtue, because just acts are not only just but also temperate (on some occasions), courageous (on other occasions), and so on; and every other virtue exercised for the sake of the good of the political community is at the same time an act of justice.

Here, then, is the final contrast I wish to draw: For Plato, justice is a single psychological condition, a harmony between reason, spirit, and appetite. But for Aristotle, justice in the broad sense is not a unitary psychological state. The motives that lead to injustice are many and diverse: excessive anger, fear, appetite, love of money, love of honour, and so on. A just person has learned how to avoid all of these extreme states (as well as the corresponding deficiencies), but that is not because there is some single emotional skill that he has developed. There is no one fund of energy on which the just person draws, no unitary psychological state that explains why he is able to master his anger, his fear, and other such emotions. Justice in the broad sense is not related to some single emotional condition, as courage is to fear, temperance to pleasure, and so on. Rather, the unity of justice lies in one's external relations: it is the skill that allows us to promote the good of the political community by respecting social norms.

Plato's attitude towards the political realities of the fourth century made him seek justice in a unitary state that lies within the human soul. By Aristotle's lights, Plato's attempt to understand what justice is makes the mistake of looking for unity where there is multiplicity, and of failing to acknowledge the many ways in which a just human being can and must make improvements in already existing communities. That, I think, is the deep significance of Aristotle's remark that justice is complete or perfect justice – not without qualification, but only in relation to others (*NE* 1129b26-7).

Reply to Richard Kraut

Christopher Rowe

Richard Kraut's paper is richly ambitious, and I need not apologize for any failure on my part to cover all of its aspects. What I propose to do is, first, to try to describe the main points in the paper that I wish to discuss, and then to single out those parts that I find difficult to accept, and why. If I devote most of the space available to criticism, that is not for the sake of it, but because there is a fundamental difference between us: while Kraut sees an essential discontinuity between Plato and Aristotle on the question of political involvement, I find an essential *continuity*.

Kraut's position can, I believe, be summed up roughly like this. Both Plato and Aristotle subscribe to (what is summed up in) the slogan 'statecraft as soulcraft': that is, for both thinkers, the role of political expertise in the proper sense is to make the citizens better, to improve them. But this similarity between the Platonic and Aristotelian camps hides a massive, and fundamental, divergence, namely that while 'Plato advises his readers to withdraw from politics in all but the most unusual circumstances ... Aristotle, as I read him, holds that justice requires a significant degree of engagement in political activity' (153). Real 'statecraft', in the Platonic view, will operate only, or mainly, in ideal circumstances, i.e. in circumstances where either it is possible to build Callipolis, or to found a colony like Magnesia; otherwise its practitioners, who are by implication philosophers in the Platonic/Socratic mould, will keep out of politics, though with proper regard to their responsibilities as citizens, and 'the description of the ideal city [will] serve no practical purpose other than to be the model we look to, as we withdraw from politics in order to save our souls' (155, with reference to the end of *Republic* IX). For Aristotle, by contrast, political expertise has a role in any city; people's lives can be made better *anywhere*. (That is why he has all those researchers studying constitutions.) And 'this contrast in political orientation corresponds to differences in the way Plato and Aristotle conceive of the virtue of justice' (159). Plato's conception of justice – that is, in the *Republic* – allows the possibility of one's performing an act of justice even 'in social isolation', that is, 'provided that one's act flows from a proper understanding of one's good and a balance among the parts of one's soul' (*ibid.*); thus does Plato make 'room for his conviction that a just person must withdraw from ordinary politics' (*ibid.*). Aristotle, however, implicitly but firmly rejects this view of justice, especially when he insists that justice, in its broader sense, has essentially to do with our relationship to other people. Rejecting Platonic metaphysics as he does, he has no time for the idea that doing philosophy might be 'just', e.g. by relating to some supra-sensible 'just' object (i.e. like the

Form of Justice); only human beings, cities and constitutions, and actions can be just (161). Again, according to Kraut, Aristotle rejects Plato's view that ordinary cities 'are incapable of significant improvement': 'some are far worse than others', and 'he also believes that there are ways for a good person to make improvements in these constitutions, or to prevent them from becoming even worse, without corrupting his soul' (162). And we find the same view reflected in the *Ethics*, insofar as 'Aristotle's definition of justice in *NE* V [and so *Eudemian Ethics* IV] makes it clear that the just person must be politically active' (*ibid.*), sc. in his own city, whether ideal or otherwise. Finally, Kraut discusses some further ways in which, as he alleges, the Aristotelian conception of justice distances itself from the Platonic.

One of Kraut's starting-points here is clearly the idea of Platonic justice as 'intra-personal': it is a matter of the relationship of the three parts of one's soul to each other – such that any action flowing from a soul whose parts are in the right relationship to each other, and 'doing their own proper thing', will count as 'just': so e.g. a philosopher's philosophizing ('contemplating the Forms', 159), or, presumably, a cobbler's making a pair of shoes, may themselves count as just. Now it might be that Aristotle found such a view of justice in the *Republic*, and was responding to such a view in the *Ethics*. But I think that if he was doing any such thing, under the impression that that was in fact Plato's view of the matter, then he was radically misreading Plato. That is, I think it a mistake to suppose that Plato meant to define justice in such terms.

My argument goes as follows. What he most urgently wants to do is to undermine the view, represented both by Thrasymachus in *Republic* I and in the challenge put to Socrates at the beginning of Book II, that justice is simply and exclusively a matter of just actions. No, this is an incorrect notion of justice, and of being just: being just is a matter of having a just soul, and, insofar as 'being just' is a matter of actually doing things, it is also – and crucially – a matter of performing the actions that flow from having that kind of soul. All of this so far looks to me a pretty uncontroversial reading; the controversial part comes when one asks what sorts of actions those are, i.e. these ones that are supposed to flow from a just soul, so being themselves appropriately labelled as 'just'. Is it, as Kraut supposes, any and every action that might be performed by someone in whose soul each 'part' is 'doing its own proper thing', 'doing what belongs to it'; or is it rather, as I propose, those actions that are indicated by Socrates when he introduces his 'absolute confirmation' that he and Glaucon have identified justice properly, at 442d10-e2?

> 'Well then', I said, 'it isn't the case at all, is it, that our view of justice is being blunted so as to make it seem to be something different from what it appeared as being in the city?'[1]
> 'It doesn't seem so to me', he said.

---

[1] I would not like to be pressed too hard on this translation of 442d7-8, but it will suffice – since nothing much hangs on it – in this context.

'No, because (*gar*)', I said, 'we could confirm it absolutely, if some [aspect of us] still, in the soul, disputes it, by applying the vulgar things to it [i.e. to the case in point?].'
'What are *they*?'

'The vulgar things' turn out, of course, to be standard examples of unjust actions: it is agreed to be a soul not of the sort described which would be most likely to do such things as embezzling gold and silver deposited with him, robbing temples, thieving, betraying friends or cities, breaking oaths or contracts, committing adultery, or neglecting parents or gods.

The sentence in question is sometimes under-translated: it is not merely 'If there are still any doubts in our soul about this, we could dispel them altogether by appealing to ordinary cases',[2] but something much stronger than that – introducing *ta phortika*, i.e. those things vulgarly identified with justice and injustice, will *altogether confirm* the account of justice that has been given, in terms of 'doing one's own proper thing'.[3] It is not merely a matter of 'dispelling' residual 'doubts', but apparently of giving direct confirmation. How so? Because, or so I claim, what Socrates has been searching for all along is precisely that state of the soul which will reliably lead to our doing and not doing the sorts of things typically regarded as just and unjust. These things are 'vulgar' only in the sense that people commonly suppose that doing/not doing them is all there is to justice. It would be vulgar to use them as the sole criterion; as it is, Socrates and the others claim to have established another aspect of justice, and now the 'vulgar' criterion can be applied precisely in order to test whether or not that claim is justified.

What I am proposing, in short, is that 'Platonic justice' here in the *Republic* is not the strange thing it is often supposed to be. Yes, it is distinct from 'vulgar' justice, justice as conceived by the common person. But Socrates does not want to substitute it for 'vulgar' justice in the sense of displacing the latter entirely; rather, he wants to deepen the 'vulgar' conception by adding to a set of descriptions of mere actions a description of a state of the soul whose presence will be necessary for those mere actions to count as 'just' at all.[4] His point is that it is not how one

---

[2] This version is to be found in the revised version of the Hackett translation of Plato's *Republic* (C.D.C. Reeve, revising the version of G.M.A. Grube); Desmond Lee's Penguin translation is similar. (Grube's original, by contrast, had 'If any part of our soul still disputes this, we could altogether confirm it ...'.)

[3] 'If something in the soul still disputes it': i.e., as perhaps Grube's translation implies (see n. 2), if some individual part of the soul wants to claim justice as belonging exclusively to it?

[4] I have no space here to discuss the implications of this, if any, for the long debate started by David Sachs' 'A Fallacy in Plato's *Republic*', (*Philosophical Review* 72 (1963), 141-58; reprinted in G. Vlastos (ed.), *Plato: A Collection of Critical Essays*, II (Notre Dame: University of Notre Dame Press, 1978), 35-51). But Kraut's view of 'Platonic justice' seems at any rate to have its roots in that debate. Cf. Raphael Demos' reply to Sachs, also reprinted in the Vlastos volume: 'Platonic justice is an individual virtue – how a person behaves toward himself; in fact, it is the harmonious realization of the soul in all its parts. But so defined, justice is self-regarding' ('A Fallacy in Plato's *Republic*?', 52-6 at 54). Or is it

acts that makes one just, but one's internal state. But that is perfectly consistent with there being, still, a particular set of actions that are just, i.e. (at least?) the sort people ordinarily call just.

The obvious objection will be that having one's soul-parts arranged in the required fashion will lead to all sorts of actions, not just to standardly just ones – and that is indeed, I take it, Kraut's thought. But then, in the very next passage, Plato seems to me to act to prevent this thought.

> But in truth, as it seems, justice was (we agreed) this sort of thing, but not in relation to a person's external activity, but in relation to that within him, truly in relation to himself in the parts of himself – his not having allowed each thing in himself, each of the kinds of thing there are in his soul, to do what belongs to another thing, or to meddle with each other's business, but in reality having set his own affairs in order and having established rule, himself over himself ... [I here omit a substantial portion of text], and going on to act on this basis, if ever he does anything either in relation to the acquisition of money or looking after his body, or indeed some political act, or in relation to individual contracts, in all these things thinking and calling a just and fine action whichever action preserves this inner harmony and indeed helps to achieve it, and (calling) wisdom the knowledge that is in charge of such action ... (443c9-e7).

What is significant here is that even while continuing (of course) to emphasize the point about the internal nature of justice and injustice, Socrates clearly marks off a particular sphere for them – and one that looks remarkably like, and recalls, that 'vulgar' list of unjust actions he adverted to in 442e-443a. If justice is relevant to things like the philosopher's contemplation and the cobbler's cobbling, I suggest that it is so only insofar as justice in the city depends on everyone's 'doing their own' (but most of all, of course, on philosophers' and not anyone else's doing the ruling: 434a-c), and insofar as there are questions about when it is just for a philosopher to contemplate (519b-521b).

What underlies the whole account of justice in the individual soul is the *Republic*'s diagnosis of the cause of vice: the capacity of non-rational desires to outgrow their proper limits. To say that 'Platonic justice' is an ordered, harmonious state in which each part of the soul keeps to its own patch (as it were) is an accurate but in my view incomplete description: what it hides is the dynamic character that Socrates attributes to the appetitive desires above all, which makes them permanently liable – unless kept in check – to get out of hand. As he tells us later, at the beginning of Book IX (see especially 572b), even the best people are

fairer to say that Kraut, like Demos, is simply paraphrasing Socrates himself at *Republic* IV, 443c9ff.? If so, my response is that the paraphrase is misleading to the extent that it leaves out the last part of the sentence that begins at 443c9, where justice as a state of the soul is linked to external and other-regarding actions. (But even in the part of the sentence before that, how exactly is each part supposed to do or not do 'its own' in isolation from action? The description of early education in Books II-III scarcely insists on it, and it is not clear in any case why it should.) See further below.

still at risk. This is what primarily explains why in 443e the titles 'just' and 'fine' are said to attach to those actions that preserve and help to bring about the relevant internal state. No doubt a soul in that state will perform all sorts of different actions. But it will not be enough that an action merely flows from an appropriate disposition of soul-parts; it must also maintain and bring about that disposition. Nor is this a purely arbitrary demand. The trouble with unjust actions, even or especially standardly unjust ones, is precisely that they stem from and bring about the wrong internal condition, in which the parts of the soul do not keep to their own: once one has robbed one temple, or killed one person, the easier it will be to rob or kill another, contrary to what reason demands. (Again, that is just what the appetitive part is like: give it the slightest encouragement, and everything starts to go wrong, or goes on going wrong.) From this point of view, which is that of 443c-444a, contemplating Forms and cobbling might well be things that are done by just people, but they hardly seem to count as just actions. What it is to act justly is to act in such a way, in contexts where unreason might begin to get some encouragement, that it actually gets none.

In all of this – as I shall go on to suggest – there is hardly anything with which Aristotle would disagree, though he would and does put it differently, and with different emphases (in different kinds of contexts). But equally, there is surely little to provide the basis for the allegedly un-Aristotelian quietude with respect to non-ideal politics that Kraut discovers in the *Republic*.[5] Indeed, the list here in 443-4 of spheres in which 'just and fine action' will be found specifically includes the political; and this is all the more significant to the extent that Socrates seems suddenly to have started talking about the ordinary world, not the world of Callipolis: no single person in Callipolis, after all, will be found doing all the things in question – acquiring money, looking after his body, doing politics, making contracts. Perhaps Socrates has forgotten himself for the moment; certainly he has become all of a sudden rather passionate. But it does look rather as if he is, now, implicitly extending his definition of justice beyond the bounds of the ideal city. What will make anyone, anywhere, count as 'just' will be his or her doing those things that produce the right order among the parts of his or her soul; but also, conversely, those actions will count as just, in any relevant contexts (including the political), that flow from such an order among the soul-parts.[6]

Thus I myself find nothing in Plato's notion of justice, even as portrayed in the *Republic*, that points in the direction of political quietism. Whether or not Plato thought philosophers ought to involve themselves in the politics of non-ideal states, I do not believe it has much to do with his view of justice. Kraut argues that Plato's definition of justice 'makes room for his conviction that a just person must

---

[5] I am struck, too, by the fact that nothing like the *Republic*'s definition of justice, if that is understood *simply*, or primarily, in terms of the soul's internal state, without or with only secondary reference to action, seems to play a significant role anywhere else in Plato; indeed, whenever we have that familiar Platonic triad, 'the just, the fine and the good' – all neuter plurals – the things referred to will surely always at least include actions.

[6] But these too could be described as actions that 'preserve' the internal order of the soul.

withdraw from ordinary politics': that is, as I understand this, a person will be just simply by showing the right sense of priorities that will go with philosophizing (in the case of a natural philosopher), or with cobbling, or farming (in the case of someone at any rate not endowed by nature with the qualities required for philosophy). My own reconstruction of the argument of the *Republic* in this case is rather that justice will be displayed in any and every relevant area that a person is involved in; but that – and this is the point that is added, quite separately from the argument of Book IV, at the end of Book IX – the best sort of people had better stay away from politics, in the same way that they will keep away from any other sort of activity (money-making, the pursuit of honours) that might disturb and corrupt the correct state of their souls (591b-592b).

Is there any difference here from what Aristotle tells us? I think not. Kraut's claim that Aristotle's just man is presupposed to be politically involved is hard to defend. For one thing, *Nicomachean Ethics* VI (= *Eudemian* V).8 clearly distinguishes political expertise from 'practical wisdom' (or, as Sarah Broadie and I prefer, just 'wisdom'),[7] while calling it the same disposition; the chapter generally indicates that politicians are a specific group of experts, by no means co-extensive with the 'wise'. In other words, there is – at least so far – no more expectation that the Aristotelian good man will take a leading role in debates in the assembly than a Socrates.[8]

Aristotle's own writing, Kraut claims, might itself count as an example of the involvement of the good man in non-ideal politics; at the same time he (Aristotle: I quote Kraut, 156) 'is willing, as Plato is not, to advise his readers about how to take any political situation, no matter how bad, and make significant improvements in it'. Now this seems, on the face of it, to be a real moment of difference between Plato and Aristotle. Plato, after all, seems only too willing to give up on any existing forms of political arrangement, and refuse even to call them 'constitutions' – even so being roundly criticized by Aristotle for not going far enough (*he* says that the three 'deviant' types of constitution are all totally 'mistaken', or just

---

[7] See Sarah Broadie and Christopher Rowe, *Aristotle: Nicomachean Ethics* (translation by Rowe, philosophical commentary by Broadie) (Oxford: Oxford University Press, 2002).

[8] Contrast Kraut (163):

> Justice [as equality] is a virtue that enables one to make astute judgements about how to distribute goods and to make good decisions about how to correct matters when they have gone wrong. Aristotle's analysis of this skill presupposes that justice as equality operates in a political context: the kind of distribution he is talking about is one that takes place in the assembly, and the kind of correction he is talking about takes place in the courts. In other words, anyone who possesses the virtue of justice is active in the assembly and the courts.

This looks an insecure set of inferences from Aristotle's text: (a) if 'correction' involves the courts, I see no reason to suppose that Aristotelian man has to display all the aspects of all the 'virtues'; it is simply that, if he does find himself in such-and-such a situation, he will behave in such-and-such a way. (b) 'Distribution' might take place in the assembly, but need not be restricted to that arena; what about arbitrations (e.g.)? We need more evidence that Aristotle's man will be found in the assembly. (And without such evidence, he does not look too different from the apolitical Socrates that Kraut describes on 153-4 of his paper.)

'mistaken as a class': *holôs ... exêmartêmenas, Politics* 1289b9).[9] But I still wonder why, then, Plato kept writing about politics, and not just about ideal states. If the *Republic* is really about our souls and how to improve them, what are we to say about the *Politicus* and the *Laws*? Why exactly should we suppose that Plato's only aim in going on describing ideal states, ideal cities, is to say what they would look like, if only they could come into existence, without any hope that he might encourage them to do so? *Republic* VI, indeed, does suggest how even Callipolis – or something like it – might come into existence. True, an approximation to the ideal would surely have to have ceased to be a democracy, or an oligarchy. But does that mean that no existing state could be mended, i.e. by being transformed? If not, Plato will after all have something to say to his readers about ordinary cities. (In general, I should like to claim that Plato's purpose, in the political sense, is in fact something like that of trying to persuade existing governments to become more philosophical. To defend such a notion in Plato, I should refer above all to the first part of *Republic* V.)

To be sure, Aristotle appears to have a much more direct interest in the non-ideal. He is also more evidently a believer in the possibility of gradualism. (Plato, paradoxically, is perhaps an implicit advocate of revolution.) But there are contrary signs here too. One can perhaps write off that remark in *Politics* IV.2 as a piece of rhetoric (in the event, Aristotle does not seem to regard all existing forms of constitution as simply 'mistaken'). But it is much more difficult to deal with *Politics* III.4 (my final topic). Kraut takes this chapter as favouring his general interpretation of Aristotle's view of politics, as having 'the inculcation of virtue' as its goal – with the qualification that 'in corrupt regimes nothing better can be expected of most citizens than "some share of virtue"' (158):

> When we turn to the *Politics* to see whether we can find Aristotle carrying forward this project [sc. the inculcation of virtue?], we find plenty of evidence that this is precisely what he is doing. In [III.4], he makes a distinction between being a good man and being a good citizen: the former requires practical wisdom and does not vary from one place to another; whereas the latter merely requires right opinion, and involves skills that vary according to the kind of constitution that prevails in one's city. The virtue of a good citizen is apparently less demanding and impressive than the virtue of a good human being. It is, in other words, the best kind of virtue that one can reasonably expect the leading citizens of a democracy or an oligarchy to acquire.

This reading of III.4, however, seems to me optimistic. Most of the chapter, I think, is openly concerned with the difference between the good man and the good citizen

---

[9] My analysis of the tasks assigned to the 'statesman' (the *politikos*) in IV.1 is different from Kraut's; see e.g. Rowe, *Classical Quarterly* 27 (1977), 159-72, an essay which also takes a different line from Kraut's on some other significant issues in the *Politics* (particularly on the aim of the so-called 'empirical' books IV-VI); more recently, Rowe, 'Aristotelian Constitutions', in C.J. Rowe and M. Schofield (eds.), *The Cambridge History of Greek and Roman Political Thought* (Cambridge: Cambridge University Press, 2000), 366-89.

under the *best* constitution (1276b35-7); and when it turns to 'political' rule, i.e. where rule alternates between citizens (1277b8-9), it presupposes 'virtue' among those citizens – and so, evidently, to go by III.5, a better form of 'citizen' constitution, i.e. what will be called a *politeia*. Democracies and oligarchies will be declared deviations in III.6-7, because they do not look to the common good, but only to the good of the rulers; and this by itself entails the presence of a different conception of justice (specifically, given Aristotle's definition of citizenship, among the leaders). The classic text on democratic and oligarchic conceptions of justice is, of course, III.9. It seems to me that on this account, Aristotle ought to regard full political involvement in an oligarchic or democratic regime as every bit as corrupting as Plato did.[10] We are here surely not at all far from that idea of withdrawal from politics that Plato expresses, in different ways, in a whole variety of dialogues. If there is no place for a Socrates at the head of some democratic or oligarchic party, so neither is there for Aristotle's man. Writing about inferior constitutions is one thing (whether dialogues or treatises), participation another.

And yet: one might well ask how the gradualism Aristotle apparently envisages in *Politics* IV-VI is to be effected, if good men stand back from political activity as such. Presumably these books must presuppose a kind of descent from the more austere and theoretical thought-world of Book III. There will, after all, be decent people even in deviant regimes, who can make a difference. And again, as Books IV-VI recognize (and III does not), there are all sorts of different *kinds* of democracies and oligarchies. The world of the *Ethics*, whether *Nicomachean* or *Eudemian*, evidently belongs to this same less austere perspective. But Plato's recognition of the possibility of greater or lesser approximations to the ideal – even, as I claim, in the *Republic* – seem to me to leave him headed in the same direction.

To sum up, and in brief: I propose that, rather than possessing different 'political orientations' in Kraut's sense, Plato and Aristotle have orientations which are – despite the old myth about them, that the one has his head in the clouds and the other his feet on the ground – remarkably *similar*. It is not for nothing, in my view, that the *Politics* begins by resembling a continuation of, or commentary on, Plato's *Politicus*; but that is another story. Both philosophers propose that ordinary sorts of

---

[10] On the 'middle' (class) constitution, and specifically on IV.11, 1295a25-9 (which makes this constitution the best 'for most cities and most human beings, judging neither by a virtue that is beyond the reach of ordinary people, nor by a kind of education that requires natural gifts and resources that depend on luck ...'), Kraut comments (158):

> Here it is unmistakable that Aristotle is lowering his sights: if one can create conditions favourable to the growth of a large middle class, then many citizens will have something that is similar to, though less impressive than, perfect virtue. And Aristotle's general formula for the reform of democracies and oligarchies is to make them resemble a city in which the middle class is dominant: the rich and the poor must be balanced against each other, so that the dominance of one class over the other is made less extreme.

But this immediately raises the crucial question: what have democracy and oligarchy to do, and so what has any compromise version of them to do, with *virtue*? And the same question is surely raised just by Aristotle's classification of democracy and oligarchy as 'deviant'.

cities and constitutions must be corrupting, and that good, thinking people should not get involved in helping to run them. Yet both are in fact in the business of reforming existing political arrangements, insofar as both write (presumably, at least in part) in order to try to help them reform. Again, even if the Platonic good man will not *willingly* be involved in politics, unless an extraordinary chance for total reform offers itself (if this is what *Republic* 592a means), nevertheless if it comes to it he will do it justly, and will be the sort of person to do it justly – as Socrates did as a member of the Council, when he stood out against an illegal motion. And for Aristotle too, there seems to be plenty of room for the good person to be involved politically, even if, strictly, he cannot become a politician, whether oligarchic or democratic. And sadly there appears a lot to be said for the view that, insofar as it necessarily involves compromise, any sort of political career must, in the end, to some extent corrupt anyone.

Index Locorum

Index of Names

General Index

unimpeded exercise of what? 12-20,
  21
value of pleasure 2, 21, 117-24, 140-
  42, 150-51
and virtue 2, 16, 18-19, 22-4, 149-52
political engagement 153-67, 168-76
  Aristotle 156-64, 173-6
  corrupting influence 154, 155, 156,
    162, 165, 174-6
  and defective constitutions 162, 165,
    168, 173-6
  and justice 159-65, 168-73
  Plato 154-5, 159-60, 162, 168-73, 175-
    6
  Socrates 154
Politics 52, 156-8, 162, 163, 173-6
Protagoras 41, 56

reason
  and choiceworthiness 137-9, 141-3
  and happiness 68-71, 74-5, 80-5, 117-
    24, 127-32, 137-47, 149, 150
  and improvability 141-3
  practical reason and theoretical reason
    145, 161-2
  and virtue of character 138, 143-7
reasons for action 64-6, 75-6, 79-80,
  112, 114; also *see* eudaimonism
Republic 3, 6, 9, 29, 31, 32, 34, 37-8, 41,
  44, 45, 46, 51-4, 59n14, 61n21, 62-3,
  68-71, 88-9, 92, 93, 98, 103, 106, 154-
  5, 159-62, 169-74
  happiness 71
  justice 29, 31, 32, 37, 42, 46, 109-10,
    159-62, 169-72
Rhetoric 43, 71-3, 75-6, 86, 97n29
  happiness 43, 71-3
rules 40-41, 48-51
ruling by the philosopher-kings 68-71,
  81-5

self-love 96-7, 102-3, 105-7
self-predication 36-8
self-sacrifice 67-71, 73-5, 81-5
self-sufficiency 117-47, 148
  and choiceworthiness 119-20, 127-9,
    131-2, 133-4
  and external goods 130
  and finality 119-20, 126-7, 131, 148-9
  and happiness 126-43
  Nicomachean Ethics 117-19, 124-43
  Philebus 117-24, 127-32, 138-43
  and sufficiency 126-32
Socrates
  political engagement 153-4
statecraft as soulcraft 153, 157-8, 168
study of constitutions 156-9, 163-4, 168
sufficiency, 118-20; also *see* self-
  sufficiency
  and self-sufficiency 126-32
supervenience 36-8
Symposium 36, 37, 42-3

temperance 16, 29, 32, 49, 166

vicious people 87, 93, 96, 106
virtue of character 33-4, 109-15, 158,
  163
  activity and state 109-14
  and fortune 94
  and happiness 55-63, 67, 71-5, 79-80,
    87-108, 111-15, 143-7
  imperfect virtue 158
  and pleasure 2, 16, 18-19, 22-4, 149-52
  and reason 138, 143-7
  unity 34, 39n26, 165-7

wisdom 34, 43, 163
  practical and theoretical 161-2, 163-4
withdrawal, *see* political engagement